Photographic Rendering with V-Ray for SketchUp

An all-inclusive guide to creating a photo quality
V-Ray render for SketchUp

Brian Bradley

[PACKT]
PUBLISHING

BIRMINGHAM - MUMBAI

Photographic Rendering with V-Ray for SketchUp

First published: March 2014

Production Reference: 1100314

Published by Packt Publishing Ltd.
Livery Place
35 Livery Street
Birmingham B3 2PB, UK.

ISBN 978-1-84969-322-6

www.packtpub.com

Cover Image by Brian Bradley (brian@vrayelite.co.uk)

Credits

Author

Brian Bradley

Reviewers

Matthew Bohne

Joel Bradley

Ross Cantrell

Mathieu Godet

Tom Hankins

Acquisition Editors

Martin Bell

Rebecca Pedley

Content Development Editor

Arvind Koul

Technical Editors

Pragnesh Bilimoria

Pooja Nair

Nikhil Potdukhe

Project Coordinator

Wendell Palmer

Copy Editors

Roshni Banerjee

Sarang Chari

Adithi Shetty

Proofreaders

Simran Bhogal

Maria Gould

Ameesha Green

Paul Hindle

Indexer

Mehreen Deshmukh

Graphics

Yuvraj Mannari

Abhinash Sahu

Production Coordinator

Manu Joseph

Cover Work

Manu Joseph

About the Author

Brian Bradley is a self-taught 3D artist and Training Author who started experimenting with creative software and 3D applications back in 1993. By the mid 90s, he was running his own small multimedia business working on projects as diverse as corporate logos, graphic design for clothing and vehicles, as well as developing full product and architectural visualization projects.

In 2007, he turned the attention of his family-run studio toward full-time production of CG Training, focusing initially on 3ds Max along with the mental ray and V-Ray render engines. In 2012, he joined the ranks of Training Authors producing course for the lynda.com online training library, producing (among others) V-Ray-based courses for 3ds Max, Maya, and of course, SketchUp.

Recently, Brian and his team have completed a revamp of the vrayelite.com website that they run and they plan to work at slowly but surely expanding both the level and quality of training and content that it houses.

Acknowledgement

While there are a lot of people that I could sincerely acknowledge as having played a part in my being able to ultimately write this book, many of them of course coming from the world wide CG community, I am going to keep things simple and say a huge and heartfelt thank you to anyone and everyone that has had a positive influence on my life.

At the top of that list would of course come my wife Karen and son Joel who have borne the brunt of many frustrating days and nights spent trying to get computer hardware and software to work in perfect harmony in the pursuit of art and creativity. Not only have they themselves been an inspiration as regards perseverance, but also in terms of creativity, providing a never ending flow of observations, suggestions, and where ever beneficial, even criticisms. To you, I say, "Drinks all round".

There is also one honorable mention that I would like to make with regards to our own inspiration in becoming trainers and educators in the CG world. Many years ago we stumbled across, what was at the time a brand new site, giving away high quality computer graphics training to anyone who would write and ask for it. The site was 3dbuzz.com and in the years that followed, the inspiration from that team, especially Jason Busby and Zak Parrish, is something for which I will always be grateful and remember fondly.

Thank you all for reading; this is Brian Bradley saying take care, and bye for now.

About the Reviewers

Matthew Bohne is currently a fourth year architecture student at the Rhode Island School of Design. His interests include interdisciplinary methods of working, including conceptual architectural drawing, as a vehicle to subvert and expand upon architectural discourse and ideas of imagination, ritual, and narration. He recently was a finalist in the international Ken Roberts Memorial Delineation Competition.

Joel Bradley is a self-taught 3D generalist and training instructor, who has been using 3D, image editing, and graphic design applications since the age of nine.

Spending 10 years working as a partner in his family-run multimedia and training business has given him the opportunity to develop skills and insight into the way people and production processes work, as well as affording the opportunity to work in a diverse number of industry areas including the production of content for the web, print, video, and interactive applications to name just a few.

In recent years, he has been enjoying the focus and challenge of helping others get to grips with the software tools and design principles that he loves as a full-time Training Author producing 3ds Max and Blender titles for both lynda.com and infiniteskills.com.

Ross Cantrell graduated from SCAD (Savannah College of Art and Design) in 2012 with his BFA in Animation. He is a 3D digital artist with a focus on lighting, compositing, modeling, and rigging. Since his graduation from SCAD, he has worked as a 3D artist and compositor within the television industry on shows and commercials for Cartoon Network, TNT, TBS, and Sprout. He has also worked within the film industry producing 3D stereoscopic animation for National Geographic. Ross currently works for TRICK 3D producing photorealistic images and animations for Delta depicting commercial airline interiors for marketing and advertising use.

Mathieu Godet is a French 3D artist specialized in modeling, texturing, and shading. He graduated from the ESIAJ in Namur, Belgium, in 2012 and has been working in the industry for about two years.

Tom Hankins developed an interest in drawing, animation, and creation at a very young age. Film and animations have always been a big part of his life. At the age of 18, he had his first 3D lessons at the Utrecht School of Arts, shortly after which he changed courses and enrolled into the 3D Computer Animation and Visual Effects program.

In his third year, he was an intern at Rosto A.D. in Amsterdam, working on the film *The Monster of Nix*, character designing, and developing one of the leading characters of the film, voiced by Terry Gilliam.

In his fourth and final year at the academy, Tom and three of his fellow students created the successful animated short *Mac 'n' Cheese* as his graduation film. He graduated with honors as a bachelor of Art and Technology.

He is now running a small Holland-based CG company called Colorbleed along with Roy Nieterau and Gijs van Kooten.

Their production and creative experience ranges from animated shorts to commercials and visual effects for films. Tom works as their Creative Director.

www.PacktPub.com

Support files, eBooks, discount offers and more

You might want to visit www.PacktPub.com for support files and downloads related to your book.

Did you know that Packt offers eBook versions of every book published, with PDF and ePub files available? You can upgrade to the eBook version at www.PacktPub.com and as a print book customer, you are entitled to a discount on the eBook copy. Get in touch with us at service@packtpub.com for more details.

At www.PacktPub.com, you can also read a collection of free technical articles, sign up for a range of free newsletters and receive exclusive discounts and offers on Packt books and eBooks.

http://PacktLib.PacktPub.com

Do you need instant solutions to your IT questions? PacktLib is Packt's online digital book library. Here, you can access, read and search across Packt's entire library of books.

Why Subscribe?

- Fully searchable across every book published by Packt
- Copy and paste, print and bookmark content
- On demand and accessible via web browser

Free Access for Packt account holders

If you have an account with Packt at www.PacktPub.com, you can use this to access PacktLib today and view nine entirely free books. Simply use your login credentials for immediate access.

Table of Contents

Preface

The art of capturing or interpreting reality is one that has been around in one form or another for hundreds of years. First it resided with painters, many of whom took the study of light play and interaction with the world around them to new heights. Next came photographers, who quickly realized that this incredible new medium was not only capable of capturing a snapshot of the world, but also of interpreting and presenting it in a manner that made it a genuine art form.

Today, a computer graphics artist can use the tools at his or her disposal to create or recreate anything that real life or imagination can conjure up. And while artistic interpretation and style has been used in visualizing such creations, the pursuit of genuine photographic-looking images has long been a goal towards which many have striven.

With the ever increasing hardware power and the availability of feature-rich render engines, such as V-Ray for SketchUp, that pursuit is no longer quite as arduous as it once was. With an appetite for learning and a willingness to apply ourselves in a workman-like manner, anyone with a mind can now learn how to produce photographic-looking renders of virtual objects in what (just a few short years ago) would have seemed like an impossible time frame.

If the ability to produce such images is an artistic pursuit that sounds appealing to you, then you have a lot of cool stuff to look forward to in this book.

What this book covers

Chapter 1, Diving Straight into Photographic Rendering, gets us nicely up and running with V-Ray in SketchUp as it fast tracks us through with the use of many key areas in the render engine, all of which need to be utilized by an artist if they want to produce photographic renders using V-Ray.

Chapter 2, Lighting an Interior Daytime Scene, gives us a thorough grounding in lighting a daytime interior scene in SketchUp. A variety of potential lighting approaches introduce us to a wide range of V-Ray light types available for use in a similar scenario. As we explore these approaches, we will also see the pros and cons that go along with using them.

Chapter 3, Lighting an Interior Nighttime Scene Using IES Lights, naturally presents a different set of lighting challenges to us and thus, introduces us to some more specialized tools such as the IES light type, which has been provided to help us recreate the energy output and complex light throw patterns that often come from man-made light fixtures.

Chapter 4, Lighting an Exterior Daylight Scene, revisits the V-Ray Sun & Sky tools that we touched on in *Chapter 1, Diving Straight into Photographic Rendering*. Here though we take a much more detailed look at how these procedural lighting tools can be used to effectively recreate very natural-looking daytime lighting conditions.

Chapter 5, Understanding the Principles of Light Behavior, introduces us to some key lighting concepts and theory that in and of themselves are not essential to our being able to use the V-Ray render engine, but will certainly help us understand how we can use light in a more realistic manner and thus, produce increasingly photographic-looking renders.

Chapter 6, Creating Believable Materials, moves us into the area of realistic material creation. In order to produce photographic-looking renders, the materials we apply to the geometry in our scenes will need to both look and react to light in the same manner as their real-world counterparts. In this chapter, we explore the creation of a number of common architectural material types as well as consider a number of possible workflow options for ourselves.

Chapter 7, Important Materials Theory, reminds us that as with lighting, understanding how and why materials behave the way they do can, go a long way towards helping us make informed texturing choices that will contribute greatly to the quality of the finished piece. In this chapter, we explore the *how* and *why* regarding a number of important material concepts such as reflectance and transmittance, all of which ultimately needs to combine in order to create realistic looking surfaces for our objects.

Chapter 8, Composition and Cameras, covers some extremely important and yet often overlooked aspects of photographic rendering in the form of composition and framing. Closely linked to these subjects are the choices that need to be made in our camera settings, such as aspect ratio, focal length, and output resolution, all of which can and will significantly affect the photographic quality of our final renders.

Chapter 9, Quality Control, introduces us to the lighting, global illumination, image sampling, and material controls that can help us produce clean, high quality photographic-looking output. The goal in this chapter is to show how (as much as possible) we are able to balance high quality output with the overall render time taken to produce it. High quality and high resolution rendering will always be a time consuming process, but we can avoid adding unnecessary time burdens to the process.

Chapter 10, Adding Photographic Touches in Post-production, takes us away from the 3D world of SketchUp and V-Ray and into the 2D world of post production. Here we use Adobe After Effects but of course, any good image editing or compositing application should suffice. The aim is to add a few extra *photographic* touches to the image rendered out of V-Ray, in order to add a final bit of polish to the good work that we have already done there.

What you need for this book

You'll need SketchUp Version 8 or higher and V-Ray for SketchUp Version 2.0 or higher (although many steps can be completed using Version 1.49 as well). An image editing application such as Adobe Photoshop and a compositing/post-production finishing application such as Adobe After Effects is also required.

Who this book is for

If you are a SketchUp user who would love to turn your favorite modeling application into a *virtual photography studio*, this book has been designed and written with you in mind. However, we are confident that even existing V-Ray users will find plenty to enjoy and benefit from this book.

Basic experience with SketchUp is expected, meaning you should be able to navigate around a 3D scene in the application, as well as know where the standard SketchUp tools can be located in the UI.

[
While having some familiarity with photography would certainly be helpful, it is by no means required as we will walk you step-by-step through using all of the V-Ray tools necessary for the creation of genuinely photographic renders.
]

Conventions

In this book, you will find a number of styles of text that distinguish between different kinds of information. Here are some examples of these styles, and an explanation of their meaning.

Code words in text, database table names, folder names, filenames, file extensions, pathnames, dummy URLs, user input, and Twitter handles are shown as follows: "To take a look at the first of the scene files that we will be working with throughout the duration of this book, you may want to load the `Daylight_Interior_01.skp` file from the `Exercise Files` folder that have been provided as a downloadable resource."

New terms and **important words** are shown in bold. Words that you see on the screen, in menus or dialog boxes for example, appear in the text like this: "Open up the **Indirect Illumination** rollout".

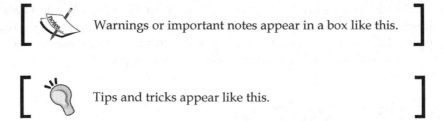

[Warnings or important notes appear in a box like this.]

[Tips and tricks appear like this.]

Reader feedback

Feedback from our readers is always welcome. Let us know what you think about this book—what you liked or may have disliked. Reader feedback is important for us to develop titles that you really get the most out of.

To send us general feedback, simply send an e-mail to `feedback@packtpub.com`, and mention the book title via the subject of your message.

If there is a topic that you have expertise in and you are interested in either writing or contributing to a book, see our author guide on `www.packtpub.com/authors`.

Customer support

Now that you are the proud owner of a Packt book, we have a number of things to help you to get the most from your purchase.

Downloading the example code

You can download the example code files for all Packt books you have purchased from your account at `http://www.packtpub.com`. If you purchased this book elsewhere, you can visit `http://www.packtpub.com/support` and register to have the files e-mailed directly to you. The files can also be downloaded from `www.vrayelite.co.uk/Books/VrfSu/Photographic_Rendering/Exercise_Files.zip`.

Downloading color versions of the images for this book

For your convenience we have also provided a PDF that contains higher resolution color versions of the images used in this book. These can be extremely useful as you work through various stages of the project when working with materials or examining small detail changes as we tweak individual parameters. You can download the PDF from `https://www.packtpub.com/sites/default/files/downloads/3226OT_ColoredImages.pdf`.

Errata

Although we have taken every care to ensure the accuracy of our content, mistakes do happen. If you find a mistake in one of our books—maybe a mistake in the text or the code—we would be grateful if you would report this to us. By doing so, you can save other readers from frustration and help us improve subsequent versions of this book. If you find any errata, please report them by visiting `http://www.packtpub.com/submit-errata`, selecting your book, clicking on the **errata submission form** link, and entering the details of your errata. Once your errata are verified, your submission will be accepted and the errata will be uploaded on our website, or added to any list of existing errata, under the Errata section of that title. Any existing errata can be viewed by selecting your title from `http://www.packtpub.com/support`.

Piracy

Piracy of copyright material on the Internet is an ongoing problem across all media. At Packt, we take the protection of our copyright and licenses very seriously. If you come across any illegal copies of our works, in any form, on the Internet, please provide us with the location address or website name immediately so that we can pursue a remedy.

Please contact us at copyright@packtpub.com with a link to the suspected pirated material.

We appreciate your help in protecting our authors, and our ability to bring you valuable content.

Questions

You can contact us at questions@packtpub.com if you are having a problem with any aspect of the book, and we will do our best to address it.

1

Diving Straight into Photographic Rendering

What should the first chapter of a book looking at photographic rendering in V-Ray 2.0 for SketchUp be all about? That was the question I had to ponder as I started developing the material that would be included in this book.

Should we spend time looking at the current state of the art regarding photographic and photoreal rendering in the CG industry? Should we delve into a technical explanation of exactly what it is that people are referring to when they make use of the terms photographic and photoreal rendering?

What this chapter is all about

Well, after quite a bit of deliberation, much of which was shaped and brought into focus by the hands-on approach to learning that Packt Publishing themselves advocate, I decided to follow the advice of a well-worn axiom: *dive right in at the deep end*. In other words, develop an introductory exercise chapter that might typically be found at the end of a publication such as this one, often in the form of a "putting it all together" type exercise.

My reasons for opting to take this somewhat turned-around approach were three fold:

- Firstly, as already noted, this approach suits the philosophy promoted by the publishers themselves, which is that learning ought to be as much of a hands-on experience as possible; one that engages and involves the student rather than one that is passive and possibly even tedious.

- Secondly, it gives users, who are brand new to photographic rendering of any kind, the opportunity to see just how easy it can be once they have figured out how to work with the tools of the trade—in this case, SketchUp and V-Ray Version 2.0. My hope is that this chapter can help strip away the mysticism, the trepidation, and maybe even some of the frustration that can result from not understanding how something works.

- And finally, for users who may already be familiar with the general principles of photographic rendering but who are new to V-Ray in SketchUp, this book will give them an opportunity to very quickly get an overview of the process, tools, and options that can be used in a V-Ray-specific pipeline.

> If you are an experienced artist looking for an overview of how V-Ray works in SketchUp, be sure to work through the steps in this chapter rather than just skimming through them! The hands-on experience will stand you in good stead as you dig deeper into the V-Ray render engine.

So, with the general idea of what this particular chapter is all about made reasonably clear, let's go ahead and dive right in.

Good composition is the foundation of photographic rendering

Once the geometry populating a scene has been lovingly prepared, the thing that we as the render artist will be charged with is the task of turning plain scene models into a finalized, photo-realistic render. We can give ourselves a solid foundation on which to build by, first of all, giving consideration to the compositional quality of the shot (or render) that we have been tasked with creating.

In fact, when you start to give some serious thought to the subject, doesn't it stand to reason that in order to look like a photograph, a rendered image would need to be constructed in at least a similar manner as the photograph that it is seeking to mimic?

This is why compositional rules such as those listed in the following bullets need to be thought of as the foundation or starting point from which a photographic render can be constructed.

- Thirds
- Positive and negative space
- Balance
- Leading lines
- Focal point
- Symmetry and patterns
- Point of view
- Subject and background
- Depth
- Framing

As a computer artist, if we are not already familiar with the total accuracy of the statement *Put garbage in and you will get garbage out*, we will be very soon, because it is one of the most often citied and indeed accurate pieces of advice that you are likely to hear.

In other words, what we get out as the end result of a piece of work or project can only be as good as the materials, the time, and the effort that we put into it. If we start our rendering project with a weak or unstable foundation (such as poor composition), then it stands to reason that we are really going to struggle to produce any kind of high quality end result from it when all is said and done.

Of course, not all of the compositional rules listed can be applied to every single image that we will ever shoot or render. Still, it should be our aim to make good use of the ones that can be applied, so as to help create a composition that presents our work in the best possible manner.

Improving our opening scene

Let's jump into our quick start lesson by loading the Ch01_01_Start.skp file from the downloadable Exercise_Files folder into the SketchUp application. As you can see, what we have at this moment is a very uninteresting view of a simple interior scene, as shown in the following screenshot:

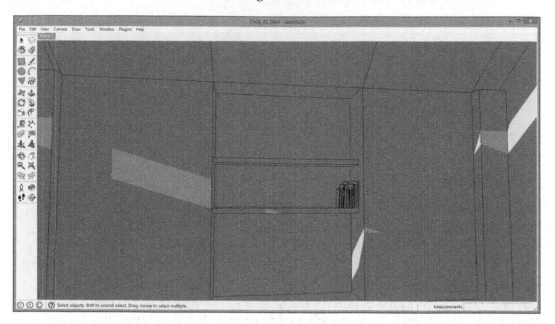

Downloading the example code

You can download the example code files for all Packt books you have purchased from your account at http://www.packtpub.com. If you purchased this book elsewhere, you can visit http://www.packtpub.com/support and register to have the files e-mailed directly to you.

Our first task is to immediately improve the visual engagement of our scene by finding some interesting **Points Of View (POV)** from which to take our renders. While setting these up, we will need to look for ways to apply as many of our rules of composition to the camera view as necessary in order to obtain a visually stronger and more engaging final shot.

One extremely important thing to bear in mind at this stage of the process, and something that I will be repeating throughout the pages of this book, is the fact that experimentation is really one of the *keys* to success! The more views or camera angles we try, the more likely we are to find something that not only evokes the feel or mood we want to convey, but also presents the scene in the manner we need.

As a skill-building exercise, let's use the start scene that we have already opened and find as many interesting POV as possible from which the environment can be rendered.

To help with this, we will need to make use of some key SketchUp tools. The major view finding options that are typically used are shown in the following figure:

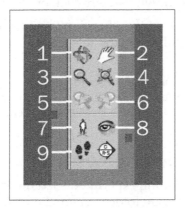

 This figure shows the tools as they appear on the SketchUp Large Toolset toolbar rather than on the default Getting Started toolbar.

The following tools are represented by the numbers shown in the preceding figure:

- **Orbit (1)**
- **Pan (2)**
- **Zoom (3)**
- **Zoom Extents (4)**
- **Previous View (5)**
- **Next View (6)**
- **Position Camera (7)**
- **Look Around (8)**
- **Walk (9)**

As we look around the scene using these tools, we will hopefully find a number of views that we like. As we do so, we will want to use the following steps to save each of those scene views so that we can return to them at any time we like and take renders from them:

1. Left-click on the **Window** menu found at the top of the SketchUp user interface. In the drop-down list, left-click on the **Scenes** option.

2. In the dialog box, click on the plus sign to add a new scene. Be sure to give each view a useful name and description.

 If we need to make changes to our scene views at a later stage, be sure to hit the **Update** button in this dialog box once the alterations are complete so as to lock them into place.

Working with six new views

To see where my own view-finding experiments led me, open up the Ch01_02_Views. skp file from the Exercise_Files folder, where the views that are available should match the screenshots that follow.

 You can of course continue to work through this chapter, adding your own scene views if you prefer. Just be sure to save your work to a differently named scene file to avoid overwriting the provided one.

I eventually decided on six different views to produce my renders. Each one of them focuses on a different element or elements in the room, and each one of them employs one or more of the compositional rules listed earlier.

Another exercise you might want to try before going any further at this point would be to take down some notes regarding which of the previously listed compositional elements are visibly at work in each of the scene views that I have chosen here. The goal will be to develop your ability to observe and break down the compositional elements being used in any of the given images. Take your time to do this and then compare your own notes with the brief description that accompanies each of the scene view images.

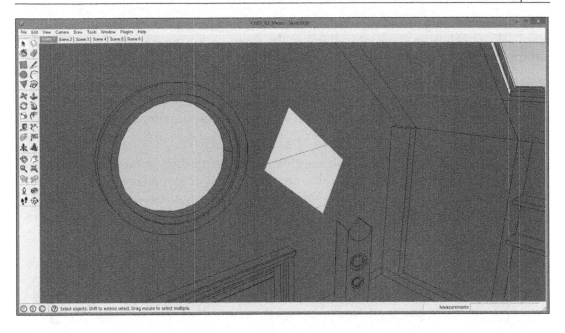

Scene 1 makes use of a very specific focal point in the form of the circular window, using a somewhat unusual POV. The scene is given a sense of balance by placing both the window and corner of the room roughly on the vertical third lines, which of course helps us add to the figure's balance.

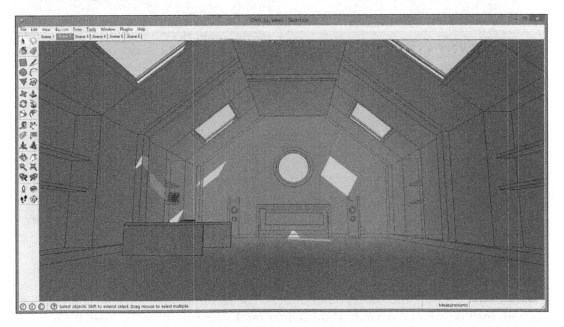

In **Scene 2**, the first deliberate choice made for the view was to use a wide shot for the POV. This lets us show everything in the room in one go, essentially making the environment itself a general focal point in the render.

We can also see both symmetry and balance at work. Both of these elements come about as a consequence of the initial choice for the POV. Looking straight down the center of the room gives us a natural sense of both symmetry and balance that hopefully feels unforced.

The fireplace and speakers both sit roughly on the lower horizontal third line, which helps draw our eyes to them naturally, creating a kind of secondary focal point that is a little more specific in nature. At the same time, having these elements placed around the lower third also adds to the sense of balance in the scene.

[As the table is the only fly in the ointment for both symmetry and balance in this view, it would be perfectly acceptable for us to do a little furniture rearranging here and place the table in a more central location. This relocation of elements in a view is typically referred to as Staging.]

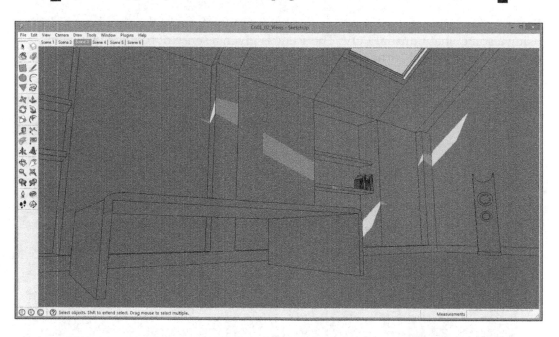

Our **Scene 3** view makes use of a very specific focal point in the table, with the POV being deliberately chosen so as to give us the ability to create depth in the scene by means of foreground and background objects. The fact that this keeps the table placed on both the vertical and horizontal third lines reinforces its role as the main focal point.

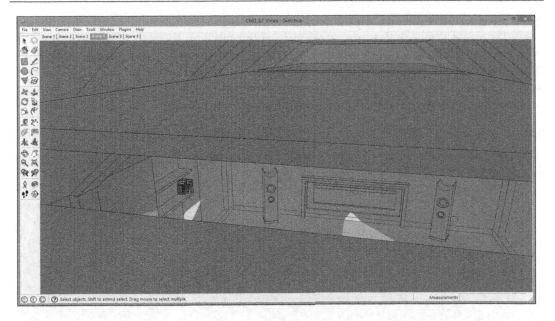

Scene 4 gives us an unusual POV on the environment that, although a little gimmicky, is a device that can give an image a very unique feel when used well. In this instance, the choice of POV directly influences what we can use as a focal point in the scene, which becomes the fireplace and speakers in this case. We also, by default, get to make a good use of framing and depth as both are created automatically by the ceiling panels that we are sitting above.

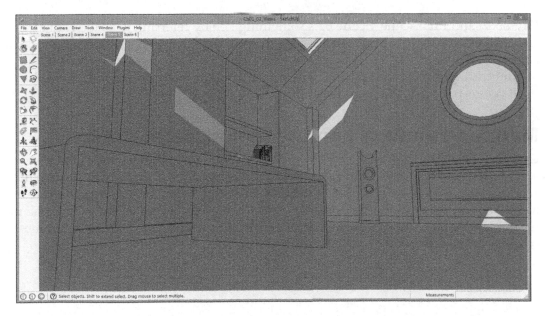

Scene 5 is a deliberate attempt to make use of balance by forcing a diagonal line of visual interest through the image, starting at the table on the left, then travelling left to right through the speaker in the center, and on to the window in the upper right. The line you will notice travels through the vertical and horizontal thirds, creating visual connectivity. We also get a measure of depth in the shot as this POV gives us some natural foreground and background object separation.

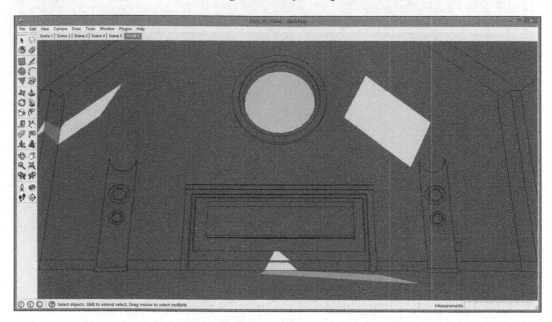

Our sixth and final scene, **Scene 6**, is something I enjoy referring to as the cathedral shot. An extremely low POV causes everything in the scene to take on a presence that can make the viewer feel somewhat small and insignificant. By placing everything symmetrically in the view, we make use of framing to create a sense of balance that itself seems to add to the grandness of our view.

Matching viewport and render aspect ratios

One final thing that we need to do before we leave composition behind is to make certain that our actual V-Ray renders match more closely with what we are currently seeing in the SketchUp viewport. It would be a shame to have worked hard to create a good composition in our camera view only to find that our render doesn't frame up in the same way. In fact, to show that currently our viewport and the V-Ray frame buffer renders are out of sync, let's take our first render.

If you don't already have the V-Ray toolbars present in the interface, now would be a good time to bring those up. To do that, let's perform the given steps:

1. On the main menu, navigate to **View** | **Toolbars…** and select the **VfS: Main Toolbar** and **VfS: Lights** options from the flyout menu.

2. I would also suggest that you dock these at the top of the SketchUp user interface as I have. This will keep us on the same wavelength when I talk about going up to the V-Ray toolbars throughout the rest of this book!

To initiate a render in V-Ray, all that we need to do is hit the big **R** (for render) button on the main toolbar and V-Ray will begin to process the scene for us.

 If this takes a while, don't be alarmed. Depending on the complexity of your scene and the power available in your computer, this process can take anything from a few seconds to a few hours before our scene begins to render.

Once the render is complete, as you can see in the following screenshot, the framing we have in the V-Ray frame buffer window does not match that seen in the SketchUp viewport at all. This is because my SketchUp interface is currently set 1600 x 900 (currently giving us a viewport aspect ratio of 2.01:1), whereas V-Ray by default is rendering at 800 x 600 (which is a 1.333:1 ratio).

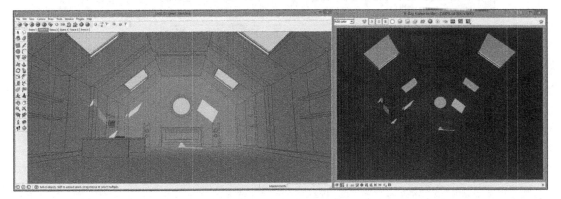

This obviously requires a bit of correction. To do that, we need to open up our V-Ray option editor by clicking on the **O** (for Option) button on the toolbar. Don't be intimidated by the sight of all the rollouts and parameters that confront us; we will become quite comfortable with these as we move through the various chapters in this book.

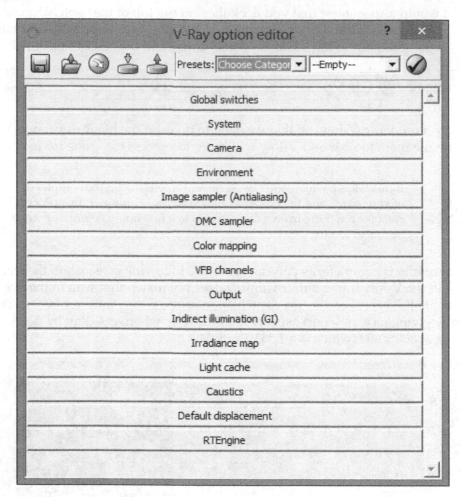

To align the framing of our renders a little more closely, let's perform the following steps:

1. Click on the **Output** rollout to open it.

2. Change the **Width** and **Height** settings to a resolution that uses something closer to a 2.01:1 ratio, such as 853 x 480, 1280 x 720, or 1920 x 1080.

 These standard HD resolutions use an aspect ratio of 1.777:1, which is close enough to help us. If the talk of aspect ratios here leaves you a little confused, don't worry. All you need to do for now is keep the preceding steps in mind and we will discuss the subject in more depth in *Chapter 8, Composition and Cameras.*

To keep things moving along quickly, I am going to employ a good workflow practice and render at a reduced, low-end HD resolution of 853 x 480. This approach to the testing phase means that we can make broad revisions without having to wait for full quality renders to finish. On average, an image rendered at half resolution will be completed four times faster than a full resolution render, which is logical since only one-fourth of the overall rendered content is being produced.

Lighting that sets the mood!

While a good composition gives us a solid foundation on which to build a photographic render, if we try to render a scene that has no lighting, well let's just say the end results will fall quite a way short of those desired.

The brilliant thing about lighting a scene with V-Ray in SketchUp is that a complete day-lighting system that consists of both the Sun and Sky elements is, by default, set up and ready to render with as soon as we start creating geometry in the scene. For newer users, this can obviously help tremendously when it comes to getting up and running with the software.

Controlling the placement of the Sun is extremely easy as we simply need to make use of SketchUp's built-in shadow controls, wherein we set the month of the year along with the time of day and time zone, and then we can render. What we instantly get is natural-looking daylight without having to do anything at all!

Better still is the fact that V-Ray also sets up a basic indirect (or global) illumination system for us automatically. This means we can even render interior Arch Viz shots right out of the box without having to do any extra set up work beyond, of course, getting our geometry created and then positioned in the scene.

Global illumination is a general name for a group of algorithms used in 3D computer graphics that are meant to add more realistic lighting to 3D scenes. Such algorithms take into account not only the light which comes directly from a light source (direct illumination), but also subsequent cases in which light rays from the same source are reflected by other surfaces in the scene, reflective as well as non-reflective (indirect illumination). The source of this content is Wikipedia.

To look at the kind of renders we can get from V-Ray without doing any real lighting setup at all, either continue to work with your current scene or open up the Ch01_03_Lighting.skp file from your Exercise_Files folder, if you prefer to work with the same scene as I will be using.

Stepping through the render process

The scene or camera angle we are using here (**Scene 2**) has been deliberately chosen to help us properly evaluate the quality and level of lighting that we are getting in our scene. It can do this because it affords us a full view of the environment.

With our camera view set to **Scene 2**, let's take a render by clicking the render button on the V-Ray toolbar. Once the initial translation phase is complete, V-Ray opens up its own frame buffer window and starts the rendering phase.

 One of the very nice features of V-Ray Version 2.0 is the fact that translation times in scenes are now significantly faster (in the vast majority of cases) than rendering the same scene in V-Ray Version 1.49.

The first activity we see in the frame buffer window will be V-Ray's indirect illumination calculations. First of all, the light cache and then the irradiance mapping engines calculate the level of illumination and light bounce requirements for the scene. This is based on the parameters set up in the **V-Ray option editor** and the materials applied through the materials editor.

 Irradiance mapping and light cache are the two indirect illumination engines set up by default in V-Ray Version 2.0 for SketchUp.

The final part of this process is the rendering of the image itself. In this instance, what we get, as we no doubt could discern from the GI calculations, is way too dark for the type of bright and airy feel in the interior that we are looking for. This brings us to a critical aspect of lighting in V-Ray, exposure!

Using V-Ray's physical camera model

Another default aspect of the V-Ray setup in SketchUp is that it makes use of a physical camera model for rendering. This means that real-world parameters such as shutter speed, F numbers (or F stops), and ISO (or film speed) values are used to control various aspects of the render, such as exposure, motion blur, and depth of field.

Basically, if we understand how to control these elements on a real-world camera, be it film or digital, then we already have a big head start when it comes to rendering using the V-Ray physical camera model. To access the physical camera controls, we need to revisit the V-Ray toolbar and click on the option editor button once more.

Then, if we open the **Camera** rollout, you can see in the following screenshot that we now have access to a wealth of camera controls and parameters. As we have already noted that our render is quite a bit darker than desired, the controls we are interested in would be those capable of affecting the exposure levels, which would be as follows:

- Shutter Speed
- F Number
- Film Speed (ISO)

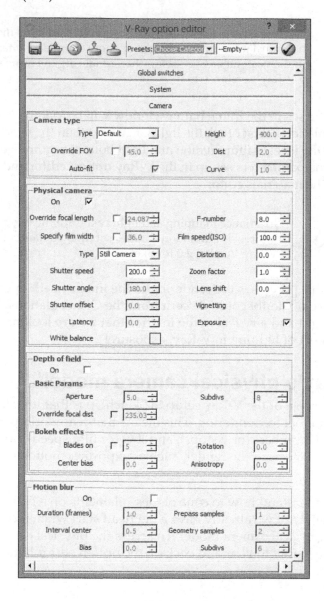

As a general rule, I prefer to handle exposure levels using only the film speed value as much as I possibly can. This is due to the fact that it is the only one of the three controls in what is often referred to as the *exposure triangle* that isn't used to control some other aspect of the physical camera model. Shutter speed is also used to control motion blur while the F number (or F stop) value will typically be the control mechanism for any **Depth of Field (DOF)** effects in our render.

To get some nice brightness levels in this instance, let's adjust the film speed or ISO value and set it to 1200. Taking another render by hitting the render button on the far right of the V-Ray frame buffer's top toolbar will show us that our illumination levels are now much more appropriate for the bright, airy feel we want to create.

The higher the ISO number we use in a render, the more sensitive V-Ray becomes to light, thereby producing a brighter final image. Unlike the ISO setting on a digital camera, we can increase this value as much as we like in V-Ray without the fear of introducing artifacts or noise into our rendered images.

Global illumination controls

The next aspect of our lighting setup that needs a little attention is the quality of the indirect illumination solution. At this moment, we can see quite a bit of dark splotching on our nice clean geometry. This often happens when we work with scenes that present a little bit of a challenge to the indirect illumination engines, which, of course, interiors nearly always do. Couple this with the reasonably low-quality default settings that V-Ray sets up, and we get splotches or noise patches in our render.

To clean this up a little, let's perform the following steps:

1. Jump into the **Irradiance map** rollout in the **option editor**, and in the **Basic Parameters** section, set the minimum and maximum rate values to -2 and -1 respectively.

2. We can also increase the **HSph. subdivs** value to 125 and the **Interp. samples** value to 35.

3. Next, we can jump into the **Light cache** rollout and increase the **Subdivs** (or subdivisions) value to 1200.

If we take another render by hitting the button on the toolbar, we should see a marked improvement in the level of splotchiness present in the image; not that every trace of it will be gone, mind you. When working with interior scenes, creating completely noise-free **Global Illumination (GI)** renders can prove to be quite costly in terms of the time it takes to render the final image.

What we often have to aim for then is a situation that would generally be considered free enough of noise to be called an acceptable final solution. One reason why we can often get away with this is the fact that once materials get applied to the geometry, any slight levels of splotchiness still found in the scene tend to oftentimes just blend into the materials themselves.

We do need to bear in mind that every increase in quality settings inside a render engine, such as those we have just applied to the indirect illumination controls, will result in a corresponding increase in the time it takes for the render to complete! This is typically referred to as the speed verses quality conundrum.

Materials that make us believe!

This, of course, leads us nicely onto the subject of creating believable materials for our models. Because this is just a quick start exercise and we will be devoting an entire chapter to the development of some very specific materials in V-Ray, we will deal with just two things here. First, we will demonstrate how to apply existing materials to various geometry elements in the scene. And second, we will walk through the creation of a new floor material just to get a feel of how the V-Ray standard material works.

To get started, we can either continue with our current file or open up the Ch01_04_ Materials.skp file from the downloadable Exercise_Files folder. This file essentially picks up where our lighting tweaks have left off. Let's introduce ourselves straight away to the V-Ray material editor by going back to the V-Ray toolbar and clicking on the **M** (for material editor) button. This, of course, will open up the editor window for us.

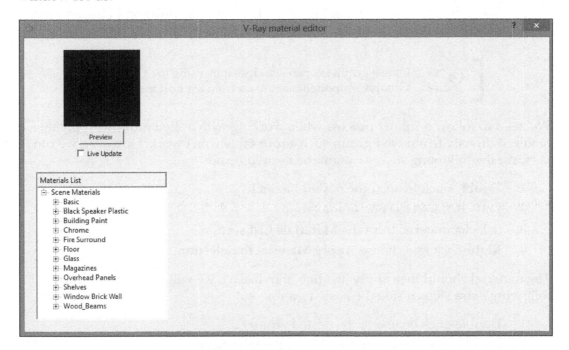

Looking in the **Materials List** section, you can see that we have a material named **Basic**. This is the plain grey material currently assigned to all the geometry in the scene. As we want to alter this arrangement, we need to briefly cover the setup or current state of geometry in the scene.

What I am referring to is the fact that everything in our scene at this moment in time has been turned into either a group or a nested group. This, for those who may be unfamiliar with SketchUp, will affect how we go about applying materials to the geometry. For instance, with one of the shelf objects selected, I can right-click on **Shelves material** in the **Materials List** section and choose the **Apply Material to Selection** option.

The selected material is then applied to that geometry. However, if I select a geometry group such as the main building itself, those same steps will no longer work and the material application would fail.

To apply a material to this type of geometry, we need to perform the following steps:

1. Double-click on the main building geometry to open up the group.
2. In the **Edit** menu, use the **Select All** command.
3. Right-click on a material in **Materials List**, such as **Building Paint**, and then choose the **Apply Material to Selection** option.

 Once a group is open, we close it by using the **Close Group/Component** command from the **Edit** menu.

We need to follow a similar process when working with nested groups. Applying a material directly to a nested group such as our table won't work. However, we can perform the following steps to attain the desired result:

1. Double-click to open the nested hierarchy.
2. Left-click to select one of the groups.
3. Select a material from the **Materials List** section.
4. Right-click and choose **Apply Material to Selection**.

The material should then apply just fine. If it doesn't, we will need to perform the following extra steps inside the nested group:

1. Double-click on one of the nested groups.
2. Use the **Select All** command from the **Edit** menu.
3. Select a material from the **Materials List** section.
4. Right-click and choose **Apply Material to Selection**.

This may seem like a clunky way to get things done, especially if we are coming to SketchUp from other 3D applications. However, once the process becomes familiar to us, it really does become second nature and flows quite freely.

Now that we understand the process of applying materials, go ahead and see if you can get the named textures in **Materials List** applied to their related scene objects. This is a good way to get some practice at working with the preceding outlined steps.

To keep ourselves moving forward, let's run through the creation of a material of our own. This is what we will use to texture the floor in our scene.

 Do keep in mind that we already have a **Floor Material** in our **Materials List** that can be used as a reference at any point if you should get a little stuck.

Creating the floor material

To move forward, we can either continue with our current file or open the Ch01_05_FloorMat.skp file from our Exercise_Files folder.

The first thing we want to do here is create a new V-Ray standard material for ourselves. So, let's perform the following steps in **Materials List**:

1. Right-click on either the **Scene Materials** label itself, or with the **Scene Materials** label selected, right-click on an empty area of the **Material List** panel.
2. In the pop-up menu, hover over the **Create Material** option and select the **Standard** material from the flyout.
3. Then, we need to locate the newly created label named **DefaultMaterial** in the **Materials List**.
4. Right-click on it and choose the **Rename Material** option from the pop up.
5. In the **Rename Material** window that opens up, call the new material **My Floor** and click on **OK**.

Of course, we will want to assign this material to the floor geometry straight away. Our new material is currently using grey for its diffuse color, making it the same as the already assigned basic material; we will avoid any potential confusion by changing our new material's diffuse color to something that will enable us to tell them apart.

To change this to something more recognizable, let us perform the following steps:

1. In the **Diffuse** rollout of our **My Floor** material, click on the diffuse color swatch.

2. In the **Select Color** dialog box, choose a color that would be very noticeable in the scene, such as the burnt orange I will create here. Let's use the HSV settings of HSV **12, 240,** and **218**.

3. Then, enable the select tool from the Large Toolset toolbar.

4. Triple-click on the floor geometry in the scene to ensure that it is all selected, or we could double-click and then use the **Select All** command from the **Edit** menu.

5. Right-click on the **My Floor** material name in the editor and choose **Apply Material to Selection** from the pop up.

If our burnt orange color appears in the viewport, we know that we have successfully applied this new material to the geometry; not that we will leave it set at burnt orange of course. In fact, we won't actually use the diffuse color swatch at all. Instead, we will make use of a number of bitmap or image files to help give our floor material a little more visual interest. To do this, perform the following steps:

1. Click on the map button (**m**) to the right of the diffuse color swatch.

2. From the drop-down list that appears under the **Preview** button, select the **TexBitmap** option.

3. In the **Open Bitmap File** dialogue box that appears, navigate to your downloaded Exercise_Files folder, and from the Textures subfolder, click to open the Floor.bmp file.

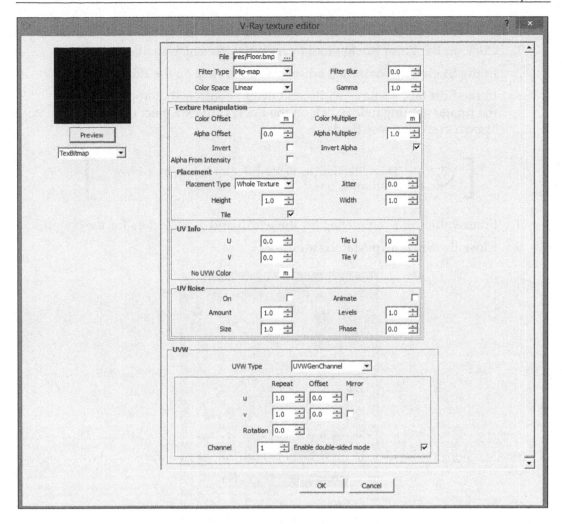

4. Then, click on **OK** to close the texture editor window.

5. And finally, let's lower the diffuse map's overall level of contribution by setting the spinner value to **0.25**.

We should now see our bitmap texture appear in the SketchUp viewport. At this moment, however, the default UV mapping coordinates are causing the bitmap to tile way too much for my liking. To rectify this, we need to use the controls found in SketchUp's own **Materials editor**.

To access that, let's perform the following steps:

1. Click on the **Paint Bucket** tool over on the SketchUp toolbar.
2. In the **SketchUp Materials editor** window, click on the **Edit** tab.
3. In the **Edit** tab, we have width and height controls that appear just below the image naming field. Click on the **Lock/Unlock aspect ratio** button that appears next to these fields.

> This will allow us to set different values for each of the dimensions.

4. Enter values of 3.00 meters for the width and 2.30 meters for the height.
5. Close the **SketchUp Materials editor**.

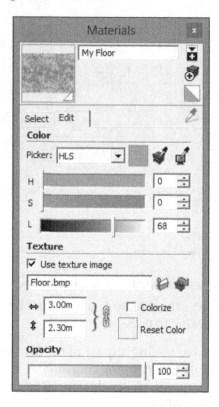

We should be able to see the difference this has made straight away in the viewport.

Adding surface properties

Next, we need to apply some parameter changes that will help us add some realism to our floor material. The first thing that we need are some reflections. To do this, we need to specifically add reflection controls to our V-Ray standard material.

> Although V-Ray Version 2.0 in SketchUp, just like other applications such as 3ds Max and Maya, now has a V-Ray Material that has all of the relevant parameter sections such as reflection and refraction set up and ready to work, there are some drawbacks to it that we will discuss in later chapters that preclude our use of it in this instance.

In the **V-Ray material editor**, let's perform the following steps:

1. Right-click on the **My Floor** material.
2. In the pop-up menu, hover over the **Create Layer** option, and from that flyout, choose the **Reflection** option.
3. Next, in the **General** area of the **Reflection** rollout, set the spinner next to the reflection color swatch to a value of **0.25**. (We can double-click and type the values in any of these fields if we want.)

   Then, we need to click on the map button (**m**) next to the reflection color swatch. In the texture editor parameters window that appears, click on the map button (**m**) for the **Perpendicular** controls.

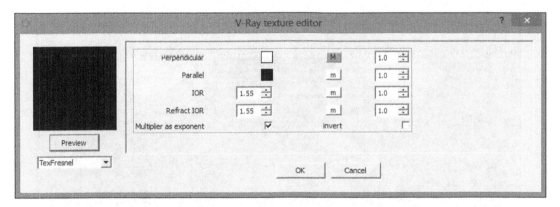

4. In the drop-down list below the **Preview** button, choose the **TextBitmap** option.
5. And, in the **Open Bitmap File** dialog box that appears, navigate to `Exercise_Files` | `Textures` and once more choose the `Floor.bmp` file.
6. Finally, click on **OK** in the two open dialogs to go back to the materials editor window.

Placing the bitmap in the perpendicular channel here will give us some nice variation in the reflection intensity, which will automatically make things feel a little more natural. Next, we need to add some breakup to those reflections. So, in the **Reflection** rollout of the **My Floor** material, go to the **Glossiness** section and set the **Hilight** and **Reflect** values to **0.85**.

Then, as a finishing touch, we can add a bit of a textured feel to the floor along with extra breakup by adding a subtle bump map to the material. To do that, let's perform the following steps:

1. Open up the **Maps** rollout at the bottom of the material controls.
2. Put a check in the **Bump** option, and at the same time, set its spinner value to **0.1**.
3. To add a map for the bump effect, click on the map button and select the **TextBitmap** option from the drop-down list beneath the **Preview** button.
4. In the **Open Bitmap File** window that appears, navigate to Exercise_Files | Textures and choose the Wall_Stucco_Bump.bmp file.
5. In the UVW section at the bottom of the texture editor controls, set **u and v Repeat values** to **4** and then click on **Ok** to exit the editor.

We can now take a render and see how things are looking by coming up to the V-Ray toolbar and clicking on the render button. Hopefully, what you have should look just like the following render:

We are closing in on a decent quick start image here. However, before we go ahead and create our final output render settings, let's just see how we can tweak things a little, now that all of our materials are fixed in place.

Final setting tweaks!

One area that I will want to address are the super bright whites that we are currently getting inside the render. You can find these by right-clicking on the image inside the V-Ray frame buffer, which should pop up a Pixel information dialog that contains RGB data readouts for varying image bit depths.

 V-Ray can do this because, by default, renders inside the frame buffer are stored at the highest bit depth possible using floating point values.

The one we are specifically interested in would be the **Color (float)** option. Whenever all three numbers in this readout go above the value of 1, which is pure white in floating point terms, then we know that what we are looking at is one or more super bright pixels in the image.

Sometimes, we can use these to good effect in our renders, especially when it comes to using the new Lens Effects feature of V-Ray Version 2.0. At other times, however, the burnout these super bright pixels cause, particularly in areas where direct light falls on an already bright texture such as our white walls, can be extremely undesirable. This means that it will always be useful to know which V-Ray tools can be used to help deal with this. One set of such tools would be the color mapping controls.

However, before we go ahead and make any changes, I am going to open up the Ch01_06_Tweaks.skp file from the Exercise_Files folder, which again picks up from where we currently have the scene. (Again, feel free to continue on using the current file, if you prefer.)

To deal with our super brights, let's perform the following steps:

1. Reopen the option editor by using the button on the V-Ray Main toolbar.
2. Inside the dialog, we want to open up the **Color Mapping** rollout and select the **Exponential** option from the **Type** drop down.
3. We also need to set **Bright Multiplier** here to a value of **1.0** instead of the default **0.8**.

This simple change in the color mapping type will prevent any of the RGB values in our image from climbing above a value of 1. Another effect of this color mapping change is that our rendered image will become a little less bright and the RGB values of our extremely blown-out sky will drop to levels below 1, meaning that we can now see a little bit of blue in there!

Another lighting tweak we might want to make at this point is in connection with the current positioning of the direct sunlight in our view. At this moment in time, the sunlight coming through the skylights is creating one or two bright spots on the left side wall, which are looking a little messy and may need cleaning. We can do that by basically shifting the Sun a little in our scene. To do that, we need to perform the following steps:

1. Open up SketchUp's **Shadows control** dialog from the **Window** menu.

2. Then, set the time of day to 11.10 a.m. by using either the spinner or clicking in the text field and typing.

 In order to apply this change to all of the scene views, we will of course need to select each one of them in turn and repeat this step. Remember that in order to have this change fixed in the scene, we will need to right-click on the scene tabs and use the **Update** option.

With that done, we will not only eliminate those distracting highlights, but we will actually create another element of symmetry in the shot in which the spots of light now fall on either side of the window opening.

One element that seems to be a little bit lacking in the scene would be occlusion or contact shadows. We may particularly expect to see these in corner areas of the room, especially the shelving recesses. At this point, we ideally want to add them without creating an extra image element that would need to be composited in another application. In this instance, we will choose the easiest route available to accomplish this and enable V-Ray's ambient occlusion option by following the given steps:

1. With the **V-Ray Options** dialog open, go to the **Indirect Illumination** rollout.

2. In the **Ambient Occlusion** section, check the **On** box.

3. Set the radius amount to **8.5**.

4. As we want the effect to be fairly subtle, let's set **Amount** to **0.35**.

With our lighting tweaks in place, a final, slightly distracting element that we may want to tackle could be the material we have applied to the shelves in the scene. I am not entirely convinced that what we have created sits well in the scene. So, I would like to experiment a little and try applying the same material that we are using for our overhead panels.

To do that, follow the given steps:

1. Select all of the shelf objects in the scene.
2. Open up **V-Ray material Editor**.
3. Right-click on the **Overhead Panel** material.
4. From the pop up, choose the **Apply Material to Selection** option.

Render settings for final output

Now, it's time to set up our final render output settings. These should ideally be dealt with as the very last step in the production process because once these are in place, the time required to complete each of the renders will increase quite dramatically.

> Bear in mind that we are referring to image sampling and final resolution settings here. Important composition elements such as the final aspect ratio for our images would need to be set up much earlier in the process.

At this point, we could increase the quality of our indirect illumination solution by upping the parameter values that we worked with earlier. In this instance though, I am going to stick with what we have as they seem to be doing a fairly decent job for us.

> It is, generally speaking, a bad idea to increase values *just because we can*. Unless there will be a visible improvement to the finished render, we will simply be increasing our render time for no apparent reason.

Let's go ahead and tackle our output image resolution first of all. In this instance, I am going to render out at full HD resolution, which means (at the time of writing) rendering is done at 1920 x 1080.

To set this up, we can perform the following steps:

1. Open up the option editor by clicking on the button on the toolbar.

2. Go into the **Output** rollout and set the width and height values to 1920 x 1080.

3. In the **Render Output** section, put a check in the **Save Output** box. Then, using the output file button next to the naming field, browse to the location where you want to save your image, such as the Exercise_Files folder that we have been working with.

4. Once there, set an appropriate file name such as Ch01_Final, which is what I will use.

5. Set the save-as type drop down to **OpenEXR image file** and then click on **Save**.

The final step here would be to improve the overall quality of the render by adjusting the image sampling settings. To do this, let's perform the following steps:

1. Open the **Image sampler** rollout in the option editor.

2. Make sure that **Adaptive DMC** is set as the **Image Sampling** type.

3. Set the **Min Subdivs** value to **1** and the **Max Subdivs** value to **16**.

4. Set the **Antialiasing** filter in the drop down to **Triangle**.

5. And finally, in the **DMC sampler** rollout, set the noise threshold value to **0.005**.

 Although we are moving very quickly over these important controls, rest assured that we will be returning to discuss them in *Chapter 9, Quality Control*.

With that, I think we are just about ready to take our final render for the chapter. So, let's visit the V-Ray toolbar one last time and click on the render button.

It is worth bearing in mind that the final settings that we have used here have the following functions:

- They represent a good, high quality starting point for renders given that they balance both quality and speed in a fairly equal manner

- They will need to be tweaked in order to suit the peculiarities of each scene on which we work

Once our image is rendered, what we end up with should hopefully look just like the render we have in the preceding screenshot, only much larger of course. Not too bad for a quick start exercise. Also, keep in mind that we haven't applied any post-production touches at all up to the final image.

Please note that your downloadable `Exercise_Files` folder contains a `Final Renders` subfolder that houses finished 1280 x 720 HD renders for this chapter, one from each of the six scenes or camera views found in the file.

Be sure to cast a critical eye over them and look for the things that do and the things that do not work in your opinion. Better still, have a go at fixing any problems you spot and then rerender the scene so that you can do a side-by-side comparison and evaluation.

Summary

Let's summarize the elements of photographic rendering that we have very quickly touched in this chapter.

As with any construction project, the crafting of a photographic render requires that we start with a solid foundation. In this instance, that means getting our basic composition in the scene right before we move on to using the tools found in the render engine itself. Solid compositional principles such as thirds, leading lines, and points of view should be considered and possibly even tried out at this phase of the project.

Once we have that in place, we can then move onto using V-Ray tools to craft a lighting setup in the scene that creates an appropriate mood for us; then, build and apply materials to scene geometry that have believable physical properties associated with them.

Add to this mix global illumination, exposure control, and then finally our finished render and output quality control settings. Now, we have a recipe for successfully creating photographic renders with V-Ray.

Of course, in this introductory chapter, we have moved incredibly quickly through the basic process of rendering an image in V-Ray. What we need to do now is break down the key processes and tools in a little more depth so that we can fully understand both the power of the tools available as well as learn how to control them. Next up is lighting; specifically, a look at how we can go about lighting an interior daytime scene from the ground up.

2

Lighting an Interior Daytime Scene

If you are using both SketchUp and V-Ray as part of your creative toolset, there is a very high probability that you are going to be producing at least some architectural renders as a part of your day-to-day work. This invariably means that at some point you will either want or need to try your hand at creating a natural-looking daylight interior render. This will require an ability to create an efficient and believable daytime lighting setup. In this chapter, we will make use of our `Daylight_Interior.skp` files to see how easy it is to create such a setup in V-Ray Version 2.0 for SketchUp.

Looking at our SketchUp scene

To take a look at the first of the scene files that we will be working with throughout the duration of this book, you may want to load the `Daylight_Interior_01.skp` file from the `Exercise_Files` folder that has been provided as a downloadable resource.

This scene contains a small gallery type building that has been designed and created to give us both interior and exterior spaces in which we can work at creating lighting, materials, camera composition, and so on, as well as providing a number of challenges that we will need to overcome as we move forward with our project.

We have also, by design, only populated one of the interior rooms in this building, leaving you free to add your own set dressing to other areas, using them to do your own exploration and experimentation with the concepts and tools that we will discuss throughout this project.

I would, at this point, encourage you to use every opportunity that you come across in this project to take the essence of what you learn in a particular chapter and then make use of it in any of the various versions of this scene that you have been supplied with. The more you experiment, the more sense the points we cover in this book will make.

Currently, all of the settings in the start scene are set to V-Ray defaults; in fact, the only work done so far has been the application of two V-Ray Standard materials to the scene geometry using RGB values of 88, 88, and 88 on the exterior material and 178, 178, and 178 for the interior version. These settings give us grayscale materials that have reflectance values of around 35 and 70 percent, respectively, which will be a big help to us as we set up our initial lighting for the scene.

Defining our goals

Now, although we have already demonstrated in our first chapter that we can pretty much jump straight in and start creating renders using the default lighting setup when using V-Ray in SketchUp, I feel the need to state quite emphatically that such an approach is in reality a long way short of ideal when it comes down to the work of creating photographic renders. Our first order of business when getting started on a project should always be to thoroughly develop the goals and aims of the project itself.

Time spent in breaking down the goals and then working out how to match our stated goals with the tools that we have available will not only save us a lot of unnecessary trial and error throughout the course of the project, but can actually lead us toward artistic choices, technical options, and even final results that may otherwise have been completely bypassed in pursuit of a quick turnaround.

Of course, at times the urgency of a project may force us to simply dive straight into V-Ray and use the default setups to produce the best results possible in the time frame allowed. This, however, should be the exception and not the rule. So if we find ourselves doing this on even a somewhat regular basis, we may need to reassess the way we evaluate the timescales required for the projects that we are undertaking.

To this end then, the first thing we have to do here is define our goals for this section of the project by creating an artistic definition that outlines exactly what we want to achieve as we work to set up the daytime lighting for our interior display room.

Once we have done that, our next task will be to break down the lighting process itself, making decisions regarding which approach will be best suited to help us reach our stated goals. Of course, we know ultimately that we are going to want to produce a photographic render, but breaking this overall goal down into smaller steps that will lead us to that end result can be very useful indeed.

Next, we will need to consider which of the lighting tools that we have available are capable of producing the desired end result. With V-Ray, there is usually more than just a single option available for creating any type of lighting effect. Identifying the options available and then making some informed choices as to which we want to use will be important if we are to fulfill the aims of our artistic definition.

Finally, we will need to put all of the generated ideas and choices made into practice and craft a finished lighting solution for the scene.

There is no doubt that what we have outlined here will indeed require a fair amount of effort from us (especially keeping in mind that we are only dealing with a single lighting set up in this chapter and have more to come). Hopefully though, this is just the kind of potential learning experience that you were looking for when you purchased this book. If that is the case, then we are ready to go ahead and start lighting up our daytime interior scene.

Obviously, a big part of creating any finished interior lighting solution will be the global illumination and material options that we ultimately use in the scene. Knowing which GI tools to use, how to refine the respective solutions, and understanding how to create realistic material properties are all must-have skills when it comes down to reaching our ultimate photographic goal.

For the next few chapters, however, we are going to work with just the default GI and sampling settings as this will help us focus on the lighting tools themselves, getting to grips with the various options we have available to us as well as coming to grips with how to make good use of them. However, tweaking the GI and sampling controls and refining the solutions we are getting from them will be something we take a look at later in the project.

Methods for defining our vision

Sitting down at a computer and starting to create scenes in an application such as SketchUp or 3ds Max without a clear goal in mind can be compared to setting off on a journey without having a fixed idea about the final destination.

While the idea of setting off on a mystery tour may sound exciting, we would never try to claim that such an approach, no matter how enjoyable, could be considered an efficient way for us to travel from one location to another.

In a similar way, while playing around with the tools available to us in our 3D application can at times be enjoyable and possibly even profitable (from a learning perspective), we would hopefully never claim that it is an efficient and cost effective way of approaching the production of a photographic rendering project. Especially so if we are looking to use the project to help take our CG skills to the next level.

In order to consistently produce high quality photographic renders using any render engines available to us, we really do need to take the time to define, in as much detail as possible, the end result that we want to create in every project that we work on. This definition can then realistically serve as the blueprint from which we work for the remainder of the project.

The idea here is not to create a fixed goal from which we can never deviate. What we need to create, is a reference point that can be used to help keep our project heading in the right direction at all times. If we do find at some stage that we need to revise or update this project blueprint, then that is fine, as long as we once again make sure that this process is done carefully and that everything gets clearly documented.

Writing a definition

How do we go about creating such a definition? Well, there are a number of possibilities open to us. If descriptive writing is a strength of ours, we could create our definition by making good use of words. The definition could be anything ranging from a single sentence mood description to a full and comprehensive document that breaks down everything we want to accomplish in the scene.

Painting a definition

On the other hand, if we have some ability with sketching and/or painting, be that with either digital or natural media, we could take the time to produce color script paintings or mood templates if you like. This can be somewhat along the lines of those used by animation studios such as Disney and Pixar in the early stages of a project when they work to develop the look and feel of the film they are making.

Compiling a definition

A third option would be to compile a collection or a scrapbook of images that epitomize the look and feel that we ourselves are hoping to create in a shot or sequence. The best way to gather these would be to head out into the world armed with a camera and shoot these images for ourselves. Physically placing ourselves inside environments that have the qualities of light and the type of materials that best represent what we want to produce in our render will give us the opportunity to analyze everything about the setting on an artistic, technical, and even emotional level.

If time or circumstances don't allow us to take such a hands-on approach, we can still do a thorough job of compiling a definition by making good use of the Internet. A couple of hours searching through images by means of a few well-chosen search phrases can yield excellent results.

We may, for instance, try searches for "wood-paneled bathroom" or "Victorian kitchen", if of course those are the type of projects we are working on. Given the scene type we will be working with here, we may want to try searching for something like "small gallery interior".

Be sure to use search phrases that are directly related to the type of project you are working on. This will keep things focused and on track. Spending many hours searching through masses of images that have little or no connection to our project's stated goals would certainly be counterproductive at this stage of the process.

Of course, just dumping a large collection of images into a folder on our hard drive, no matter how relevant they are, will not in and of itself benefit us in any great way. We will need to spend some time breaking down what we see in the images, making notes on the visual qualities that we find desirable. We can also take a look at a few quick ideas regarding how we might recreate such qualities using the SketchUp and V-Ray tools that we have at our disposal.

Ultimately, of course, which method we choose to work with for creating our definition isn't really the important thing as all of the methods mentioned here can work equally well for us. The genuinely important thing is that we both have and use some method for creating an outline that covers the expectations/requirements that we have for the project. Keep in mind that without a clear goal in view at the outset, our chances of creating a genuinely photographic solution can be greatly reduced.

Artistic exercise

As there really is no time like the present to start building such skills, a good exercise at this point in the process would be to create our own definition or blueprint for the `Daylight_Interior_01.skp` scenes lighting solution. If at all possible, I would encourage you to try creating at least one definition using each of the methods that we have outlined here, just to test which approach suits you best.

Also, keep in mind that there is no rule against having more than one mood for the scene that you would like to try and create. In fact, trying out variations in the early stages of a project, if time permits of course, can be a great way to find something that really works well for us.

My definition for the gallery interior

To show you how simple the definition for the artistic vision or definition on a project can be, we are going to make use of the first method mentioned and use a simple piece of descriptive writing that will consist of just a couple of short, simple sentences.

The goal for the lighting in this scene is to help make people feel comfortable and at ease inside the space, creating an environment in which they could easily spend a few hours without feeling closed in or claustrophobic. This effect can probably best be accomplished by using as much natural daylight as possible to light the space.

Do keep in mind that this is a description of the feel we want to create in our final lighting solution. In photographic terms, this is not necessarily connected or dependent upon the architectural design of the space we are rendering.

For instance, film makers often create completely believable exterior lighting scenarios while, in fact, working on an interior sound stage. The trick is to use the correct combination of lighting and photography tools to create the desired final effect.

The lighting workflow

Now that we have the goal for the lighting in our scene clearly defined, the next step is to outline the approach we are going to take and the tools we are going to use in order to create that lighting solution for ourselves. Again, we could quite easily jump in and probably use the default Sun and sky system in V-Ray, which has been designed with the goal of creating natural-looking daylight in mind.

The problem with *diving in* isn't necessarily the lack in quality that such an approach will produce, but rather the lack of artistic development that it can foster. Remember, a good photographer is, generally speaking, an artist first and a technician second. He/she is someone who has learned how to utilize the technology at their disposal as a means to an end in the pursuit of their artistic vision. Ultimately, it is their understanding of *what* makes a photograph good along with their artistic sensibility that will allow them to create the kind of high quality images that people love to look at.

The same should be true for you and I as rendering artists, possibly even more so, given the fact that we can be called upon to wear many different hats during a project, filling a variety of roles that each require the application of artistic know-how.

To help develop our lighting skills, we are going to take an approach to developing the lighting scheme that has been used by skilled lighting artists for many decades. This is to build our solution one light at a time, gauging and weighing the contribution that each added light makes to our overall lighting effect.

To do this, we will, of course, need a blank slate or completely dark scene into which we can add each light, building the solution as we go. This will mean doing a little bit of tweaking in our start scene as V-Ray in SketchUp automatically makes use of a V-Ray Sun & Sky system in order to produce a readymade daylight system.

To make the required tweaks, let's perform the following steps:

1. Open the V-Ray option editor from the V-Ray toolbar.

2. In the **Environment** rollout, uncheck the **On** box that can be found in the **GI (skylight)** options.

This disables the V-Ray Sun & Sky lighting elements in the scene, while still leaving us with the V-Ray sky rendered as a visual backdrop by virtue of the fact that it is still applied as a map in the **Reflection/refraction (background)** option.

> This handy ability to separate the lighting and background elements of an environment in the scene means that we can go ahead and use a completely different image (such as an HDRI) for the background and/or reflections in our renders while still making use of the V-Ray Sun & Sky to take care of lighting, or vice versa, if we so desired.

In fact, while we have the option editor open, we might as well turn the GI systems off for now as we are only interested (at this moment in time) in creating the direct light contribution coming from the Sun. To do this, perform the following steps:

1. Open up the **Indirect Illumination** rollout.

2. Uncheck the **On** box found in the top-right corner.

If we now hit the render button up on the V-Ray toolbar, we can see that our scene is in total darkness, which of course is the perfect point from which to begin crafting the lighting solution we want.

> In V-Ray for SketchUp, the V-Ray Sun is not an actual light object as it is in other V-Ray versions such as for 3ds Max and Maya, but rather exists only as a part of the TexSky map control set. For the sake of accuracy and continuity, however, I will continue to refer to it as a separate entity called the V-Ray Sun. This is entirely appropriate, as the V-Ray Sun can be set up in SketchUp to function as a solitary light source if we should need it to be.

Sunlight is our key light

The place to start when working on any kind of lighting design is to decide exactly what will constitute the key light in the environment. This is the light that provides the main source of illumination for the render and is also, generally speaking, the main shadow casting light.

In a daylight setting, it doesn't take a lot of figuring to realize that our key light would most likely be the Sun. The question is, which of the available V-Ray light types should we be using as our Sun? This, I suppose, could seem like a silly question given that we have already highlighted the availability of the V-Ray Sun light type.

Well, V-Ray does offer other light types that could almost as easily be used as a sunlight in the scene. In V-Ray Version 2.0, we have the Omni, Rectangle, Spot, Dome, Sphere, and IES light types, which are all readily available at the click of a button in the VfS:Lights toolbar.

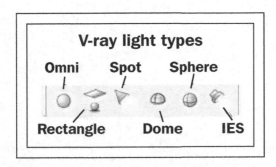

The beauty of these particular light objects is that they are free of the inherent restrictions and limitations that come with the V-Ray Sun, given that it has been designed to be a *physically* accurate light source. This means that the position of the V-Ray Sun in a scene can only be set according to what is physically possible in the real world given a particular time of day at a particular time of year.

SketchUp shadow settings – positioning the V-Ray Sun

To demonstrate the possible difficulties this could present, let's close any open dialogue windows and then open up the SketchUp's shadow settings window by performing the following steps:

1. Left-click on the **Window** menu at the top of the SketchUp UI.
2. Select the **Shadows** option from the drop-down menu.

With the **Shadow Settings** dialog box open, left-click on the show/hide shadows toggle in the upper-left corner of the dialogue box to see how the direct sunlight will fall in the scene. Then, if we grab the time slider and gently drag it left and right, we should see circles of direct sunlight in the SketchUp viewport traveling across the walls.

Now, from a purely compositional point of view, I would like to have those circles fall on the floor somewhere just in front of the camera, but making this happen is not as easy as it may sound. However, let's give it a go by altering the time sliders value, setting it to read **11:20 AM**. Then, we can move the date slider so that it is set to July 18. (Be sure to leave the time zone set at the default of **UTC-07:00**.) This should achieve the desired effect, creating three circles of sunlight on the floor in front of the camera as shown in the following screenshot. So far so good.

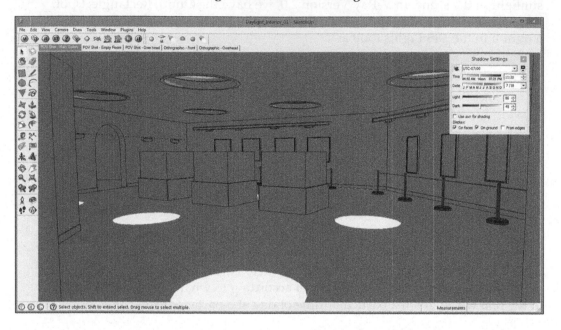

Let's switch over to the **POV Shot - Empty Room** scene tab now and see if what we are getting from this view will also work for us.

Unfortunately, as you can see, we have no direct light entering this room with our current time and date settings. Even more unfortunate is the fact that even if we alter our time and date, in this instance to **6:50 AM** on July 8, the best we can manage (with our building in its current location) would be a couple of small splashes of direct sunlight on the inside of the room, as shown in the following screenshot.

The problem is that, in creating this new setup, we have now completely altered the placement of direct light that we have just worked to set up in the main gallery view.

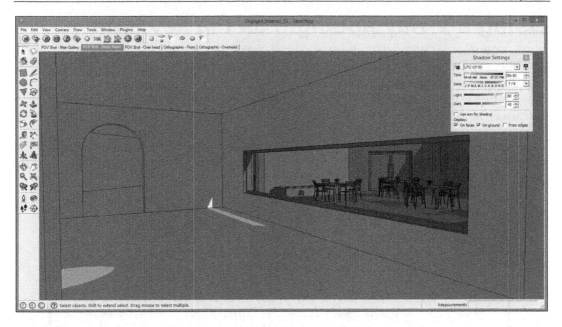

Of course, one thing we could do to get around this problem would be to set up our lighting as desired and then save the **Shadow** settings with each specific scene view, thereby allowing us to switch back and forth between the scene views and having the **Shadow/Sunlight** settings update automatically.

Doing that, though, would only cause us to run into a different problem. The V-Ray Sun & Sky system produces physically accurate light levels and sky coloration according to the time of day and the month of year settings that we have dialed in. This means that the individual renders from each of these rooms would look drastically different due to the fact that the lighting conditions found at these differing times of the day are completely different.

By lighting conditions, I mean the level or brightness of illumination found in an environment as well as the coloration coming from the sky itself.

Clearly, the realism built into SketchUp's shadow controls, along with its direct control over the positioning of the V-Ray Sun in a scene, can be a hindrance to the development of an artistically crafted photographic render in some circumstances.

To get around such limitations (and, of course, as a means of demonstrating alternative lighting options using the V-Ray render engine), we are instead going to make use of a different V-Ray light type as our key light, specifically a V-Ray spotlight.

Using a V-Ray spotlight as the key light

Now, you may be wondering why we don't make use of the V-Ray Omni or Sphere light types instead, given that the Sun itself is a roughly spherical and omni-directional light source? The answer to that question would be our continuing need to make the best or most efficient use of the computing resources available to us.

Creating a photographic render will always give the processing and memory resources of our computer a good workout, and in some cases it may even tax them to their limit. It is simply the way of things that as our workstations get faster, we just add more quality, more effects, and more everything into our final renders with the goal of producing an ever more realistic final result.

 Certainly, an image that we would have considered to have photographic realism some 10 or so years ago would no longer be viewed as such today. Take as an example the work (both character and environment) undertaken by Square pictures on the movie *Final Fantasy: The Spirits Within*. Upon release, it was hailed as a genuinely photorealistic piece of CG, but when compared to more recent efforts such as James Cameron's *Avatar*, it unfortunately doesn't hold up quite so well anymore.

All of this means that we need to be as conscientious as ever concerning the demands that we place on our system, taking care that we are not adding more computational load on to a scene than is really necessary.

In this instance, if we were to use an Omni light as our Sun, we would really be making use of just a small fraction of the 360 degrees of light that it would be emitting. Even when not directly lighting scene geometry, V-Ray still has to calculate the light emitted from it. So, in this situation, making use of a directional spotlight would seem to be a much more sensible use of resources.

To add a V-Ray spotlight to the scene that can function as our Sun, we first of all need to perform the following steps:

1. Switch our view by clicking on the **Orthographic – Front Scene** tab.
2. Now, we can click on the spotlight button up on the V-Ray Lights toolbar.
3. Then, left-click on the upper-right corner of the viewport to create our spotlight.

As positioning and rotating a spotlight into the required location can take a little bit of time, you can use the following screenshots to place your own spotlight at the same location as mine:

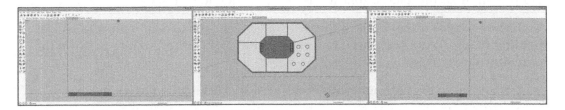

Alternatively, for the sake of speed, open the `Daylight_Interior_02.skp` scene file from the `Exercise_Files` folder that has the spotlight already in position. With that taken care of, if we switch back now to our POV (which is the main gallery view) and take a render, we should see that we have (to a reasonable degree) recreated the spots of direct light in front of the camera on our main gallery floor.

The added benefit of taking this approach to create our sunlight is that we can now move and rotate our spotlight to any position in the scene that we like, without affecting anything else, other than the position and direction of the direct light source itself.

However, to more closely mimic a camera's exposure for an interior shot on a bright sunny day, our sky should render as an extremely bright element in the scene at this point, heading towards being white in color.

We also need a little bit of color in our Sun. Although sunlight can be considered to be almost white at midday, viewers will typically expect to see varying degrees of yellow, orange, and even red in the sunlight, depending on the exact time of day and prevailing atmospheric conditions we are trying to recreate.

As the Sun's color is the easier of the two stated elements to deal with, let's tackle that first of all. To do so we need to use the V-Ray light editor, so let's perform the following steps:

1. Switch to the **Orthographic-Front** view by clicking on the scene tab.

2. Right-click on the V-Ray spotlight in the view, and then click on the **Edit light** option in the **V-Ray for Sketchup** flyout.

3. In the **Intensity** section, click on the color swatch and set the HSV color values to **60**, **40**, and **250**.

4. Then, click on **OK** to exit the color dialog box.

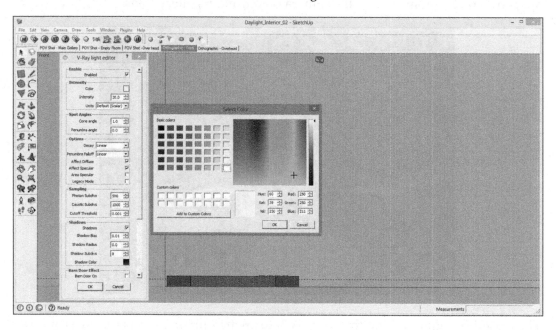

While we are in the light editor, I think it would probably be a good idea to add a little bit of softness to the edges of our shadows.

1. Scrolling down to the **Shadows** section of the light editor, let's set our **Shadow Radius** value to **45**.

2. Then, click on **OK** to exit the light editor.

 Although the default shadow sampling settings do (as you can see in the preceding screenshot) produce noisy edges in the shadows, we don't, at this point, want to make any changes to the sampling quality as we are, after all, still only in the setup phase for our lighting. Increasing the sampling quality now would only slow down the test renders that we need to be taking.

With the Sun color taken care of, we are now ready to tackle our scene's exposure settings. So, let's perform the following steps:

1. Open the V-Ray option editor from the V-Ray toolbar.

2. Click to open up the **Camera** rollout.

3. In the **Physical Camera** section, set **Cameras Shutter Speed** to a value of **125**.

4. Set **F Number** to a value of **8**.

5. And finally we can settle, for now at least, on a **Film Speed (or ISO)** setting of **325**.

With these adjustments in place, let's switch to the **POV – Main Gallery** scene view and take a look at what we have by hitting the render button on the V-Ray lights toolbar.

Obviously, we are quite a long way from creating anything that looks pretty just yet, but we have managed to set our sunlight up with some very specific properties that we will perhaps want to come back and tweak a little as we get closer to finalizing the lighting solution.

With the Sun set up then, let's stick to our process of working with only a single light source at a time and disable our spotlight so that we can focus on creating the fill light that we need in the scene. This, of course, would come from the Sky. To disable the spotlight, we need to perform the following steps:

1. Switch to the **Orthographic – Front Scene** view and right-click on the spotlight.

2. From the drop-down menu, select V-Ray for SketchUp and then the **Edit Light** option.

3. In the light editor, uncheck the **Enabled** option and click on **OK** to exit.

Turning the spotlight off takes us right back to working with a completely blacked out scene, which again is the perfect starting point from which to build our fill or skylight solution.

Skylight is our fill light

Just as it is obvious that in most daylight scenarios the Sun will be the dominant and therefore key light, it is also very clear that without the secondary or Fill light that comes from the Sky, what we call "natural daylight" would probably not look so natural at all.

Essentially the Sky acts as a giant diffuse reflector that is able to cast at least some level of illumination even into areas of an environment that direct Sunlight could never hope to reach. In this respect, the Sun & Sky system form a perfect lighting partnership—one that we often fail to fully appreciate for both its technical complexity as well as its aesthetic beauty.

Besides adding almost perfect illumination coverage for an environment, we also need to take into account the fact that Skylight can and often does add quite a strong color cast. Again this is not something that we generally appreciate or possibly even notice due to the automatic color balancing that our eyes and brain typically perform.

However, once we start to examine a naturally lit environment by means of photographic reference, especially when making use of varying exposure levels on the camera, we start to see that the color cast added by a skylight can often be quite significant.

Of course, in order to create our final render we are not obliged to stick rigidly to the physics of real-world light, but if we are serious about creating a genuinely photographic image, such realities certainly need to figure (at least to some degree) in our final lighting solution. It is, after all, the attention that goes into the sometimes subtler details that will often times create a feeling or sense of genuine quality in a finished piece of art.

To create a Skylight effect for an interior render we can again use a number of approaches in V-Ray by means of the different light tools available. The first option that we will explore here is an older technique that involves making extensive use of V-Ray's Rectangle light type.

Using Rectangle lights

The basic premise of this approach is that we place a V-Ray rectangle light over every opening that leads from an interior room to the outside environment. In the case of our project scene, this would mean giving coverage to the circular skylights, the doors and also the elongated windows we see in the two long gallery rooms.

Obviously, setting up all of the 12 required lights in the scene would take quite a while and result in a lot of unnecessary repetition in our text here. So, for the sake of speed I have prepared a scene that already has most of the work done. I have, however, left us with just one final light to add to the mix. This will give us an opportunity to take a look at how we both create and set up the options for the V-Ray Rectangle light type.

[
If you prefer, however, it would be perfectly fine for you to go ahead and place all of the rectangle lights in the scene using the same basic steps that we will cover in the next section.
]

From your `Exercise_Files` folder, open up the `Daylight_Interior_03.skp` file.

A quick examination of the scene shows that we already have lights placed over the skylights, the doors, and in one of the long gallery windows (north facing). All that remains is to add one last rectangle light to the south-facing gallery window. To do just that, let's first of all perform the following steps:

1. Select the **South Facing Gallery Exterior Scene** tab to get ourselves into a good position to place the light.

2. Then, select the **Rectangle light** button from the V-Ray lights toolbar to enter light creation mode.

3. Now, we can move our mouse cursor to the outer upper-left corner of the gallery window and left-click once to start creating the light.

4. Then, we want to move the cursor to the point in the outer bottom-right corner of the window and left-click a final time to both finish creating the light and at the same time exit the create mode.

Although this initial positioning should work just fine, the last thing we want from our V-Ray light objects would be to create any extra noise or render artifacts due to having them inter-penetrating the geometry in the scene. To make certain this does not happen in this instance, let's perform the following steps:

1. With the light still selected, click on the **Over the Window Scene** tab to switch.

2. From the SketchUp toolbar, select the **Move** tool and then hover the mouse cursor over the far-left or far-right corner of the light object.

3. When a snap point highlights, press and hold the left arrow key on the keyboard to constrain movement to the green axis, and then move the light away from the window by about two foot.

As our light object was created at exactly the same size as the window opening, we do have a little bit of scaling that we need to do in order to get proper illumination coverage for the interior. To scale our light up, we can perform the following steps:

1. Switch back to our **South Facing Gallery Exterior Scene** tab.

2. With the Rectangle light still highlighted, select the scale tool from the V-Ray toolbar.

3. In each of its four dimensions, scale the light source up enough to ensure that it easily covers the window opening, as shown in the following screenshot:

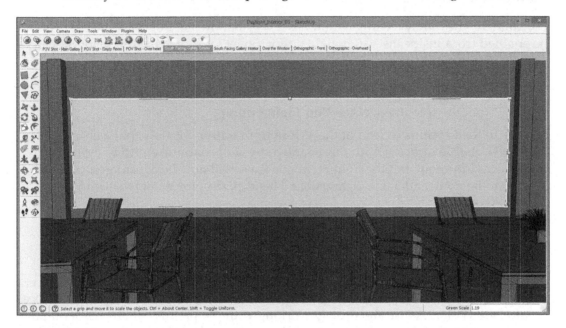

There are a couple of points to keep in mind regarding the V-Ray Rectangle light. Firstly, as this is a genuine area light, the larger it is, the more light it will emit even though the intensity value may remain unchanged. Secondly, the bigger the area light, the softer and more diffused the shadows we get from it. The inverse of this is also true; a small rectangle light will tend to give us very sharp shadows much like the defaults we get from point light sources such as V-Ray's Omni lights and Spotlights.

Having run through its creation, we will obviously want to check that everything is working correctly on the light. So, let's switch over to the **South Facing Gallery Interior** view by clicking on the tab, which will of course put us on the inside of the room. (If from this vantage point it seems to you that a little more scaling on the light object wouldn't go amiss, now would be the time to make that correction.)

One problem that we currently have is that our window is completely covered by the light object, giving us no ability to see through to the outside environment. Indeed, if we were to take a render at this point, our window opening would simply show as solid white.

Fortunately, the V-Ray rectangle light has a very handy piece of functionality that can be enabled from inside the V-Ray light editor. So let's perform the following steps:

1. Right-click on our rectangle light and come down to the **V-Ray for Sketchup** option.

2. From the flyout, select the **Edit Light** option.

3. In the **Options** section of the **V-Ray light editor** window, put a check in the **Invisible** option. (With this enabled, we will continue emitting light in the environment, but the light rectangle itself will now be considered by V-Ray to be non-renderable or invisible. This is perfect for what we need.)

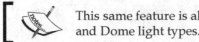 This same feature is also available on the V-Ray Sphere and Dome light types.

Another option that we may well want to tweak while we are in the Light Editor, one that can help us more closely emulate the look and feel of light coming from the sky, would be its color. As we are already working with the premise of our render taking place on a clear sunny day, we would perhaps expect the color contribution from the sky to be quite strong, having quite an obvious blue cast to it. To set this up, let's perform the following steps:

1. Click on the color swatch in the **Intensity** section to bring up the **Select Color** dialogue box.

2. To create a nice blue sky, we can set the HSV values to around **224**, **55**, **255**. (This same color has already been added to the other V-Ray Rectangle lights in the scene. However, feel free to experiment and create your own sky color at this point, if you would like to.)

3. When done, click on **OK** to accept the color change.

4. And finally, click on **OK** to exit the light editor.

Testing our shot views

Having walked through the basic process of adding and configuring a V-Ray rectangle light in a scene, our next job is to enable them all and take some test renders from our interior POV shot cameras. To do this, we could go into the V-Ray light editor and place a check in the **Enabled** option for each of the lights, one at a time. Or, to speed things up a little, we could just load the `Daylight_Interior_04.skp` file from the `Exercise_Files` folder which has all of the lights already turned on.

To get a clear idea of what our V-Ray Rectangle lights are contributing to the scene (in terms of illumination), we ideally need to take a number of renders from our interior views. Initially, I think we can take them using only the direct light contribution from the rectangle lights, but then it may also be worth taking a couple with the global illumination systems enabled. This will give us an idea of just how much light energy these substitute skylights are going to bounce around the interior environment.

As a final test, perhaps we can then take a render that adds the key or sunlight into the mix as well, giving us an opportunity to evaluate the ratio of key to fill light in the scene. This will show us whether or not any final tweaks will be required.

In order to save our test renders for comparison, we could set things up so that the images are saved directly to the hard disk using controls found in the **Output** rollout of the options editor. However, we will take this opportunity to look at a very cool option that can be enabled on the **V-Ray frame buffer** window itself.

With the **POV – Main Gallery Scene** view selected, let's click on the render button on the V-Ray toolbar to render our direct light image. Once that is finished, we can go ahead and save it to the hard disk by using the render history feature of V-Ray Version 2.0. This is a very handy set of tools that lets us quickly save the image shown inside the **V-Ray frame buffer** window to the hard disk and then, at a later point in time, load it back into the frame buffer for comparison with a different render. To show how this works, perform the following steps:

1. Click on the **H** button found among the icons along the bottom of the **V-Ray Frame Buffer** window.

2. In the **Render History** window, click on the **Save** icon to write a temporary V-Ray image file to your hard drive.

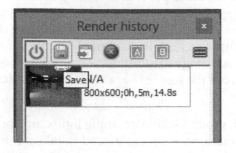

 If you want to change the default location where these images are saved, click on the **Settings** icon found on the far-right corner of the **Render History** window. In the history settings dialogue box, set a new file path.

3. Next click on the **POV – Empty Room Scene** tab and then hit the render button found on the far-right corner of the V-Ray frame buffer's top toolbar. Again, once that is finished, we can run through the process of saving it by means of the **V-Ray Render history** window.

Next, we need to turn on our GI systems. So, let's perform the following steps:

1. Open up the V-Ray options editor from the V-Ray toolbar.

2. In the **Indirect Illumination** rollout, put a check in the **On** box.

3. Once again, hit the render button, and when done, save it using **Render history**.

4. Repeat the render and save process for the **POV – Main Gallery** view as well, if required.

For the final test render, we need to enable our key light. We can do this by performing the following steps:

1. Select the **Orthographic - Front scene** tab.

2. Right-click on the V-Ray spotlight.

3. From the **V-Ray for SketchUp** flyout, select the **Edit Light** option.

4. In the V-Ray light editor, put a check in the **Enabled** option and click on **OK** to exit.

5.   Switch back to the **POV – Main Gallery** view by clicking on the scene tab.

6.   Finally, hit the render button and again save to the hard disk using the **Render history** window.

The evaluation time

With the renders completed and saved, one thing that we really should follow as a standard practice would be to always perform a comparative evaluation by examining and measuring what we are seeing in the images against the artistic definition that we created at the outset of our chapter. Ultimately, the questions we need to answer are: *am I (or are we) heading in the right direction with the lighting by using this particular approach? Can it produce the end result that we are after?*

To show how we can use the render history feature on the V-Ray frame buffer to make such an evaluation, let's perform the following steps:

1.   In the **Render history** window, click to select our initial render that should be right at the bottom of the stack by now.

2.   Then, on the toolbar of the same window, click on the **A** button to set this render as the **A** channel in the **V-Ray frame buffer** window.

Instantly, we get a split screen in the **V-Ray frame buffer** window with our newly selected **A** channel render showing up on the left while the currently rendered frame is shown on the right.

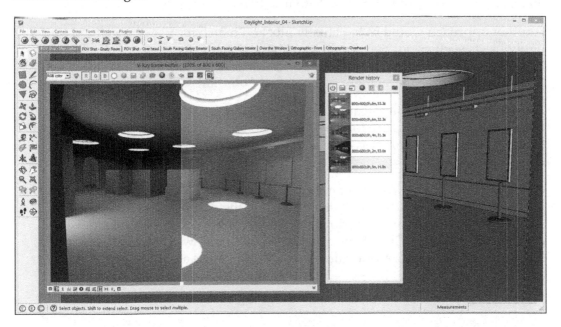

The divider line between the two in the frame buffer window gives us the ability to slide left and right over the two renders. This means that we can compare various elements of the two and decide whether or not the changes we have made have brought about an improvement in the newer render.

In this instance, clearly the final result with both GI and sunlight enabled looks far more natural than the original Rectangle light-only render. Obviously, we do need to keep in mind here that we are working with all of our quality settings as per V-Ray's default settings, and also that we haven't applied any actual surface properties to our materials as of yet.

Using the GI skylight

Our rectangle light setup is clearly capable of helping us add a daylight feel to our interior; one big drawback besides the required setup time would be the fact that there are quite obviously a lot of direct lights now required in the scene, all of which need to draw on processing power in order to create light and shadow effects. This, as you have probably already experienced, can slow down our renders by quite a significant amount.

These kinds of drawbacks have to be carefully weighed against the quality and flexibility (or indeed lack of such) that we get from the fill light solution when we use this particular approach. Such considerations become especially important given that, as we have already noted, this particular method for creating a skylight effect is not the only option available to us when using V-Ray.

Another approach would be to actually mix and match the use of specific V-Ray light objects such as our Sun spotlight with the default environment GI (skylight) that we used in the previous chapter. To test that out with this scene we will need to first of all disable the sunlight component of our Sun & Sky system.

To help us explore this approach, open up the `Daylight_Interior_05.skp` file from your `Exercise_Files` folder. This version of our interior scene takes us back to being in complete darkness once again, ready to build up a lighting solution using the GI (skylight).

One important difference between this and the rectangle light approach, one that we need to think carefully about, is the fact that the rectangle lights we were dealing with initially are recognized as direct light sources by V-Ray. This means we get light whether V-Rays GI systems are enabled or not. However, the GI (skylight) is an indirect light source, and as such, can give no light at all unless the GI systems are enabled.

Clearly, the first thing that we need to do in order to work with that option would be to turn the GI systems on. To do that, perform the following steps:

1. Open up the options editor from the V-Ray toolbar.
2. In the **Indirect Illumination** rollout, put a check in the **On** box.
3. Next, click to open up the **Environment** rollout.
4. Put a check in the **On** box for the **GI (skylight)** option.

By default, the GI skylight (with the TexSky map applied) has a V-Ray Sun element already enabled, which, of course, we are not using in this instance. To disable that, we need to perform the following steps:

1. Click on the map button next to the **GI (skylight) multiplier** spinner.
2. In the V-Ray texture editor, inside the **Default Sky Options** area, click on the **Sun** drop down and then choose the **None** option.
3. Click on **OK** to exit the **V-Ray texture editor** dialog box.

With those steps taken care of we are, believe it or not, ready to render with our GI (skylight) enabled.

As you can appreciate, this approach is far quicker and easier to set up than the V-Ray rectangle light solution, which is definitely a big plus. Let's click on the render button on the V-Ray toolbar then.

In a very short while, you will see another advantage of this particular skylight approach: it also renders far quicker than our array of V-Ray rectangle lights. This, of course, doesn't mean that there aren't drawbacks to this particular approach as well.

For one thing, our render shows that the occlusion or contact shadows in the scene are nowhere near as defined as they were with our V-Ray rectangle lights, and we also see a much stronger color cast in the environment that is not as simple to control as it was on the rectangle lights. There we had a simple color swatch, whereas here, because the V-Ray sky (or TexSky) map has been designed to be physically accurate with respect to both its light energy and the coloration it adds to an environment, the V-Ray sky map has no direct color control option as such.

As you can see, this option's physical accuracy can sometimes limit our ability to exercise artistic license in setting up a lighting solution. One quick and easy way to make a big change to the color coming from the sky map would be to change the algorithms being used to compute the sky model itself. To do this, we would need to perform the following steps:

1. Go back into the V-Ray texture editor by clicking on the GI (skylight) map button again.

2. In the **Default Sky Options** area, click on the **Sky Model** drop down and select **CIE Overcast** from the list.

3. Click **OK** to exit the texture editor.

If we click the render button on the toolbar now, we get (as you can see in the render) a much less saturated look from our skylight.

One potential drawback of using this option, however, is that because this color model has been designed to mimic an overcast sky, we do see a noticeable drop in the light energy levels that it outputs.

We could compensate for this drop by using the intensity multiplier value next to the map button. In all honesty though, if we want or need more control over the color quality of the skylight we are creating, we may decide that using the V-Ray Sky (TexSky) map is not really the best approach. Instead, we could decide to make use of a solid sky color, as we were in fact doing when using our rectangle light setup. To do this using the GI (skylight), let's follow the given steps:

1. Go back to **V-Ray texture editor** by clicking on the GI (skylight) map button.

2. In the drop down underneath the **Preview** button, select the **None** option found at the top of the list.

3. Click on **OK** to exit the V-Ray texture editor.

4. Click on the color swatch next to the **GI (skylight)** label and set the same sky blue color as used in our rectangle light setup (HSV values of around **224, 55, 255**).

If we were to take a render now, we would see that the level of color saturation added to the environment has been greatly reduced. Unfortunately, our level of illumination has also been greatly reduced, which is not really what we want. To counteract this, we can enter a value of 15 in the GI (skylight) multiplier field. This will take us back to roughly the same illumination level that we were getting from our V-Ray sky map.

At the end of this series of steps, we should end up with a render that looks like the following screenshot:

Again, with our Sun spotlight enabled, the GI (skylight) option would give us a very acceptable natural daylight simulation. One of the drawbacks of using just the GI (skylight) color swatch, however, (a drawback that also applied to our rectangle light setup) would be the fact that we are lacking any real variation from the skylights color contribution. When using the V-Ray sky map, we automatically get color shift and variation in the sky map as defined by the position of the V-Ray Sun in the sky. This is not so when using a flat color as we are here.

Another problem we see in this approach is the relative weakness of the occlusion or contact shadows in the scene. As this was one of the strengths of the rectangle light approach, this lack becomes very apparent here.

As with every aspect of rendering, the lighting choices available to us mean we are constantly trading the benefits of any particular approach with its drawbacks.

Trying out the Dome light

One skylight option available that would certainly improve the occlusion shadows in the scene would be the (new to V-Ray Version 2.0 for SketchUp), Dome light. This light takes its name from the fact that it provides us with a 180 degree, hemispherical dome of light that can give perfect skylight coverage to any scene. Now, of course, the **GI (skylight)** tool that we have just been working with does exactly the same thing. The big difference with the dome light, however, is that it doesn't need V-Ray's GI systems enabled in order to work given that it is, in fact, a direct light source. This, of course, is what gives it the ability to create much stronger occlusion shadows than its GI (skylight) counterpart.

To take a look at this powerful lighting tool, open up the `Daylight_Interior_06.` `skp` file from your `Exercise_Files` folder. This again resets the scene, bringing us back to complete darkness in our renders.

To create a Dome light in the scene, we need to perform the following steps:

1. Click to switch to the **Orthographic – Front Scene** view.

2. On the V-Ray lights toolbar, click on the Dome light option.

3. Left-click once in the viewport to set a starting point for the light's creation (somewhere around the midpoint of the building will be good).

4. Then move up in the blue axis and click a second time on a point roughly halfway between our building and the spotlight.

> These two points simply set the scale at which the dome light gizmo will be created in the scene. We need to be aware that both the scale and positioning of this gizmo in the scene make no difference at all to either the level or type of illumination that we get from the dome light. The only thing we need to take into account is the fact that its orientation does matter. Indeed, because this is a direct light, turning the dome on its side will in fact give us a sideways dome of directional light, which can in some instances be quite a handy trick to have available.

Once created, you should have something that looks pretty close to the screenshot we have here:

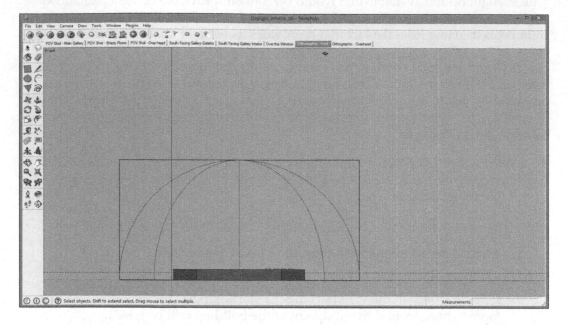

To set up our dome light's color and intensity options so that they match up with those of our previous skylight attempts, let's follow the steps given here:

1. Right-click on the dome light gizmo and select the **Edit light** option from the **V-Ray for Sketchup** flyout.

2. In the **Intensity** section of the controls, click on the color swatch and again set the HSV colors to **224**, **55**, and **255**.

3. While here, let's also set the intensity control to a value of **25** and then click on **Ok** to exit.

If we were to take a render at this point, I am pretty certain that you would feel a little disappointed with the final result, as the completely dark areas and the noise levels present in the image would present us with a very ugly-looking render. To improve things considerably, let's again add GI into the mix by performing the following steps:

1. Open up the option editor from the V-Ray toolbar.

2. Open up the **Indirect Illumination** rollout and put a check in the **On** box.

If we now switch back to the **POV – Main Gallery** view and take a render, we can see that things are starting to look reasonably promising.

Of course, we still have a number of issues that would need to be dealt with here, not least of which is the high level of noise still present in the scene. At some point we are going to have to work with V-Ray's sampling controls to clean things up considerably here.

Adding a High Dynamic Range Image to the mix

We are also still lacking any color variation in our sky model due to the fact that we are once again only working with a solid color in the dome lights controls. There is, however, one more option available to us that can help add a little bit of color variation back into this shot, one that just happens to work exceptionally well with the dome light: the use of a **High Dynamic Range Image** (HDRI) in the dome lights texture map slot.

> HDRI is a multi-exposure format (typically created in floating point) that is used to reproduce a much higher luminosity range than would be possible using standard non-float or 8 bit image file formats. HDR images give artists the ability to more accurately reproduce the range of intensity levels found in typical real-world environments.

To demonstrate how this works, I am going to make use of the fantastic IBL spherical map resources that can be found at http://www.hdrlabs.com/sibl/archive.html. The specific archive or set of maps that I will be working with are entitled **Etnies Skatepark**, so if you want to follow along with me over the next steps, feel free to download and make use of this same free HDRI archive.

The specific map from the set that I will use here is one that has been especially prepared for use in lighting. It is a much smaller file (both in terms of resolution and disk space) that has had a blur operation applied to it so as to help prevent adding any unnecessary artifacts to the render.

To add the HDRI to our dome light, let's perform the following steps:

1. Jump into the **Orthographic – Front view** scene by clicking on the scene tab.

2. Right-click once more on the dome light gizmo and from the **V-Ray for Sketchup** flyout, choose the **Edit light** option.

3. In the **Dome Settings** section, put a check in the **Use Dome Texture** box and then left-click on the **Dome Texture** map button.

4. From the drop-down under the **Preview** button in the V-Ray texture editor, select the **TexBitmap** option.

5. In the **Open Bitmap File** dialog box that appears, browse for the HDR image that you are wanting to use, (in my case, I will be using the Etnies_Park_Center_Env.hdr file) and then select and open it.

6. We need to gamma correct this image a little in order to lighten the color cast that it will add to the renders. So, in the controls found at the top of the options window, make certain that the **Color Space** option is set to **Gamma Corrected**.

7. Set the **Gamma** value, which is present just to the right, to **2.0**.

8. In the **UVW** section found at the bottom of the **V-Ray texure editor** window, select the **UVWGenEnvironment** option from the **UVW Type** drop-down.

 The **UVWGenEnvironment** option tells V-Ray that the HDRI map we are using is an Environment map, with a default mapping type of spherical setup, which is the format in which this particular light probe comes.

One major issue that would arise if we were to render the scene using our current setup would be the fact that the HDRI we are using was captured with the Sun high in the sky and in plain view. This means that we have inadvertently created a situation in which (with our V-Ray spotlight enabled) we will essentially have two Suns in the scene, both potentially casting conflicting shadows. (As our interior is not meant to be set in a galaxy far far away, this problem could seriously detract from the photographic quality of our final render.)

We can, however, create a little bit of a workaround by placing the Sun found in the HDRI at roughly the same location in world space as that occupied by our V-Ray spotlight. Now, while this is clearly not a perfect solution, it will hopefully cut out the chance of having two sets of shadows being cast in differing directions. To set this up, let's perform the following steps:

1. In the UVW controls of our HDRI, set the **Horizontal Rotation** field to a value of **260**.

2. Click on **OK** twice to exit both the texture and light editors.

3. Finally, switch back to the **POV – Main Gallery** view and hit the render button on the V-Ray toolbar.

What we get now (as the render clearly shows) is an image that has a very natural looking range of colors, especially in the areas where the sunlight from the HDRI is coming through the skylights, adding slightly warmer tones to the floor. We may feel that the blue color cast we get from our sky is still a little strong, but before we go ahead and make a final evaluation of that, we need to turn our Sun spotlight back on. To do that, we need to perform the following steps:

1. Jump back into our **Orthographic – Front Scene** view.

2. Right-click on the V-Ray spotlight and select the **Edit light** option from the **V-Ray for Sketchup** flyout.

3. Put a check in the **Enabled** option and click on **Ok** to exit the light editor.

4. Finally, switch back to our **POV – Main Gallery** scene view and hit the render button up on the V-Ray toolbar.

As we can see, doing so evens out the color cast in the scene quite a bit. This means that we can probably leave any final analysis and possible alterations until we have gone ahead and added materials to the scene as these will make a difference to the way that color from our light sources behaves in the environment.

Bringing the sky back into the view

One thing you may have noticed with the dome light renders that we have been taking here is the fact that our sky color (as seen through the circular skylights in the ceiling) has remained pretty much white, which may or may not be acceptable depending on what we are wanting from the scene. For my part, even though we could technically take care of this issue during postproduction, I would prefer to have a little more control over the coloration of the sky *in render* as it were so as to introduce a little more blue into the environment. To do that, let's follow the given steps:

1. Jump back into the **Orthographic – Front Scene** view.

2. Right-click on the V-Ray dome light and from the **V-Ray for Sketchup** flyout, select the **Edit light** option.

3. In the **Options** section, we need to put a check in the **Invisible** option.

4. Click on **Ok** to exit the light editor.

We can now go ahead and make use of V-Ray's **Reflection/refraction (background)** control to set up an image as the backdrop for our render. We can, of course, use any image we want here, but my personal preference would be to use either a non-blurred version of the same HDRI that is providing the skylight in the scene, or use a nice clean V-Ray sky map. To do the latter, we need to perform the following steps:

1. Open up the V-Ray option editor from the V-Ray toolbar.

2. In the **Environment** rollout, click on the map button for the **Reflection/ refraction (background)** control so as to open up the V-Ray texture editor window.

3. In the drop down below the **Preview** button, switch the **TexSky** map over to using a **TexBitmap**.

4. In the **Open Bitmap File** dialog box that appears, navigate to your EtniesPark_Center folder and this time select the Etnies_Park_ Center_3k.hdr file.

5. With **Gamma Corrected** set as the **Color Space** option, set the **Gamma** value to **2.0**.

6. Down in the **UVW** options, set the **UVW** type in the drop down to **UVWGenEnvironment** and set the **Horizontal Rotation** value to **260** (this means the location of the Sun in our background HDRI will match that being used by the lighting).

7. Click on **OK** to exit the texture editor and then set the multiplier value for the **Reflection/refraction (background)** control to **4.0**.

This value has no effect whatsoever on the lighting levels in the scene as it only controls the brightness of the image being rendered as the scene backdrop.

8. Finally, we can switch back to the **POV – Main Gallery** view and hit the render button one last time.

Our render shows that we now have some blue back in our sky that can easily be controlled and made lighter or darker whenever we wish.

Wrap up

Having run through a number of approaches then with regards to creating fill or skylight in the scene, I feel that this final combination of the V-Ray dome light and HDRI gives us the most versatile option to create the kind of lighting mood that we settled on in our artistic definition at the start of the chapter.

For this reason, I am going to save this file just where it is so that we can come back and use it when we get to the point of creating realistic materials for our scene geometry.

Summary

Let's quickly summarize the elements of creating a daylight solution for photographic rendering that we have covered in this chapter.

The first thing we need to keep in mind is that unless we approach every aspect of creating a photographic render with a clear, well thought out plan, there is a very good chance that we will fail to hit the required mark, whether that is one we set personally or by our client. We also need to make certain that our plan is put down as a permanent record somehow, be that written, painted, photographed, or compiled.

We also need to work smart. Rather than trying to reinvent the wheel each and every time we work on a new project, we should already have learned to work with a few tried and tested workflows that will get us most of the way towards a finished solution in a very short space of time. We also need to note that when working on lighting, every new light added to a scene should be test rendered in isolation, giving us a clear view of the illumination that particular light is adding to the environment. My preferred starting point is to have a completely dark scene into which we add and test each light.

The points we have mentioned here will become even more important as we move on to the next phase of learning to light with V-Ray, where we take a look at the options available to light a nighttime interior shot.

3

Lighting an Interior Nighttime Scene Using IES Lights

When it comes to creating visually compelling images, it is generally acknowledged that photographers always have to work that little bit harder and perhaps be a little more skillful in their craft when it comes to creating nighttime shots. This, in part, is because the whole image capture process becomes much more reliant on the photographer being able to configure the tools and technology at his or her disposal. Only then will they be able to get the best out of whatever shooting situation they find themselves in.

When working in nighttime conditions, camera settings and exposure options have to be configured with much more care and consideration than is necessary at other times. Insight and understanding have to be applied to the situation in order to get the best out of available light sources, be they natural or artificial. It may even be that photographers will find themselves needing to skillfully create or at the very least augment the existing lighting found in the environment.

In many ways, much the same can be said about creating genuinely photographic nighttime renders, be they the interior or the exterior type. In these scenarios, the role or skillset of both the CG render artist and the photographer can become somewhat interchangeable given that much of the same knowhow and understanding will need to be applied to the final setup in order to get the best possible image solution from it.

Taking a look at our SketchUp file

To work along with me as we look at creating a nighttime interior lighting setup, load the `Night_Time_Interior_01.skp` file from your `Exercise Files` folder so that we can go ahead and take a look at how the scene is currently set up. Take a look at the following screenshot:

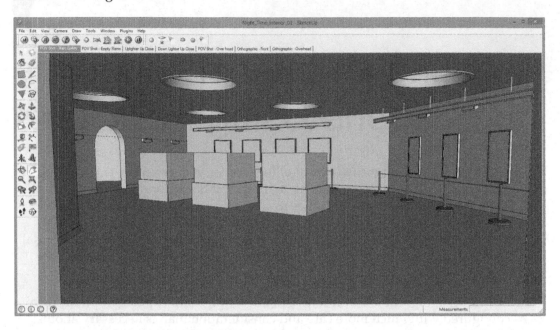

As you can see, we once again have a number of different camera views already available in the scene, all of which we will be making good use of as we work through the lighting setup in this chapter. They are for the most part identical to the daytime version of this file that we have already worked with, other than the fact that we now have a couple of extra working views that can help us with both the placement and checking of light objects in the scene.

Defining our goals

Before we create any kind of lighting setup in the scene, we need to first of all create our definition or vision regarding what we want to accomplish in our final render(s). At the risk of starting to sound a little repetitive, it is important that we get this created so that it can serve as the guide or blueprint that we use as we move through creating this somewhat different lighting setup.

Observation is crucial

Now, while a definition created entirely from our own imagination can be used as a blueprint for our scene, it isn't generally speaking the best way to go about creating a document that, as we have noted a few times already, is fairly important with regards to the success of the project.

Even if we are working at creating a completely fantastical lighting setup — something that doesn't exist in the real world — we still need to create it based on the reality of how light works. The behavior of light is something that those who view our images will be incredibly familiar with; after all, they see and make use of it every day of their lives, and even though they may not fully understand the physics of how it works, they will instinctively spot mistakes in its behavior.

Once again then, before fixing on the definition that we will use to create the mood or feel for a particular scene, going ahead and gathering reference notes and photographs should be considered an essential part of the process.

In regards to this particular scene, if you have a local gallery or exhibition space that has nighttime sessions (ones that are open to the public, of course), be sure to go along and take notes regarding important elements such as the style of the lighting used and the mood it appears designed to create.

Make a note of the number of light fixtures in the space, the positioning, and even their coloration. If you do find a very particular lighting effect that you realize would look very nice in the render you are trying to create, be sure to document as much about its setup and apparent creation as you possibly can.

If a field trip such as this is not an option, then we can make good use of image searches on the internet, taking the time to compile a varied collection of images that contain different types of lighting fixtures, styles, and feels that we like and that we think will suit the space we are currently working on.

Another option would be to describe in writing or perhaps even capture using a vocal recording, the mood we see being created inside the photographs we are viewing. Keep in mind that one very powerful tool overlooked by many visualization artists is their own emotional reaction to a particular environment or photograph of an environment. By that, I simply mean the way an image strikes you and the feel or mood it suggests to you.

Interior lighting is designed to evoke an automatic emotional response of some sort from us whenever we are present in that space. Obviously, when we are using photographs as a source of reference and inspiration, something of the "automatic" aspect of that response may be missing, which means we may have to work a little harder to capture the feeling that a given lighting solution has been designed to elicit. What we end up with in our lighting designs, however, will often make that little bit of extra effort well worth our while.

My definition for interior nighttime scene lighting

For the sake of speed here, as in the previous chapter, we are going to simply create a very brief text outline of what we want to accomplish with the lighting in this particular chapter.

For this particular space, I would like our renders to have a kind of "after hours" feel to them. The kind of lighting that perhaps only the night guard or maybe VIP's on a special evening tour of the gallery would be likely to see. Indeed, what I have in mind to create will contain way too many areas of shadow or darkness for the lighting scheme to be used when the gallery is open to the public.

This will hopefully give us a nice atmospheric contrast to the bright and airy feel of our previous daylight setup and will also require us to make use of V-Ray's lighting and **Global Illumination (GI)** tools in quite a different way. This, of course, can only be good practice for us as we work towards becoming familiar with the workings of the V-Ray engine and its tools.

The lighting process

Having defined the kind of mood we want to create inside our space, our next set of considerations would need to be based around the tools available to us in our render engine of choice. They should be focused on figuring out how the tools can be used to bring our definition to life. In other words, what kind of approaches can we and will we take given the tools that we have available?

Contrasting artistic and realistic indoor lighting

We could decide to take a more artistic rather than realistic approach to the lighting; maybe you have in your mind the creation of a render that has a bit of a suspenseful atmosphere about it—something along the lines of a film noir feel perhaps.

While such a lighting scheme would still need to be based at least somewhat in reality, the contrast between light and shadowed areas would need to be artificially enhanced, generally creating very bright pools of light that are starkly contrasted with darker-than-usual shadowed areas.

Such artistic approaches are certainly possible using the lighting tools that V-Ray provides. For this reason, we may want to spend time in our reference gathering phase looking not just at still-image photography of real world interior lighting, but also at cinematic and possibly stage lighting setups as well.

Of course in our case, the brief for the project, which is to create a series of photographic renders, instantly tells us that we need to be focused here on a more realistic rather than artistic approach to our lighting.

Do we have a key light?

One important consideration with regard to the design of an interior lighting scheme would be the decision as to whether or not there should be a key light in the scene. Remember, the key light would be the main source of illumination and shadow casting in the scene—the one that tends to provide a measure of directionality and, indeed, motivation for the illumination in the environment.

 The term **motivation** when applied to lighting setups, generally refers to the fact that the light in the scene has an obvious source that it is coming from or is motivated by.

While in a domestic setting, rooms may often have a key or main light source, this typically isn't the case with spaces such as the one we are working with here. In this kind of environment, the idea is generally speaking to achieve the required level and spread of illumination by means of lots of smaller, strategically placed light sources rather than having just a few extremely bright ones.

To make the definition that we created a few moments ago work for us, we will probably want to forego a key light in this instance and work instead to create more contrast in the scene by using a number of low-level light sources. Now, I use the word *probably* because as we are creating the lighting solution for any scene, we should always be open to possibilities and be ready to try out new ideas as and when the opportunity arises. If we suddenly see some where a key light could be used, maybe to create a unique point of focus in the scene, then we should certainly be prepared to test that out and evaluate the new idea's potential.

While having a blueprint to work with helps to keep us focused and organized, sticking to it so rigidly that we lock ourselves out of any possible improvements to the lighting of a scene would be a very bad mistake to make indeed.

Understanding the IES files

All of that having been said, I am thinking that for the most part, we can probably stick to using V-Ray's IES light type here as this will both simplify the workflow for us while at the same time enhancing the realism of the lighting setup we are creating.

Having chosen this as the approach we are going to take, it would probably be a good idea to take a moment or two here to outline exactly what a V-Ray IES light is, as well as pointing out why they make an excellent light choice given the type of scenario we are working with here.

Illuminating Engineering Society (IES) are in fact the originators of the IES file format. The file type was created as a means of digitally profiling the photometric data for any light fixture as well as then having the ability to both easily view and distribute the data to anyone who wanted or needed it. The IES format is widely used by many of the industry's leading lighting manufacturers at the time of this writing and has become one of the, if not *the* industry standard in photometric data distribution.

Because they contain a digital profile of a real-world light unit (in 3D software packages that support them), the IES files can be used to create light sources that have physically accurate energy distribution and throw patterns attached, giving them an extremely realistic look and feel when used inside our 3D scenes.

Downloading and viewing IES profiles

One of the brilliant things about IES files is that lighting manufacturers such as ERCO often make them freely available for the light fixtures that they create. This of course is extremely good news for 3D artists and lighting engineers, who can put them to very good use on both visualization and lighting analysis projects.

[Visit http://www.erco.com for more details.   ]

Take a look at the following screenshot:

As well as being able to download IES files themselves, IES viewer applications on the **World Wide Web** (**WWW**) may also be found, which can be extremely useful when it comes to figuring out the type of effect that a given IES file will produce. Again, these are often freely available and will be extremely useful when the time comes to assess the usefulness of a specific IES profile to our project.

With these viewer applications, we typically get to see a two-dimensional representation of the light energy and distribution patterns contained inside any given IES file. This comes in the form of a polar diagram that shows the angular spread of the fixtures' luminous intensity.

The following screenshot that you see is taken from an online photometric viewer by Acuity Brands found at their Visual-3d website (`www.visual-3d.com/tools/photometricviewer/`).

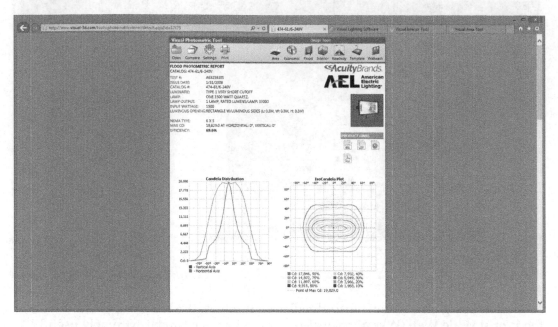

One extremely helpful tool and a particular favorite of mine is the Photometric Toolbox that can be freely downloaded from Cooper Industries website at `http://www.cooperindustries.com/content/public/en/lighting/resources/design_center_tools/photometric_tool_box.html`.

As seen in the following screenshot, this toolbox has lots of data options available, with one particularly useful aspect of the application being the fact that it has an IES viewer that is capable of giving us both a 2D and a 3D representation of the light distribution pattern contained in the IES file along with all sorts of data regarding the likes of lumen and candela output from the file. This makes it extremely useful when it comes to evaluating which IES profiles we may want to use in a particular scene.

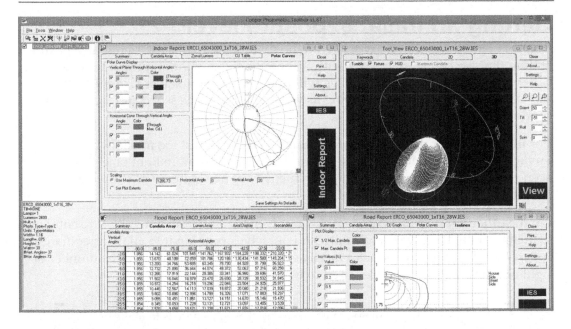

When it comes to creating photorealism in our renders, there is no doubt that having a collection of IES files (preferably categorized and catalogued) along with at least one viewer application can often prove to be an invaluable source of help when it comes to setting up realistic interior lighting rigs.

Starting with a blank canvas

Armed with a fairly good idea of the direction we want to take as well as having some thoughts in mind regarding the lighting tools that we will use, it's time to move on to the creation of our lighting solution in the scene.

We would typically want to start our lighting scheme using what I refer to as a blank canvas, by which I mean a totally dark scene. In this instance though, as we will be making use of the V-Ray Sun and Sky system in a little while, we will skip this so as to avoid performing unnecessary steps.

Setting an initial exposure level

The very first thing that we will need to do then is set up at least an initial exposure setting that we can start to work with. Without a fixed point of reference in the form of some typical exposure values, we will probably find ourselves struggling to make any sense out of what we are seeing as we add lights to the scene and make our test renders.

For instance, if our initial exposure settings were to cut out too much light from the environment, we could find ourselves adding more and more light objects to the scene or possibly even cranking up the intensity of our lights so as to create enough illumination to see by.

On the other hand, if our exposure settings were to allow too much light to enter our virtual camera, then we could easily find ourselves running into all manner of ugly hotspot and/or burnout issues as well as probably having to reduce the number of light objects and/or intensities so as to not over-illuminate the scene.

 As the whole point of our using IES lights here is to make use of real-world lighting data for the intensities, any solution that involves artificially altering the light intensities would probably be extremely counterproductive.

It is true though that as photography and 3D rendering are both forms of art, the whole question of which setting gives us the correct exposure could well be described as being somewhat subjective. This means anything we set up here should only be used as a suggested starting point, one that works well for this particular scene. Indeed, in this case, we will start off using some very middle-of-the-road settings for our exposure as this will hopefully give us quite a bit of flexibility when the time comes to settle on definite exposure values for use in the final renders.

That said, let's perform the following steps to set the exposure level:

1. In the **Option** editor, open the **Camera** rollout.
2. Set the **Shutter Speed** value to **250**.
3. After that, we can set **F Number** as **8**.
4. Finally, use a **Film Speed** or **ISO** setting of **1200**.

Unlike a real-world camera, we can go as high or low as we want with the ISO setting in V-Ray as it will never affect the amount of noise or grain present in the final image.

If we need a quick introduction to working with exposure settings on real-world cameras, you may want to check out this excellent article on the wikihow website `http://www.wikihow.com/Understand-Camera-Exposure`.

Adding some much-needed ambience

Now, before we proceed with our first lighting step, I do need to add a disclaimer here. The choice regarding whether or not to add this step is purely a matter of personal preference. Not all visualization artists include it in their personal workflow, and so I would recommend that you try lighting the scene both with and without it. In the end, simply weigh the time it takes to include it against the extra (if any) quality that you feel it adds.

Having gotten that out of the way, one thing I always like to try and do when starting an interior lighting setup such as this one is get at least a hint of the outdoor lighting conditions to show up on the interior render. In this instance, this would mean bringing some of the ambient light from the exterior moonlit sky to the inside. This generally speaking amounts to a subtle effect that should add just a small measure of purple and blue tones to the dark or shadowed areas of an interior image.

It is, to be honest, a difficult effect to achieve to a satisfactory degree in any render engine, which is why (as we noted) lots of render artists tend to skip it altogether and instead let a background color or even an image added in post production suggest ambient lighting conditions rather than trying to include them in the V-Ray render itself.

As this is meant to be a learning experience, however, we are going to see how such a lighting effect could potentially be approached using the tools and options that V-Ray presents to us.

Using the V-Ray Sky

Perhaps the first option that we might think of trying would be V-Ray's Sun and Sky elements along with SketchUp's Shadow settings controls. We noted in *Chapter 2, Lighting an Interior Daytime Scene*, that this system gives us a physically accurate method for recreating lighting and sky coloration according to the time of day and the month of the year that we specify.

Well, as we already have the Sun and Sky elements enabled in the scene, let's:

1. Click on the **Window** menu at the top of the SketchUp UI and open up the **Shadows** control dialogue.

    As soon as we try to dial in a nighttime setting, however, we should instantly see the problem that we naturally run into. The **Time** slider control limits the range of time that we can work with, only allowing us to set the slider somewhere between sunrise and sunset.

     The exact times available to us for sunrise and sunset will of course vary according to the month of the year and the time zone settings that we are working with.

    Now it may occur to us to bypass the slider altogether and try typing more suitable values into the numeric fields themselves, maybe setting the time of day to, for example, **23:00** hours. If we do that, be prepared to see some very strange color effects going on in any test renders that we may make. More than likely, we will end up with odd results that make it look as though we have entered into some kind of alternate dimension.

    One way that we could get something along the lines of what we are looking for would be to make some changes to the V-Ray Sky map itself. To take a look at just what we could do there, let's continue with the following steps:

2. In the **Environment** rollout of the V-Ray option editor, Click on the **GI (skylight)** map button.

3. In the V-Ray **texture editor** that pops up, disable the **sun** plugin by clicking on the dropdown in the **Default Sky Options** section and selecting the **None** option.

4. We can then access the **Sky Model** dropdown in the same section and set that to use **CIE Overcast**.

5. Set the **Horizon Illum** value all the way down to **125**.

6. After that, click on **OK** to exit **texture editor**.

7. We also need to click on the **Map** button for the **Reflection/refraction (background)** option and this time in the **Sun** controls section, set the **Sky Model** to **CIE Overcast**.

8. With the **Horizon Illum** value set at **2**, finally click on **Ok** to exit.

If we now go ahead and render, we should see a very small amount of ambient lighting in the scene that could be used as a starting point from which to build an interior lighting setup. I say *could* because for me, this particular approach, while working of a fashion, is a little bit limited in that it really gives us only a single level of control with which to work, that being the level or amount of illumination that gets added to the scene by means of the GI (skylight) control.. Ideally, I would like to have at least a little control over the coloration that gets added into the environment as well.

It is true that we could use the **Ozone**, **Turbidity**, and **Water Vapor** parameters in the GI (skylight) TexSky controls to get a little bit of color variation going on here, but from a control perspective these options are neither very intuitive to work with, nor do they offer a great deal of control when it comes to doing any kind of real color correction work.

The GI skylight

What then about trying just the GI (skylight) option on its own, taking the V-Ray Sky map out of the equation? That would at least give us the ability to make use of the **Color** swatch control, just as we did in our earlier daylight setup.

Well, let's try that approach and see what we can come up with. To do so, we need to perform the following steps:

1. Click on the **GI (skylight) map** button to open up the V-Ray **texture editor**.
2. In the map dropdown, just below the **Preview** button, choose the **None** option that can be found at the top of the list.
3. Click on **OK** to exit the **texture editor**.
4. Repeat the process for the **Reflection/refraction (background)** controls, also setting the **map** option to **None**.
5. Again, click on **OK** to exit the **texture editor**.
6. Next, we need to click on the **Color swatch** control for the GI (skylight) and set the color as follows: **Hue** as **240**, **S** as **146**, **V** as **14**.
7. Finally, click on **OK** to exit the **Select Color** dialog.

If we were to take a render at this point, we would again see a very faint level of ambient illumination in the scene. Now while this also could be used, the fact that we are working with just a flat color in itself detracts a little bit from the potential realism of the lighting setup as we aren't really getting any of the subtle color variations that naturally exist even on a fairly dark, moonlit night.

Also, a little less saturation than we currently have would probably be good, but of course, the truth is that when working with such dark values, subtle color variations are very difficult to dial in using only a 0 to 255 color range.

HDRI to the rescue

What about trying one final option. Let's see if it is possible to create the ambient light we want by again making use of a **High Dynamic Range Image (HDRI)**. To do this, of course we will need a HDRI that is suitable for our purposes, so once again I am going to make use of the HDRI resources found over at `hdrlabs.com`. And although it may sound a little strange, I am in fact going to make use of the same Etnies Skatepark image set that we used in our previous daylight setup.

Remember if you want to follow along with the steps we are taking in this section, feel free to download the same HDRI archive from http://www.hdrlabs.com/sibl/archive.html.

Now you may be wondering how we can use a daytime HDRI to create low-level, nighttime ambient lighting? Well it is one of the beauties of the HDRI format that, due to the fact that it contains such a wide range of illumination information in its dynamic range, it can still be extremely usable even when effectively turned down to very low-intensity levels. To demonstrate what we mean, let's perform the following steps:

1. In the **Environment** rollout of the option editor, click on the **GI (skylight) map** button.
2. From the dropdown underneath the **Preview** button, select the **TexBitmap** option.
3. In the **Open Bitmap File** window that pops up, browse for and select the HDRI file that you will be using. (In my case, the `Etnies_Park_Center_Env.hdr` file.)
4. In the **UVW** section at the bottom of the editor controls, set **UVW Type** to **UVWGenEnvironment**.
5. Click on **OK** to exit **Editor**.

Let's take a render at this point to see how things are shaping up by clicking on the **Render** button up on V-Ray's main toolbar.

As you can see in the finished image, while producing a reasonably decent overall effect, the current GI (skylight) intensity value of 1.0 is perhaps just a little too bright for what we are trying to create here. We also have more color saturation showing up in the scene than is perhaps necessary or desirable.

To fix the problems that I am seeing, let's first of all reduce the intensity of the HDRI by effectively dialing down its brightness:

1. We can do this by setting the **GI (skylight) intensity spinner** value to **0.05**.

2. And we can then adjust the saturation of the image a little by clicking on the **GI (skylight) map** button and with the **Color Space** value in the controls at the top set to **Gamma Corrected**, set the **Gamma** value just to the right to a value of **2.0**, and click on **OK** to exit the editor.

As always, whenever making subtle changes we really need to see how effective they are by taking yet another test render. Take a look at the following screenshot:

Not only does that alteration give us a much subtler ambient lighting effect, but we also get (although both effects may be a little difficult to see here), a reduction in the perceived saturation of color bounce in the scene. As what we have here is pretty much exactly what I wanted from this basic ambient light setup, I am going to stick with the GI (skylight) and HDRI option for now and build the rest of my interior light rig on top.

If you are wondering why we are not trying out the V-Ray Dome light on this occasion, the simple truth is that in such low-light conditions, the extra noise generated by the dome light on interior renders would be extremely difficult to clean up and would certainly prove costly in terms of the render time required. I would again though, for the sake of experimentation that leads to understanding, encourage you by all means to give the Dome light a try and evaluate the results that you get from it.

Layering up our IES lights

As we are going to be working exclusively with V-Ray's IES light type from this point on, the first thing we will want to do is get one of them placed in the scene. This will give us the ability to take a look at its controls and also see how we go about attaching one of the IES profiles we discussed earlier. Before we just jump into that and in the spirit of keeping our scene as organized and easy to work with as possible, we are just going to create some layers that we can add our lights to as we go. At this point, you can either continue working with the scene file you currently have open or from the `Exercise Files` folder, load the `Night_Time_Interior_02.skp` file.

The approach I have decided to use is to create specific light layers for the different types of geometry light fixtures that are present in the scene. As you can see in the viewport, we have up lighters that will be used for general illumination purposes, and we also have down lighters or wash lights that are being used to illuminate the wall hanging exhibits.

As it would be good to have the ability to control and evaluate both light types separately (remember, in SketchUp, a hidden layer effectively turns off all light objects that are placed on it), we are going to create a layer for each light type. To set our layers up, perform the following steps:

1. From the **Window** menu, click to open the **Layers** dialog.
2. Click on the plus icon at the top of the dialog twice to create two new layers.
3. Let's name the already highlighted layer `Up Lights`.
4. After that, double-click on the second layer, and rename it `Down Lights`.

With the required layers in place, we can now create an IES light object and then take a look at how it can be controlled and put to work as a usable light source in the scene.

Adding the IES down lighters

To get into position to add our first IES light, let's click on the **Down Lighter Up Close** scene tab, which has been set up to give us a nice close-up view of the ceiling-based light fixtures in the scene. The IES light objects themselves, like all V-Ray lights, can be created directly from the **VfS: Lights** toolbar. To do this, perform the following steps:

1. Click on the **IES** button on the toolbar to engage the create mode.
2. Click on a point on the fixture geometry to create an IES light at that point in 3D space.

3. Next, select SketchUp's **Scale** tool, and scale the light to 50 percent of its initial size.

4. Finally, move it into position using SketchUp's **Move and Rotate** tools as required (match the lights position to the screenshot images as closely as possible):

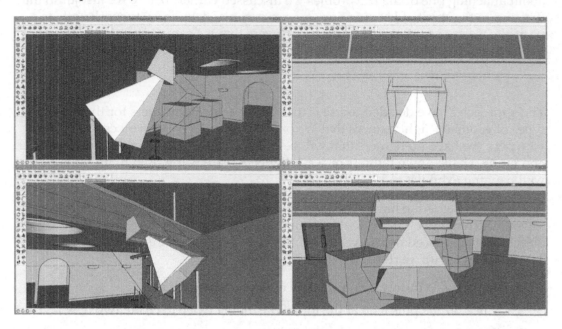

With our first IES light in place, it is (generally speaking) a good practice to perform as much setup on the lights' properties as we reasonably can at this point before copying it to create the full complement of exhibit lights that we require.

As the light's scaling has already been taken care of, what we need to do now is to attach an IES profile to the light and then tweak whatever options we feel would be appropriate.

As with HDRI files, the Web offers lots of freely available IES files, most of them, as we have mentioned, come from light fixture manufacturers themselves. In this instance though, the IES files I will be using in the scene come from `http://mayazest.blogspot.co.uk/2012/02/free-light-ies-files.html`.

To add an IES profile to our light, with the SketchUp **Select** tool active, we need to perform the following steps:

1. Right-click on the light object.

2. From the list, select the **V-Ray for Sketchup** option.

3. From the flyout, select **Edit light**.

4. In the **V-Ray light editor**, click on the **File** browse button in the **Options** section, and navigate to the IES file you want to attach (I will be using the file entitled `30.ies`).

5. Highlight the file and then click on **Open**.

6. Click on **OK** to exit the **V-Ray light editor**.

   As easily as that we have attached real-world lighting data that includes both intensity and distribution patterns to the V-Ray IES light object, and so we are now ready to give it a test render. To do that, follow the next steps.

7. Make certain we are looking through the **POV Shot - Main Gallery** camera.

8. Next, click on the **Render** button up on the V-Ray toolbar.

Take a look at the following screenshot:

As you can see in the render, what we get looks pretty good, given that we are shooting for a subdued, after-hours feel to the lighting. However, it may well be that once a number of these lights are added into the scene (along also with the up lighters that we will be putting in place in just a little while), we could possibly end up with more illumination in the environment than we really want. That, however, is a bridge we will cross when we come to it.

What we need to do right now of course is replicate our light by placing a copy in front of each of the wall-mounted frames that need illuminating. Unfortunately, even though turning our light into a component would be the ideal way to proceed at this point, this option hasn't worked very well since before V-Ray Version 1.49. with certain light types only correctly updating intermittently once they are turned into components. In fact, the IES light itself seems to only update the IES profile attached to it, ignoring other light properties.

Still, as this is a minor glitch that will no doubt be taken care of in due course, we will go ahead regardless and walk you through the process of turning a V-Ray light object into a component. The only thing we need to do at the moment is make sure that all of the relevant light properties are set exactly as we want them before we go ahead and actually create a new component from the light.

 Having our light as a component will give us the ability to quickly and easily update all of the lights at the same time by simply editing just a single instance of them.

The first thing we may want to do is warm the color of our lighting up a touch by performing the following steps:

1. Right-click on the light object itself, and then from the menu list select the **V-Ray for Sketchup** option.

2. From the flyout, select **Edit light**, and in the **V-Ray light editor**, click on the **Filter Color** option in the **Intensity** section.

3. Now we alter the HSV color settings to read: **Hue 17**, **Sat 31**, and **Val 255**, which gives us pretty much the color produced by a 5500 Kelvin lamp.

4. Click on **Ok** to exit the **V-Ray light editor**.

Once that is taken care of, with the SketchUp Select tool active, we can go ahead and set up our light as a component with the help of the following steps:

1. Right-click on the IES light object in the scene, and then select the **Make Component** option from the menu.

2. From the **Window** menu, select the **Components** option.

3. In the editor, make sure that you are viewing the **In Model** components by clicking on the **In Model** button.

4. Locate the new **V-Ray Light** entry and select it.

5. In the naming field right at the top of the editor, modify the component name slightly so that it reads, `V-Ray IES Down Light`. (If you like, you can also add a useful description to the **Component Definition Description** box just below it.)

6. Finally, hit the escape key on your keyboard to exit the **Component** placement mode.

If we now right-click on our light object, we may become concerned about the fact that we appear to have lost the ability to actually edit its properties. This happens due to the fact that the light object as a group has been placed inside a component node. To make the light group editable, we will first need to double-click on the light component and then right-click on the now-exposed light group in order to get to the light editor in the usual way. Again, the workflow may be a little confusing at first, but it all makes perfect sense once you get into the flow.

Now we are ready to create two banks of our down lights, with each individual light object pointing straight at the wall-mounted frames. To start the process, we need to perform the following steps:

1. Click on the **Down Lighter Up Close Scene** tab to get ourselves into a better position.

2. After doing so, we can then use the viewport navigation tools to focus on a currently unoccupied piece of down light geometry.

3. Now, we can again click to select the **V-Ray IES Down Light** component in the editor and follow exactly the same placement procedure as per our initial IES light.

We will of course need to repeat this process for each of the unoccupied down light fixtures, but as this is really a function of SketchUp and not V-Ray itself, we are going to jump ahead a little and load the `Night_Time_Interior_03.skp` file from the `Exercise files` folder.

Of course, if as a means of practice you want to keep going with the current scene and place each of the light components yourself, please feel free to do so, and then continue from this point once you have them all placed correctly.

 Just be aware that in the `Night_Time_Interior_03.skp` version of this scene, all of the lights are unique objects rather than components, and so will require individual rather than collective editing.

Once the lights are replicated, this would seem as good a point as any to take a test render and see how things are looking. To do this, let's go up to the V-Ray toolbar and hit the render button. Take a look at the following screenshot:

Our final task for this group of IES lights is to make sure that we have them all assigned to the correct layer. Doing that is very easy in SketchUp; all we need to do is perform some simple steps shown as follows:

1. Select all of the IES light objects by holding down the *Ctrl* key and clicking on each of them in turn (be sure to get all eight).
2. Right-click on the selection, and select **Entity Info** from the list.
3. In the **Layer** drop-down list, select the **Down Lights** layer we created earlier.
4. Close the Info box by clicking on the X (exit option) in the top right-hand corner.

All of our exhibit's down lights are now nicely organized on their own layer, which we can go ahead and hide while we work at setting up our second set of IES lights. To do this, perform the following steps:

1. From the **Window** menu, select the **Layers** option.
2. Remove the check from the **Down Light** layers visible column to hide it. (Keep in mind that the **Scene** tab will need updating if we want these lights to remain hidden; otherwise, we will need to hide them again each time we switch back to this view).

With that done, it is now time to add our up lighters.

Creating the IES up lighters

As adding these into the scene will follow our previous set of steps pretty closely, we can go ahead here and move through this process fairly quickly. The first thing we need to do is create a new IES light object, one that can serve as the **Up Lighter** template for a whole group. To do this, perform the following steps:

1. Click on the **Up Lighter Up Close** scene tab to get up close to one of the **Up Lighter** fixtures.

2. Select the **IES Light** button on the **V-Ray** toolbar.

3. Click on a point on the light fixture to create and position the IES light object.

4. Rescale to about 20 percent of the original size.

5. In this case. We will be using a down lighter IES file to create the effect we want we will have to rotate the light object by 90 degrees, effectively turning it upside down. (We can do this using either SketchUp's **Move** or **Rotate** tools.)

6. Once rotated, we want to place it inside our fixture geometry, making sure that the light cone stays above the internal face of the geometry. (This ensures that light emission is not blocked.)

7. Perform a final check to ensure that your light is positioned to match the screenshot images:

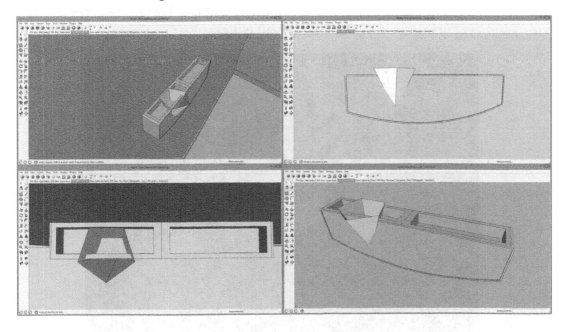

As with our down lights, we will want to add an IES profile to our light so as to get an interesting throw pattern on the wall. To do that, let's perform the following steps:

1. Right-click on the light object, and choose the **V-Ray for Sketchup | Edit light** options.

 Now you may find at this point that your light already has an IES profile attached to it. This again seems to be a part of the components glitch with V-Ray lights that I mentioned a few moments ago. As this can be ignored without causing problems, let's just go ahead.

2. From **V-Ray light editor**, select the browse button for the **File** option.

3. Again we need to browse to the IES file we wish to attach to this light. (In my case, the IES file entitled `7.ies` taken from the archive found at `http://mayazest.blogspot.co.uk/2012/02/free-light-ies-files.html`.)

4. Click on **Open**, and then click on **OK** to exit **V-Ray light editor**.

Once again, we will want to test the results we are getting from the IES file and the positioning of the light, so let's click on the **POV Shot - Main Gallery** scene tab to get our render view back, hiding the down lights again if we want to, and then going up to the V-Ray toolbar, let's click on the **Render** button.

As you can see in the screenshot, with our current settings, this is a small (from this view) and yet fairly interesting looking spread of light.

As the geometry for the light fixture is clearly split into two compartments, we will need to create a copy of the light to sit in the second section as well as then replicating both lights so that each of the **Up Lighter** fixtures has a pair of IES light objects associated with it.

This of course means turning our light into a component, although before we go ahead and do that, we will want to make sure that any final tweaks have all been applied to the light. As we will more than likely want the same, or at least a similar, warm color as our down lights, let's continue by performing the following steps:

1. Right-click on the light object itself, and then from the menu list, select the **V-Ray for Sketchup** option.

2. From the flyout, select **Edit light**, and in the **Light Editor**, click on the **Filter Color** option in the **Intensity** section.

3. In this instance, let's alter the HSV color settings to make the lamps resemble a 4500 Kelvin light source. This means using the settings: **Hue** as **20**, **Sat** as **69**, and **Val** as **255**.

4. Click on **OK** to exit **V-Ray light editor**.

It's time then to replicate our lights. Again if you want to go ahead and do that in this scene, please feel free; but for the sake of speed, we will go ahead and open up `Night_Time_Interior_04.skp` from the `Exercise files` folder.

Again, as a final step, we need to make sure that we have all our up lighter IES objects assigned to their own layers. To do this, perform the following steps:

1. Select all of the up lighter IES lights by holding down the *Ctrl* key and clicking on each of them in turn.

2. Right-click on the selection, and select **Entity Info** from the list.

3. In the dropdown **Layer** list, select the **Up Lights** layer that we created earlier.

4. Close the Info box by clicking on the X sign (exit button) in the top right-hand corner.

With everything nicely organized, we probably should take another test render and see what we are getting from the up lighters in the scene. Up on the V-Ray toolbar, let's hit the **Render** button. Take a look at the following screenshot:

Evaluating the render with all lights enabled

At this point, we are probably going to want to take a render that makes use of all the IES lights that we have now added into the scene. Rendering the individual fixture types has been beneficial, but we cannot make a proper evaluation of the lighting scheme for the environment without a render that makes use of all the light sources. To do this, let's perform the following steps:

1. Go up to the **Window** menu, and open up the **Layers** dialog.
2. Put a check in the **Down Lights** layer to make it visible.
3. Close the **Layers** dialog.

4. Then click on the **Render** button on the **V-Ray** toolbar.

Previsualizing image corrections using V-Ray FrameBuffer

One thing you may be questioning at this point could be the reason why we appear to have kept our renders quite so dark throughout this chapter? After all, doesn't V-Ray have lots of tools and options that could have been used to brighten things up just a little? Well the answer to that question would most certainly be yes.

We could, for instance, have altered our camera's exposure settings, or worked with non linearized materials, meaning they would bounce a lot more light around the environment. We haven't taken any of those steps however so that we could give you a taste of just how powerful V-Rays floating point rendering can be when combined with the power of image post-processing tools.

The brilliant thing about V-Ray is that we don't even have to go into an image-editing application such as Photoshop in order to actually use this workflow. We can instead do some basic image post-processing or color correction using the tools that are built right into the V-Ray frame buffer itself.

These can all be found in the first six icons that are part of the tools found along the bottom of the V-Ray frame buffer window. These buttons are, running from left to right:

- Show corrections control
- Force color clamping
- Show pixel information
- Use colors level correction
- Use colors curve correction
- Use exposure correction

If you are ever unsure which buttons are for enabling and disabling which tools, just hover your mouse over them and you will get a small tooltip that will help you out with a handy reminder.

To work with these tools, the first thing we will need to do is click on the Show corrections control toggle, which will bring up a floating window that houses all of V-Ray's color correction tools.

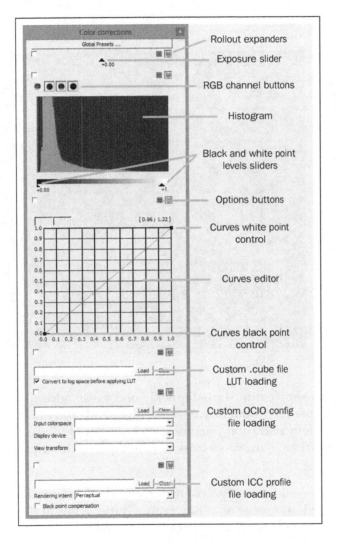

To mimic the kind of tweaks we might make in Photoshop to create a higher level of contrast in the render, let's make use of the curves controls. To enable that, as well as using the curve editor in the **Color corrections** window itself, we also need to engage the **Curves** toggle button on the V-Ray Frame Buffer itself in order to enable the feature.

On the curve editor grid, I am going to create a fairly typical color correction curve by working in turn with first the white and then the black point controls, which can be seen in the following screenshot:

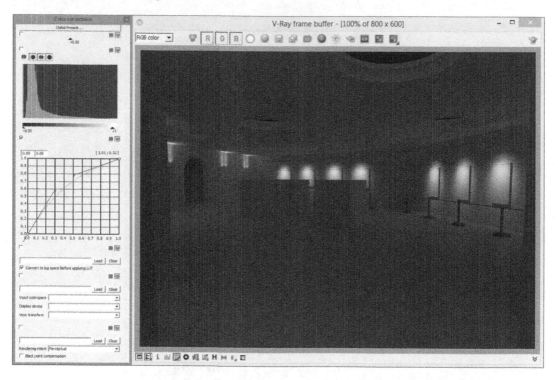

As you can see, this simple adjustment quickly and easily adds quite a bit more light to the environment without any re-rendering at all, and although this is a little overdone for demonstration purposes, you can hopefully see how we could easily use this workflow to move us closer to the lighting description given in our initial definition.

If we wanted to, we could actually save this image to disk from the frame buffer now using the **Save** button row of V-Ray Frame Buffer Icons at the top, and the adjustment we have made would be burnt into or saved as a part of the image file.

However, seeing as Compositing applications such as Photoshop or After Effects give us a much finer level of control over the color correction process compared to the relatively simple tools found on the V-Ray frame buffer, this is not a workflow that I would typically recommend following. Although the V-Ray frame buffer can certainly do the job in a pinch, final compositing and color correction operations are generally speaking, best applied in dedicated post-production applications farther down the production pipeline.

Don't forget of course that all we have done here is run through using some of the V-Ray tools available to light an interior; what we have created is by no means anything like a finished solution. Materials, final quality GI, image sampling settings, lighting and exposure corrections—all of these would need to be added before we even attempted making a final render here. Those, however, are things we will save for a little later on.

Summary

We have very importantly noted that one essential tool any serious lighter would do well to make available to himself/herself is a set (preferably an extensive one) of IES light profile files along with at least one IES viewer application. Certainly, the speed up these tools can give us in terms of lighting realism makes the time and effort given to getting them organized worthwhile.

Of course, the IES profiles by themselves would be of little use if we didn't know how to create and then work with the V-Ray IES Light type itself. Even though it is very similar in nature to other V-Ray light sources, we still explored a number of properties that make the IES light type quite unique. Not least of these was the ability to attach the aforementioned IES light profile to it, letting that control both the energy output and distribution pattern of our light source. This all of course adds up to an increased level of realism in our renders with very little (if any) extra cost in terms of the time it takes to set the IES light sources up.

Having spent the past three chapters working pretty much exclusively indoors, and having now had at least some practice working with manmade interior light sources, it's time to move outdoors. In our next chapter, we will take a look at how we might light a daytime exterior shot using V-Ray.

4
Lighting an Exterior Daylight Scene

As all parents know, spending too much time indoors is not (typically speaking) a good thing for a young person to be doing. Liberal doses of fresh air and exercise can work wonders on both the general health and temperament of young and old alike. In a way, much the same can be said regarding the effort a lighting artist needs to put in so as to be able to grow or improve in his or her ability to produce a variety of high-quality lighting setups. With that thought in mind, time for us to go ahead and move our lighting exercises to an outdoor environment.

While in many ways exterior lighting can be a much simpler proposition than its indoor counterpart, it is still true that being able to create exterior light setups is a unique skill that a lighting and render artist will need to develop. Natural daylight is a phenomenon that we need to learn to admire, study, and breakdown in order to be able to replicate the complex illumination conditions that can be found in what we might call a typical daylight environment.

Setting up our SketchUp file

If you want to work along with the steps we will be taking in this chapter, then we have a SketchUp scene file ready and waiting to be loaded up. It is called `DayTime_Exterior_01.skp`, and can be found in your `Exercise_Files | Model_Files | Chapter_04` folder.

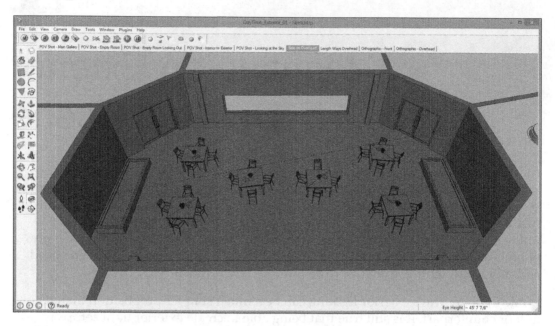

Reference and observation

Probably more so than in any of the other definition discussions we have had up to this point, it is when dealing with exterior lighting that we really need to stress the importance (to the success of the project) of careful observation and reference gathering.

Unfortunately, due to our familiarity with the subject matter, we may be tempted to try and recreate exterior lighting conditions based on memory alone. This can lead us into the trap of thinking that exterior daylight has only a handful of stereotypical scenarios with which we will need to work. Bright and sunny, cloudy and overcast, and where I come from, wet and windy would possibly be three fairly generic descriptions of outdoor weather conditions that we may generate in our mind's eye, especially so if we have not gotten into the habit of closely observing and documenting what is really going on in the world around us.

Of course, these generalizations don't really come close to giving us an accurate description of the subtleties that make up the amazing atmospheric conditions that we describe simply as daylight. And because we can so easily take something this familiar for granted, the reference gathering and observational aspects of our pre-production work will become even more critical than in our earlier indoor lighting scenarios.

If then we have a tendency to spend the majority of our time these days indoors, especially during work hours, now may be a good time to put some effort into altering that situation. This becomes especially important when we have set ourselves the goal of being able to produce photographic exterior renders when using both SketchUp and V-Ray.

The sunlight color

So what exactly are we looking for as we observe and take note of exterior daylight? Well perhaps one of the more obvious areas we can focus on is that of color. Most children will draw the sun as a big yellow circle in the sky, but to describe the sun as simply producing a yellowish light would be a vast oversimplification of the color ranges that can and do come from this phenomenal energy source.

One big recommendation that I would make right now for anyone serious about the quality of their lighting work would be that they regularly put aside a good chunk of time to make a serious study of the color properties that come from the sun. First of all perhaps from sunlight on a clear sunny day, but then also under a variety of daytime lighting and weather conditions including noting the range of sun colors that are produced due to the differing times of day, month, and year. An excellent way to approach this would be to arm ourselves with a reasonably decent digital camera that is capable of capturing images in at least a 16-bit format such as Camera RAW, with 32-bit HDR capture being even better.

Keep in mind that we will probably want to set our camera's white balance control manually when gathering references so that all of our reference shots are using the same fixed base point regarding color. If we were to leave our camera to use its auto white balance feature, we would probably find the colors in our images shifting around all over the place, which would of course seriously hamper our ability to draw any usable conclusions from the shots we take. A daylight balance of somewhere between 5,500 to 7,500 degrees Kelvin is generally recommended for this type of work, with my personal preference being a daylight white balance of 6,500 Kelvin.

Currently, the V-Ray Physical Camera doesn't use "degrees Kelvin" for its white balance controls but instead uses a standard RGB/HSV color select dialogue. Even so, we can still get a rough 6500k white balance by using HSV settings of H 320, S 6, and V 255 (RGB 255, 249, 253).

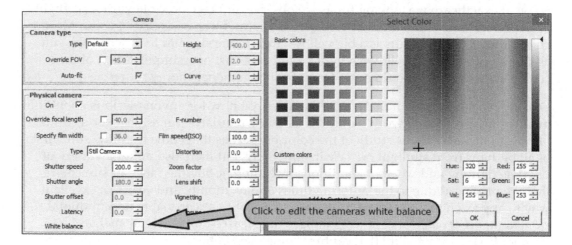

Something else that we may find useful during the capture process would be to work with just a single set of exposure settings for the duration of any single reference gathering session. This will allow our reference shots to capture the sometimes-subtle changes in illumination levels that oftentimes go hand in hand with shifts in lighting color.

Good quality components in our camera, coupled with the extra data levels that can be captured when using the RAW format, will mean that we are able to continue observing and learning from real-world day-lighting scenarios long after the sun itself has gone down and we have been forced back indoors.

Of course we do need to keep in mind that no camera will capture color information in a way that maps 100 percent to what we see with our own eyes while we are present in any given environment. This means that going to huge expense in terms of the camera equipment we use for reference gathering simply isn't required. All we need is a decent set of equipment that can help us pull together as much good quality information as possible and so gain valuable insights into what is going on, photographically speaking, whenever an environment is being lit by the sun and sky.

Another habit I would strongly recommend avoiding is the trap of using just a stock set of RGB or HSV Sunlight colors that we always apply in daylighting setups. Though fine to work with as a starting point, if we always use the same colors for sunlight in our renders then we are taking a definite step towards killing off variety in our lighting. Working with a range of colors in this area tends to be a much better idea.

One big set of questions we should be asking during our observation and reference gathering sessions would be a consideration of just how much the color information coming from the sun itself is affecting our perception of the colors found on objects in the environment around us.

For instance, in the preceding photograph of a rose, look at what happens on the right as we remove yellow tones from the color information found in the image. Our perception of the color tones or hues present alters quite a bit, as does our feeling regarding the type of environmental/lighting conditions under which the image was shot. What clearly started out as golden morning or afternoon sunshine now becomes a bit more ambiguous, perhaps looking more like a crisp autumn day.

The skylight color

Of course it isn't only the color of sunlight in an environment that we need to give attention to. Going back to our analogy of a child's drawing, we will often find that the sky is also depicted as a solid color, typically a light or pale blue. As we have already noted in our interior exercises though, block or solid colors can't really capture the variety of tones that come from skylight. Indeed often, the dominant color in a sky, depending on the time of day (and weather conditions of course), may not even be a shade of blue at all. Reds, purples, oranges, yellows, in fact pretty much every major shade available in the color spectrum may at some time or another be present as a component in the color tones of the sky.

Knowing when and how to introduce some or all of these hues into a particular piece of work will be part of the skillset that we are looking to build. We also need to keep in mind that when we talk about observing sky color, we are not just talking about the colors that can be seen up above our heads. As lighting artists, we should also be very much interested in what is happening at the ground level. How much are the colors we see up in the sky affecting the look of objects on the ground all around us?

For instance, what is happening with the colors being picked up on the buildings and roadways found in a city? What hues are being created in the shaded and dappled areas of a woodland beauty spot?

These are the questions that we do well to think about and then introduce into our renders, simply because they can make the difference between our creating a decent looking final render and a genuinely photographic one.

In fact, this brings us to another important aspect of our reference gathering and observational work: the question of location. The environment in which we make our observations and/or capture our reference images will obviously have a big impact on the type of lighting conditions and colors that are being both viewed and captured by us.

What we observe and capture in the center of a large city will obviously differ greatly in terms of the lighting and color information present compared to images taken out in the remote countryside somewhere.

Just as with our indoor research, we can gain valuable insights by doing our reference gathering in locations that are at least similar in a general sense to those that we will be trying to recreate in our V-Ray renders. The extra realism that can come from our understanding of how light is working in specific location types will be another step towards giving our finished renders a photographic feel.

Shadow properties

Another aspect of daylight that can oftentimes go somewhat unnoticed is the effect that shadows can have on the look of the world around us, which is unfortunate as the quality of shadows in a rendered image can often be the thing that will either make or break it in respect to its photographic quality. This is due to the fact that the human brain makes use of shadow information in ways that we may not even be consciously aware of.

We use shadows to judge the directionality of major light sources in an environment. We use them for depth cues to help us figure out just how close to one another two objects really are. And let's not forget that a good photographer will always be looking to make good use of shadows as compositional elements in an image, sometimes turning them into major ones. All of this ultimately means of course that when things are not looking quite right, we instinctively know it.

If then we are wanting to create a believable outdoor lighting solution, we need to understand just how our shadows ought to be working. We also need to ask where are they being generated from? How are they defining the shape or look of objects in the environment? What color or colors do they need to be? And also, what type of penumbra or edges should they have: soft and blurry or hard and crisp? All of these shadow aspects will need to be given at least some attention as they will all, to a greater or lesser degree, play a role in the photographic makeup of our rendered shot.

Now if you are perhaps new to creating CG lighting and everything we are mentioning here regarding shadows sounds a little overwhelming, we can simplify things to help us get started by initially focusing our minds on just three specific aspects: color, depth (or darkness), and penumbra (or edge). If we get those three aspects right, then we will have taken quite a big step towards producing realistic-looking directional shadows in our renders.

Ambient occlusion

There is, however, a warning that we need to sound in connection with our shadow observation and reference gathering work, and that is to avoid the trap of looking closely at only the directional shadows found in an environment. What are referred to in CG as occlusion shadows can themselves be extremely important to the photographic quality of a rendered image and will in fact oftentimes make up the larger percentage of shadows found in a given environment. The problem is, we don't always recognize that they are there, although the following woodland photograph would look very different if they weren't:

Just in case we are not entirely certain about what is meant by the term occlusion shadows, here is a brief explanation. In computer graphics, the term ambient occlusion is used to describe the shadowing effect seen on any portion of an object's surface that is not visible to the environment (or as it is often called), **ambient** lighting found in a scene.

In the following screenshot example, we have one of the tables from our exterior environment being lit by nothing more than a V-Ray Sky map that has been placed in the GI (Skylight) slot. Our Skylight is not a direct light, but rather an example of indirect environment or ambient lighting. So, the dark area we see beneath the table isn't being created by any kind of directional shadow but is instead an example of occlusion shadows at work, albeit in this case fairly weak ones.

Occlusion shadows are often referred to by animators as contact shadows due to the fact that they clearly show when two objects are either in close proximity to or actually in direct contact with one another. We see an example of this in the objects sitting on the table as well as the table and chairs themselves as they sit on the floor geometry.

Making certain that we are creating occlusion shadows in a scene that looks appropriate for the type of environment and lighting conditions that we are using will for a certainty go a long way towards giving our image believability. Again, this means we need to pay close attention in the reference gathering and observation phase of our work so as to discern just how occlusion shadows ought to be working.

A camera-matched exterior

If we are asked to work on a project that requires dropping a rendered building into an existing day-lit photographic plate, then all of the observational skills that we have discussed so far become even more critical. Today's effects-savvy audiences will of course instantly notice any discrepancies in the lighting and perspective matching of our renders.

On such a project, the reference photo (or photos) that we work with may well end up being the actual plates that we need to use in the final shots. If that is the case, I would strongly recommend that (wherever possible) we go ahead and visit the location in question, gathering reference shots and making observations of our own. There really is no substitute for the personal touch when it comes down to successfully creating work of this type.

SketchUp, of course, is capable of handling the perspective matching part of this process very nicely, which means that we can focus the majority of our attention on the lighting aspect of the shot so as to get it just right.

Again, a big requirement for this type of shot will be the need to pay particularly close attention to the settings for shadow density and color. Many times it can be these aspects of the lighting setup that ultimately let the shot down, leaving it looking anything but photographic.

Defining our exterior daylight setup

In the SketchUp scene that we are using here, we are of course trying to create a generally appealing architectural visualization render, which in most people's minds would typically equate to a bright, warm-looking sunny day. So that is what we will shoot for, specifically aiming for a mid-afternoon feel to the render.

This will require warm tones in the overall coloration of the image as well as a measure of softness to the penumbra or edges of any directional shadows coming from the sun. To give everything a nice solid feel, we will also want the occlusion shadows to be fairly obvious, but without being overly or artificially strong.

The lighting process

With all of those important considerations taken under advisement then, it is time to move forward and start defining the lighting tools that we could potentially make use of on this project.

The obvious initial choice would perhaps be to once again make use of the daylight system in the form of the V-Ray Sun and Sky (TexSky map), using them of course in conjunction with SketchUp's own shadow setting controls.

 While this is an obvious first option to explore, you have hopefully by now come to realize that when lighting in V-Ray, we have the ability to use any kind of lighting rig that we want, mixing, matching, and configuring lighting elements to suit the needs of our current project.

Having said that, the ease of use, power, and quality of the daylight system in V-Ray certainly makes it a serious contender as our lighting tool of choice when working on an exterior setup such as this. So let's go ahead then and explore its controls a little more deeply than we perhaps have up to this point.

Setting a starting exposure level

To get things started in our `DayTime_Exterior_01.skp` scene, we will of course need to once again dial in some initial exposure settings that will hopefully put us in the ball park for our final renders. In this particular instance, I am going to make use of the sunny 16 rule as a starting point and then from there tweak the exposure settings a little so as to set a solid exposure start point for the scene.

> The sunny 16 rule can basically be described as follows. On a bright sunny day, in order to get a decent exposure, one that will give us a good overall level of illumination in a shot, we can set our aperture at F16 and then simply set our shutter speed to be one over the film speed or the ISO setting being used. So if, for instance, I am shooting using an ISO value of 100, my shutter speed should be set at 1/100th of a second. With an ISO of 200, this would be 1/200th of a second, and so on.

With the V-Ray option editor open then, let's perform the following steps:

1. Click to open up the **Camera** rollout.

2. Set the **Shutter speed** to a value of **200**, **F-number** (or F Stop) to **16**, and of course **Film speed (ISO)** also to a value of **200**.

3. We can also set our camera's white balance control to match the earlier suggested values for reference capture, so H 227, S 6, and V 255 it is.

> It would be good to remember that no matter what setup values we use here, we should always fully expect to have to revisit and tweak most if not all of the camera settings once we start to approach the point of creating our final renders on the project.

Now we aren't quite finished with our exposure settings here, but before we can go ahead and finalize them, we really need to set up the first of the light sources that we will be using in this particular set of shots. Typically, this will mean setting up the key light for the scene.

Sunlight is the key

The key light here is very easy to identify as we would naturally expect it to be the sun itself. So in order to stick with our iterative lighting approach and have only direct sunlight present in the scene for now, we will need to perform the following step:

1. In the **Indirect illumination** rollout of the option editor, remove the check from the **On** box.

> As **GI (skylight)** is an indirect source rather than a direct light source in V-Ray, this leaves us able to render with just direct sunlight in the scene, which means of course that we can focus on getting this element looking good before moving onto the fill light.

Of course, before we can go ahead and take any test renders here, we will need to dial in both the time of day and month of the year settings that we want to work with. To do this we can perform the following steps:

1. From the **Window** menu, select the **Shadows** option.
2. In the dialog, click on the Show/Hide shadows toggle to the left of the time zone setting so that we can see the directional sunlight in the SketchUp viewport.
3. Leave the **Time Zone** dropdown set to UTC-07:00.
4. But set the **Time** slider to read **15:15** (03:15 PM).
5. And finally set the **Date** to August 16, and close the **Shadows Settings** dialog.

Remember that in order to make this setting stick for the particular Scene view we are working with here, we will need to:

1. Right-click on the **Side on Overhead** scene tab.
2. Click on the **Update** option.

Of course the time and date that we have just set up are currently only applied to this single camera or scene view. If we were to click on one of the other scene tabs, the shadow settings would revert to the default at which they were created. This means that in order to set things up as we want them, we will need to go through each of the remaining scene views and set up the shadow controls using the same settings we have applied here.

You can feel free to go ahead with that exercise if you wish, or if you prefer to save a little time, you may want to just jump ahead and open up the `DayTime_Exterior_02.skp` scene file from your `Exercise_Files | Model_Files | Chapter 04` folder. This version of the scene already has all of the relevant time and date settings applied to each of the scene views.

With the scene open then, let's take a render by clicking on the render button up on the V-Ray toolbar.

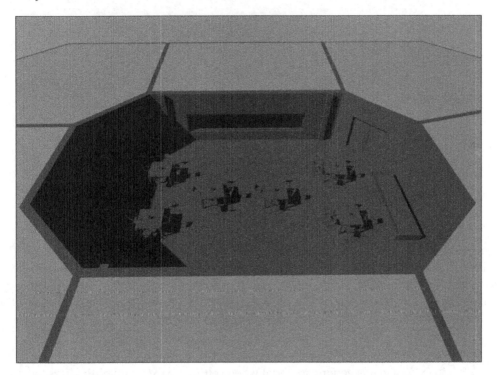

What we actually see in the finished render may be a little bit of a surprise to us given that we currently have both our lighting and camera settings using real-world tried-and tested-values that really ought to be giving us something that looks at least reasonably similar to a bright sunny day. Instead, what we are getting looks extremely dull and lifeless.

The problem is being caused by two inter-related aspects of our scene's current setup. You see if we were working in V-Ray for 3ds Max or Maya, this same scene would render much more like the following figure, which is probably much closer to what we would expect to be seeing here:

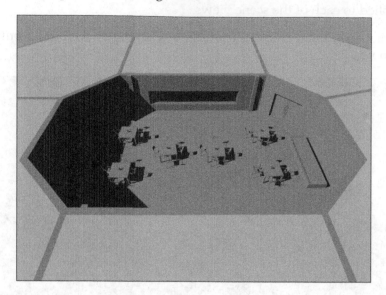

One reason for the difference can be seen if we click on the **M** icon up on the V-Ray main toolbar and open up the V-Ray specific material editor. As you can see, we currently have just two V-Ray materials assigned in the scene: one has a diffuse grey value set to give us a reflectance or light bounce value of 35 percent, while the other uses a grey diffuse color that gives us 70 percent reflectance.

> Typical target reflectance values for concrete, which I tend to use as a generic material when setting up exterior lighting rigs, would be between 40 and 60 percent.

As seen in our second render, these values used in V-Ray for 3ds Max or Maya would give us a decent, sunny-looking starting point from which we could tweak both our material and exposure settings in the scene. So what is there in our scene's current settings that would be causing things to work differently in V-Ray for SketchUp? The answer is found in a color mapping option that is on by default in V-Ray for SketchUp, but off by default in the 3ds Max and Maya versions.

To take a look at that, open up the **Color mapping** rollout in the options editor. The setting we are interested in is the **Linear workflow** checkbox which as you can see in the following screenshot is enabled by default:

Color mapping		
Type	Linear Multiply ▼	Sub-pixel mapping ☐
Dark multiplier	1.0 ⬍	Affect background ☑
Bright multiplier	1.0 ⬍	Don't affect colors (adaptation only) ☐
Gamma	2.2 ⬍	Linear workflow ☑
Input gamma	2.2 ⬍	Correct LDR textures ☐
Clamp output	☐	Correct RGB colors ☐
Clamp level	1.0 ⬍	

This checkbox was originally added to V-Ray as a quick-fix option for a "double gamma" or texture-brightening problem that many artists were running into whenever they used images or bitmaps as the diffuse component in a material.

Essentially, images that come from applications such as Photoshop, or even directly from a digital camera, already have a brightening curve or gamma correction applied to them. This is done to make the images created in a software application or taken by a digital camera (both of which are in linear color space by default), more closely match the way that our eyes and brains interpret illumination levels and color values in real life.

The Linear Workflow switch does this by reversing the gamma correction (often referred to as de-gamma or linearizing) already applied to the image. In V-Ray however, this de-gamma process doesn't just get applied to images used as the diffuse component of a material but also to any colors set by means of its diffuse color swatch.

This, in many ways, is what SketchUp users are used to seeing in their viewport. There (whenever a surface is viewed directly or head on), the bitmap or color seen in the viewport pretty much exactly matches what is being seen in the SketchUp materials editor.

Now while the SketchUp type approach produced by the **Linear workflow** option does make it much easier for an artist to recreate the same material colors seen in the viewport in the final renders also, it doesn't actually take into account the way in which both color and illumination are perceived by humans. You see if we (in real life) were to look at a grey color that has a diffuse (reflectance) value of 35 percent, we would perceive something that looks much brighter than a representation of that color given to us in V-Ray for SketchUp.

This is because the human visual system applies an automatic (logarithmic) brightening or color correction curve to the raw data that it receives. This in turn means we see the world with much brighter mid-tones than raw data alone suggests we should.

The upshot of all this technical information is that we are now left with a choice as to how we proceed with our lighting and rendering setup. We could leave the Linear Workflow option enabled and proceed to work in a technically correct manner. This would cause our color and illumination values to behave in a very predictable manner, but would at the same time leave colors, especially those found in the mid-tone range looking unnaturally dark to us.

Or we could instead disable the Linear Workflow option and work with much more numerically unpredictable shifts in color that will ultimately look and behave in a manner that feels much more natural to us given that this is the way we perceive light to be working in the real world.

Ultimately, the choice we make regarding our workflow will be up to us. Both options have strengths and weaknesses inherent in them, in fact the choice we eventually make could even on occasion be dictated by the type of work that we are doing for our clients.

In our case, even though we have up to this point been working with this V-Ray for SketchUp default option enabled, I am going to change things around and use a workflow that is fairly typical of what I do when working with V-Ray in either 3ds Max or Maya. To do that, we need to perform the following step:

1. In the options editor **Color mapping** rollout, uncheck the **Linear workflow** option.

A render at this point would produce an image identical to that shown in our previous rendered screenshot, which to my eye looks as though it could still do with just a little bit of a tweak in order to brighten things up.

As the illumination and materials in the scene are both behaving in a physically correct manner, we clearly need to revisit and tweak our exposure settings a little. In fact, the best way to do this would be to switch to one of our ground-level camera views and use the brightness of the sky in our renders as a gauge to help us get the exposure settings just right.

To do that, let's perform the following steps:

1. Click on the **POV Shot – Looking at the Sky** scene tab.
2. In the **Camera** rollout of the options editor, break away from our use of the sunny 16 rule and set our **ISO (Film speed)** value to 500.

This should give a nice, bright sky with the gradient producing a little bit of a halo effect just above the walls of the building. At the same time, the exterior dining area is now lit in a manner that makes it feel as though we are looking at mid-afternoon summer sunshine. Have a look at the following screenshot:

Of course we are getting a very stark contrast between the light and shadow areas in the image due to the fact that we don't currently have any sky or ambient light contributing to the illumination. Before we get to that though, as we now have our exposure looking about right, let's focus for a few moments on working with some of our sunlight controls, taking a look at how we can use them to alter the feel of the sunlight just a little.

The sunlight color

The first thing we will examine is the coloration we are getting from the sun. At this moment in time, we are getting a little bit of a warm, yellowish tint to our lighting, which shows up very clearly on the plain grey material applied to the geometry.

Of course, we do need to remember that the V-Ray Sun and Sky are a physically accurate, automated system, and so the colors we are already getting from the sun are based on the coloration that we would get under clear sky conditions at the times of day and year that we have set. However, every artist will most likely want the ability to exercise at least a measure of control over how the color elements in the scene are currently working.

The question we need to answer then is, how much control can we exercise over the color of our direct sunlight while making use of the TexSky environment lighting map? Well, in essence, we have two controls in the TexSky map that can be used to make color alterations. It does need to be said though that if we are not careful in our use of them, we can potentially create a situation whereby these controls actually end up cancelling each other out, possibly even creating anomalous effects in our renders at the same time.

The two controls we are interested in are Turbidity and Ozone.

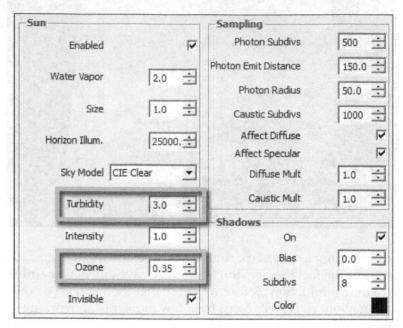

Turbidity, which affects both the Sun and Sky elements in a scene, is a control that simulates the effects of particulate matter, generally dust in our atmosphere. Lower Turbidity values denote a clearer sky, with the minimum value of 2 denoting an almost dust-free atmosphere. Interestingly, for us, this has the added effect of giving us much bluer skies. The opposite of course is also true in that higher values denote an increase in particulate matter with the maximum value of 20 creating a dust filled sky with Sun and Sky colors edging toward the orange and red part of the color spectrum.

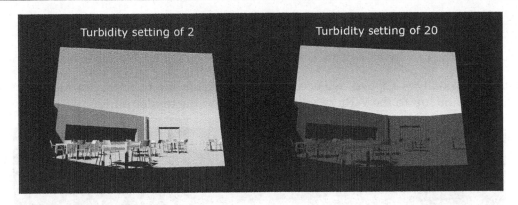

Ozone on the other hand (which only affects the color of light from the sun), when set at its minimum value of 0, produces sunlight that has more of a yellow aspect to the color, while its largest setting of 1.0 takes us in the opposite direction and pushes the sunlight towards the blue part of the spectrum.

To enhance the idea of a late afternoon on a sunny summer's day for the setting here, I am going to make the sunlight look a little warmer by performing the following steps:

1. Open up the V-Ray option editor (if it isn't already), and in the **Indirect illumination** rollout, put a check in the **On** button.

     We need to take this step so that our TexSky controls become accessible and editable.

2. In the **Environment** rollout, click on the **GI (skylight)** map button.

3. Then in the V-Ray texture editor, ensure that the **Turbidity** value in the **Sun** control section is set to **3**.

4. Set the **Ozone** value to **0.1**, and finally click on **OK** to exit the texture editor.

With those changes applied, we need to once again disable **Indirect illumination** and then come up to the V-Ray toolbar and click on the render button.

Although the differences we see in the colors of the final render are subtle, they will nevertheless alter the feel of the lighting in the final render.

The shadow quality

One thing that we can perhaps very readily perceive while focusing on the sunlight in our current render is the fact that we appear to have a bit of a problem with our shadow edges. Sunlight at this time of the day and coming from this kind of angle, tends to produce shadows that have a very obvious softness about their edges or penumbra. At this moment in time though, we have shadow edges that are looking quite hard.

You may have noticed in the TexSky options though, that our sun, unlike many V-Ray light objects, has no apparent control for altering the softness of shadow edges. The trick here is to remember that the V-Ray Sun is designed to function as a physically accurate light source, and in the real world, in order to create a diffused or softening effect on both lighting and shadows, a lighting technician would have to use lights that have a bigger surface area to them. This essentially is what we need to do in order to control the softness of shadow edges on our V-Ray Sun. To soften our shadow edges then, let's perform the following steps:

1. In the Option editor, click on the map button for the **GI (skylight)** control in the **Environment** rollout.

2. In the **Sun** section of the controls, set the **Size** value to **8**, which, although a little exaggerated, will certainly help us see the difference in shadow edge softness.

3. And then finally click on **OK** to exit the texture editor.

To get a render that lets us see our shadow edges to best advantage, let's switch back to our **Side on Overhead** scene view, and then click on the render button up on the V-Ray toolbar.

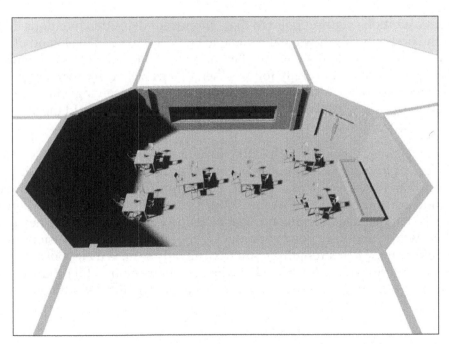

The very obvious soft edges we now get on our shadows clearly demonstrate the effect of the V-ray Sun size multiplier.

At this moment in time of course, the fact that our shadows are still completely black inside the render isn't really helping them look too realistic at all. This is something that can easily be remedied with the introduction of some fill or sky lighting to the scene.

Filling in with skylight

Before going ahead and starting work on the skylight, however, this would seem like a good time for us to go back and consult the lighting definition that we have written for the scene and see if we can get a sense of what we may want or need our skylight to do. The problem we have of course is that I didn't really add anything to the definition that specifically outlined the type of fill or skylight required.

Could we go ahead and do that now even though we are well under way with our lighting creation? Well the simple answer is yes, we should never feel that it is too late to improve any of the scene definitions that we create. If we get to a point in our project where we realize that our blueprint is missing even a single piece of information, something we feel would be useful to us, taking the time out to add it in can only be beneficial in the long run.

We do have a bit of a starting point in that our current definition mentions that we wanted the occlusion shadows in the scene to be fairly strong. This in and of itself would seem to suggest that we want a fair amount of illumination to be coming from the sky. It perhaps naturally follows then that as well as receiving a good level of illumination, our shadowed areas should also be receiving a fair amount of coloration from sky. At the suggested time of the day, that would mean seeing quite a noticeable blue tinge in the shadows.

Of course, the big question is which of the skylight options available in V-Ray should we make use of in order to accomplish our stated goals? Given that we already have the TexSky map in place, we could for instance simply turn on the indirect illumination systems and make use of the V-Ray Sky. The problem with this default daylight setup however, is that the default Irradiance Mapping and Light Cache GI engines aren't in all honesty tremendously good at producing the kind of strong occlusion shadows we are looking for. Their strength, as you have already seen, is their ability to bounce light around interior spaces very quickly while at the same time still producing very natural-looking lighting solutions even when using low quality GI settings.

Using the V-Ray Sky

This doesn't mean we couldn't make use of the V-Ray Sky if we really wanted to. It just means that we would need to make better use of the GI engine options available in V-Ray. To show the difference that a switch of engines could make, let's first of all switch to a better view by performing the following steps:

1. Left-click on the **POV Shot – Interior to Exterior** scene tab.

2. Then use the Walk and Look Around tools to position the view to match that seen in the following screenshot:

In order to see any kind of skylight contribution in a render, we will again need to turn our indirect illumination system on. To do that, perform the following step:

1. In the options editor, open up the **Indirect illumination** rollout, put a check in the **On** box for the GI systems, and take a render.

What we get back from V-Ray tells us that we are indeed now getting a skylight contribution from the TexSky map that definitely adds to the feel of mid-afternoon sunshine.

In order to compare the occlusion shadows in this irradiance map and light cache render with the changes that we will make in a moment or two, let's perform the following step:

1. Click on the **H** icon at the bottom of the frame buffer window, and then in the history window that opens up, click on the save icon found on the toolbar at the top.

What we can do now is make a switch in V-Ray and make use of a GI engine that is much more suited to picking out geometry detail in a scene and so is much more adept at creating strong occlusion shadows. In the **Indirect illumination** rollout of the options editor, perform the following steps:

1. From the dropdown in the **Primary bounces** section, choose the **Brute Force** engine.

2. Now we can take a render by either clicking on the render button found on the frame buffer window or up on the main V-Ray toolbar.

3. When done, in the **Render history** window, left-click to highlight the image we saved a few moments ago, and then click on the set **A** button found on the toolbar just above.

What you will notice as you left click-and-drag on the divider bar to scrub between the two images, is the fact that the Brute Force engine clearly produces much stronger contact shadows in the scene. We can unfortunately also see a lot of extra noise in the image that would need to be cleaned up by means of higher sampling rates, leading of course to longer render times.

So while the Brute Force engine is certainly a viable option for producing nice, strong shadow details when lighting a scene using the V-Ray Sun and Sky system, the setup actually becomes a less-than-optimum approach to rendering if we decide to make use of image-based lighting in our scene. In this instance, this is exactly what we are going to be doing, and so it would make much more sense for us to use the V-Ray Dome light. It can make full use of importance sampling techniques, and works very nicely alongside the Irradiance Map and Light Cache GI engines, both of which will help bring a little bit of speed back to our renders.

Image-based lighting for exteriors

To add a Dome light, let's load up a fresh version of our scene to both reset all of the lighting, putting us once again in total darkness, as well at the same time as re-enabling the Irradiance Map and Light Cache GI engines. The scene we want to load is the DayTime_Exterior_03.skp file that can be found in the exercise files download.

While initially set to render in complete darkness, this scene still retains all of the Camera and Color Mapping options that we have set up in the chapter thus far.

First of all, let's go ahead and get our Dome light set up and functioning as a skylight, and then we can set about choosing and adding a **High Dynamic Range Image (HDRI)** to the mix. To add the Dome light, perform the following steps:

1. Click to switch to the **Orthographic – Front** scene view, and then on the VfS: Lights toolbar, click to select the **Dome Light** option.

2. We then need to left-click and release the mouse button somewhere around the midpoint of the building geometry in the scene.

3. Next, move the mouse straight up in the view (along the blue axis), and then left-click a second time to both create and orient the Dome light in the scene, hopefully creating something that appears similar to the following screenshot:

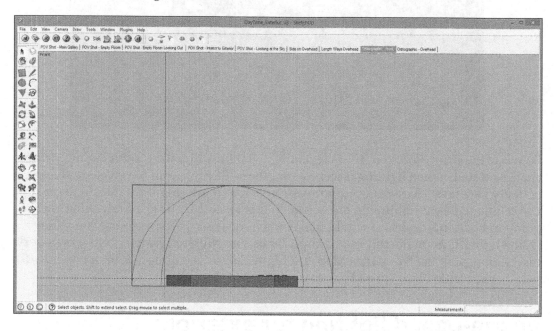

If we were to render now (given the exposure settings that we are currently working with in the scene), this default Dome light setup would give us very dim and neutral-looking lighting. To remedy this, let's perform the following steps:

1. Right-click on the Dome light, and from the **V-Ray for Sketchup** flyout found at the bottom of the menu, choose the **Edit light** option.

2. In the **V-Ray light editor** dialogue box, set the Domes **Intensity** multiplier to a value of **17**.

3. Then click on the color swatch, and set the HSV options to H 210, S 125, and V 245.

These settings should produce illumination levels and coloration similar to those that would be produced by the physically accurate V-Ray Sky while using the current exposure options.

Two big differences with regard to this setup, however, are seen in that firstly, I have chosen to dial brightness and saturation of the color back a little compared to that produced by the V-Ray Sky. And secondly (as we will shortly see), the Dome light creates much stronger occlusion shadows in the scene. Both of which in my opinion will help give the scene lighting a more natural look and feel. Have a look at the following screenshot:

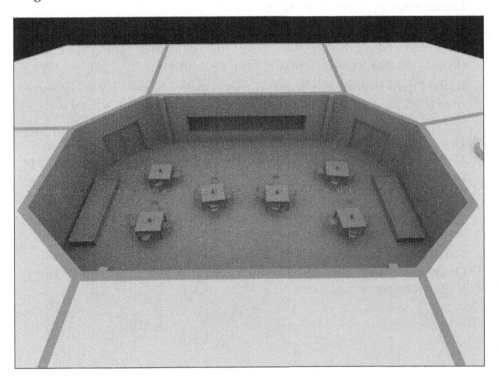

Of course both the illumination levels and color saturation will probably change quite drastically once we add our HDRI to the mix, but by setting up these initial options we can be certain that our base Dome light setup is closely matched to the physically accurate V-Ray Sky.

Adding the HDRI

Our next task is to pick out a HDRI for ourselves; one that will provide a good match regarding the kind of lighting conditions that we want in our scene. Once more, I am going to make good use of the sIBL archive found at `http://www.hdrlabs.com/sibl/archive.html`. In fact, in this particular instance, I will be making use of the **Grand Canyon C** zip archive.

Again, if you want to follow the steps we will be taking here, you can go and download this freely available resource for yourself although you can of course follow along using any spherical HDRI that you may have available.

To add the High Dynamic Range Image to our Dome light, with the V-Ray light editor still open, let's perform the following steps:

1. First of all, put a check in the **Use Dome Texture** option found in the **Dome Settings** section of the controls.

2. Then, click on the **Dome Texture** map button found just below, and in the texture editor that appears, select the **TexBitmap** option from the dropdown box found below the **Preview** button.

3. In the **Open Bitmap File** window that appears, browse for and select the HDRI file you are going to use here; in my case, this will be the `GCanyon_C_YumaPoint_Env.hdr` file.

4. Down at the bottom of the **texture editor** in the **UVW** section, set the **UVW Type** to **UVWGenEnvironment**, and ensure that **Mapping Type** is set to **Spherical**.

5. Next, in order to place the sun in our HDRI at approximately the same point on the environment dome as our already in place V-Ray Sun, set the horizontal rotation to **215** and the vertical rotation to **335**.

6. Finally, click on **OK** to exit the texture editor; switch to the **Side on Overhead** scene view; and then click on the render button up on the V-Ray toolbar.

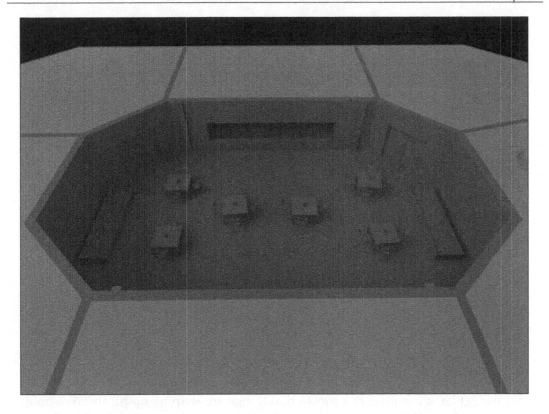

Looking at the render this produces confirms our earlier thought in that our skylight is now both a little more saturated and a little darker than was the Dome light before we added the HDRI. In this instance, our skylight is a little too dark and saturated for what we want, so let's go back into the V-Ray light editor and perform the following steps:

1. Click on the **Dome Texture** map button to access the bitmap controls for the HDRI.

2. In the initial set of controls, make certain that **Gamma Corrected** is set as the **Color Space** type, and then set the **Gamma** option to the right at a value of **2**, and click on **OK** to exit the texture editor (this applies a gamma or midtone boost to brighten the image).

3. In the **Intensity** section of the light editor, set the **Intensity** multiplier to a value of **22**, and click on **Ok** to exit the light editor.

4. Finally, switch to the **Side on Overhead** scene view, and then click on the render button up on the V-Ray toolbar.

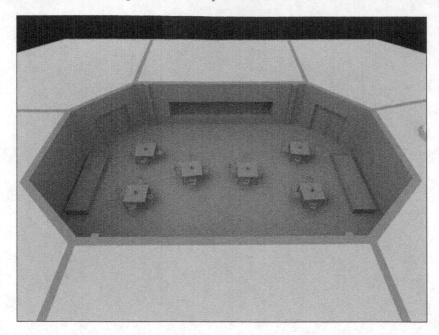

What we get back in the render shows that things are shaping up nicely. We should even be able to just about pick out the fact that the directional sunlight from the HDRI is now travelling from left to right in the render, which of course means that it now corresponds to the shadow settings at work inside the SketchUp viewport.

Adding direct sunlight to an HDRI setup

Of course, one big problem with what we see here is the fact that the lighting information coming from the HDRI doesn't really give us an appropriately strong sense of directional sunlight in the scene, nor are we getting any of the nice, clear directional shadows produced earlier while making use of the V-Ray Sun.

Ideally then, we need to turn our V-Ray Sun back on in the scene, which is something that we can in fact happily do although there are two possible ways that we could go about it. One would be to simply open up the **Environment** rollout in the V-Ray option editor, and once again turn the GI (skylight) on. The other would be to make use of the fact that in SketchUp the V-Ray Sun is considered to be the default light. This is very handy as it just so happens that V-Ray also provides a **Global Switch** that can be used to force the system to render with this light enabled irrespective of whether or not the GI (skylight) option is turned on.

The final result when using either of these approaches will be identical. However, some artists seem a little wary of using the GI (skylight) option, wondering whether or not they may in fact end up doubling their skylight illumination. To allay such fears, we will in this instance make use of the Global Switch that V-Ray provides. To do so, perform the following steps:

1. Open up the **Global switches** rollout in the option editor, and in the **Lighting** section, put a check in the box for the **Default lights** control.

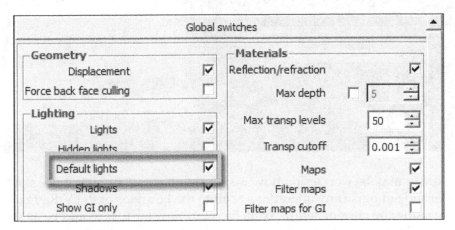

As easily as that we have now added direct sunlight back into our scene. In fact, while we have the option editor open, let's also perform the following step:

2. Open up the **Indirect illumination** rollout, and put a check in the **On** box for the GI systems.

If we switch now to one of the other camera views available in the scene, (in this instance, I will make use of both the **POV Shot – Empty Room Looking Out** and **POV Shot – Looking at the Sky** views), we can take some test renders that will help us get a feel for how the lighting in the scene is now working.

Indeed, what we can see in the finished renders is that we now have both strong direct sunlight and clear directional shadows working very nicely in the scene. You may have also noticed that even our soft shadow settings (created using a sun size of 8 earlier) have been retained.

Of course you may be wondering how we would go about altering those shadow settings or indeed make any alterations at all to the behavior of the V-Ray Sun in our scene using the current setup? Well, the workflow for that would be as simple as accessing the TexSky map options for the GI (skylight) and then making the necessary changes. To demonstrate, let's go ahead and reduce the softness of our shadow edges this time.

 In order to make a comparative evaluation, once you have finished making changes here, you may want to save your current **Looking at the Sky** render by means of the **History** window.

To alter the shadow edges, we need to perform the following steps:

1. In the **Environment** rollout of the option editor, click on the map button to open up **V-Ray texture editor**.

2. In the **Sun** controls (where we note that all of our earlier parameter edits are still in place), set the sun size parameter to a value of **4**; click on **OK** to exit the texture editor; and then, up on the V-Ray toolbar, click to initiate a new render.

A quick comparison with our previous render using the **Render History** window will show that we have shadow edges that, while still retaining a measure of softness, now appear decidedly sharper than they were.

This then is a very nice approach to creating exterior daylight that can give us a lot of flexibility regarding the way that both light and shadows work in the scene.

Creating even stronger occlusion shadows

As one final touch, just in case we feel that the occlusion shadows we are generating through the Dome light are still not quite as strong as we would like them to be, we can very easily go ahead and enable the **Ambient Occlusion** option that is a part of the GI controls.

To do that, perform the following steps:

1. In the V-Ray option editor, click to open the **Indirect illumination** rollout.
2. In the **Ambient Occlusion** section, put a check in the **On** box.
3. Set the **Radius** value to **15**.
4. Set **Amount** to **0.5**.

Of course the difference that these changes will make to the image will be subtle, but in reality, that is exactly what we want them to be—slight tweaks that help ground the render just that little bit more in reality.

Creating a better sky

Another tweak that we may want to perform *in render* as it were would be to create a better-looking sky backdrop than is currently on view. You may have noticed in your renders from the **Looking at the Sky** scene view, that our sky currently looks extremely soft and nondescript. This is not surprising as the lighting specific HDRI that we have added to the Dome light has been deliberately blurred to reduce the possibility of artifacts in the render.

The reason we see this in the background of our renders is because, by default, the Dome light that we have added to the scene is visible, meaning that it now serves as the visual environment or backdrop for any renders we take. Initially, the backdrop it provided would be white as this is the color set in the light editor. As soon as we add a Dome texture, however, that particular image now becomes the default rendered backdrop.

Now we could, if we wanted, add a clear, non-blurred version of the HDRI to the light and so get a much clearer sky in the rendered image, but as that could potentially create problems with our lighting, it seems much more sensible to take advantage of V-Ray's flexibility and take a somewhat different approach instead. To do so we need to perform the following steps:

1. Click to switch to the **Orthographic - Front** scene view.

2. Right-click on the Dome light, and from the **V-Ray for Sketchup** flyout, choose the **Edit light** option.

3. In the **light editor** dialog, in the **Options** section, put a check in the **Invisible** control, and click on **Ok** to exit the editor.

With the Dome light now invisible in our renders, we can add in a new backdrop by performing the following steps:

1. Open up the **Environment** rollout and in the options editor, turn on the **Reflection/refraction (background)** option by putting a check in the box.

2. Next, click on the map button for the same option, and in the texture editor map, type dropdown and choose the **TexBitmap** option.

3. In the **Open Bitmap File** window, navigate to and select the spherical map that you want to use as an environment backdrop.

In this instance, we will continue to make use of the GrandCanyon_C_YumaPoint archive from hdrlabs. com, this time selecting the non-blurred GCanyon_C_ YumaPoint_3k.hdr file.

We could, if we wanted, make use of the GCanyon_C_ YumaPoint_8k JPEG file, but as I would prefer to have the extra dynamic range available in the HDR version of the file, that is the one that I will be working with.

4. With that selected, make sure that the **Color space** dropdown is set to **Gamma Corrected** and that the **Gamma** value to the right is set at **1.2**.

5. Next, in the **UVW** section of the bitmap controls, set the **UVW Type** to **UVWGenEnvironment**; make sure that the **Mapping Type** is set to **Spherical** and also set **Horizontal rotation** to **215**.

6. Finally, click on **Ok** to exit the editor; set the **Reflection/refraction (background)** multiplier value to **22**; and from the POV Shot – Looking at the Sky scene view, take a render.

Now the image we have used for the environment backdrop here is essentially the same HDRI as the one used to create the sky lighting in the scene, but that doesn't necessarily have to be the case. All that really matters is that the look of the sky in the background image matches the mood or feeling seen in our environment lighting setup.

In all honesty though, the idea of including the environment background in the final render itself is an approach that I would very rarely take. My personal preference would be to instead add this during the post-production phase where I have a much greater level of control over how the image integrates with the lighting seen in the render. Still, it is good to know that these things can be done in V-Ray, should the need arise.

Tweaking exposure

As we close in on finalizing our exterior lighting setup, (at least for the time being), we have reached the point where we may want to consider revisiting the exposure settings that we been working with up to this point and see if there are any tweaks to be made that could perhaps benefit the final render in some way.

We can ask probing questions, such as, are the values being used perhaps making things a little too bright or overexposed? Do we want to push the hotspots in the image a little more, giving the suggestion that we are looking at a setting found in an extremely hot climate?

Whatever our initial answers to these questions, it would probably be a good idea at this point in time to go ahead and render out a series of shots, one from each of the available camera views so that we can make a thorough evaluation of the scenes current lighting.

In fact once we have those renders, one exercise we may want to try would be to take our images into an image editing application such as Photoshop and make use of the histogram function that can generally be found there. This can be used to visually evaluate the overall spread of tones in the scene and also experiment with brighter and darker exposures

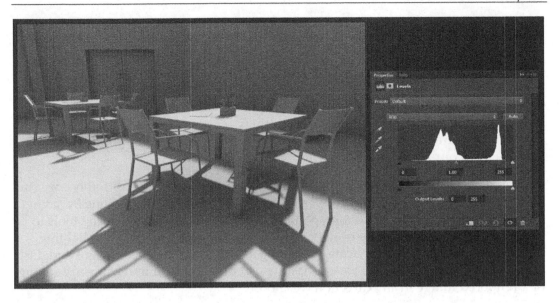

In the preceding and following screenshots, you can see two renders taken from very different locations in the environment along with the accompanying Photoshop CC histograms for them.

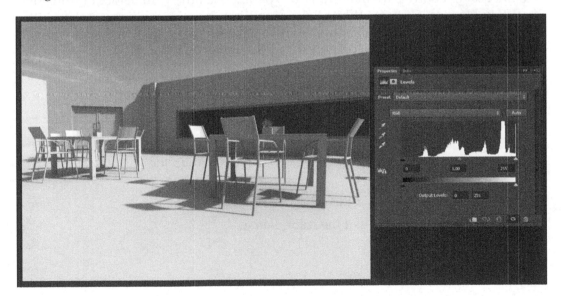

One thing we will certainly want to take into account as we make decisions on the final exposure settings for our scene lighting would be the fact that we are currently only working with plain grey materials applied to all of our objects. So while the reflectance values may be behaving as expected, the lack of any other physically correct properties in the materials will most definitely be affecting the behavior of light in the scene. Once believable materials are added, we will more than likely need to check our lighting and exposure settings once more. These steps are all a part of the iterative process that will lead us to the production of photographic renders from our 3D scenes.

One final and again very important thought to keep in mind is the difference we can make to the lighting and exposure of a shot *after the fact*. This can be done by saving our renders to 16- or 32-bit floating point files, and then use image editing tools to either manipulate or possibly even completely reimagine the look of our lighting inside a post-production application. As long as we get the balance of light and dark zones nicely set up in V-Ray, we can easily push the final color and exposure settings of a rendered image in any direction we choose.

Experimenting with white balancing

One final set of controls we may want to experiment a little with before finishing is the V-Ray Physical Cameras White Balance settings. We did, of course, make a little tweak to these earlier in the chapter, but now we need to decide whether or not we are happy with the overall coloration we are seeing in the renders.

We could, for instance, decide that we would like things to be quite a bit warmer than they currently are, making the blue/purples hues less pronounced in the render. If so, we can do that by performing the following steps:

1. Open up the **Camera** rollout in the V-Ray option editor.
2. Click on the **White balance** color swatch to open up the **Select Color** dialog.
3. In the **HSV** controls, set H – **230**, S – **50**, and V – **195**.
4. Then click on **OK** to exit the color dialog.

We do, of course, need to remember that any changes we make to the camera controls will affect our entire render including any background images we are using. To reiterate, my personal preference for handling any kind of color correction or experimentation with tones in the scene would be to do so in post-production.

Summary

As we have done in previous chapters, let's summarize what we have managed to accomplish here.

Well, we have certainly been reminded once again that good observation and reference gathering can be the factor that determines whether or not we end up with simply a nice-looking render or a genuinely photographic one at the conclusion of a project. If we have observed and so come to understand how colors ought be working in our daytime lighting setups, then not only will we be able to tell when things are looking correct in our renders, but will also know how far, and under what conditions, we might be able to mix things up and push the boundaries a little.

In terms of working with V-Ray, we have seen how we can use color control options, such as Ozone and Turbidity, in the V-Ray Sun to mimic different atmospheric effects in a daylight setup, while at the same time showing how we can add variety and realism to the skylight portion of our renders by means of **image-based lighting (IBL)**.

Having completed all three of the lighting scenarios that we wanted to explore in this first part of the book, the next phase of the pipeline moves us onto the creation of believable materials for our scene.

Before we get to that, however, we are going to take a little time out in our next chapter and consider one or two important technical aspects of lighting that we really need to grasp if we are to put ourselves in the position of being able to create good lighting setups in V-Ray.

5
Understanding the Principles of Light Behavior

Even though light is something that everyone on the planet makes use of every day, I would think it fair to say that more than a few of us are somewhat in the dark when it comes to understanding how it really works.

If my own research is anything to go by, most of us will admit that the smattering of understanding garnered when covering the basic concepts of how light works in high school Physics has, for the most part, disappeared into the black hole of disused memory with the passage of time.

While it does need to be noted that having an understanding of the physics of light isn't absolutely essential for us to become a skilled user of the lighting tools that are available in V-Ray for SketchUp, it also should be noted that understanding at least the basics of how the thing works will most definitely help. This is because most of what we learn regarding how real light works can be transferred over to working with the lighting tools in V-Ray or indeed any GI render engine of our choice.

Of course, the last thing that you may have the time or inclination to do at this point in your skill-building journey is to slog your way through an entire chapter of a book that turns out to be nothing more than a dry physics recitation. Well, hopefully, we can avoid such a situation by taking a slightly different approach to our technical learning.

Wherever possible, alongside a brief textual discussion of an important technical point that we need to understand, there will also be some hands-on exercises that will help visually reinforce the point being made in the text. Some of the exercises involve using V-Ray tools (inside SketchUp, of course), while others take a more real-world, hands-on approach. For example, we will be taking a look at the following topics:

* How light behaves
* What light decay is and how it works
* How to use the color temperature scale
* The cause of color bleed in renders and how we can control it

The SketchUp files

For this chapter, we don't have a single SketchUp scene that we will be working our way through as in the previous exercises.

Instead, we will be opening up a number of SketchUp files, each with slightly different setups that can help us visualize and therefore more fully understand the points that are being discussed.

Defining our goals

Although defining our goals for this chapter is probably not as important an exercise as with our previous hands-on lighting work, it would still be good to put something down in writing that can help us understand how the effort we put into this chapter will benefit us in our photorealistic rendering endeavors.

Our goal this time around is to make sure that by the end of the chapter we understand at least the basics of a number of aspects of the way light behaves in the real world. Taking the time to do so will hopefully help make us much more efficient in our use of the lighting tools available in V-Ray. At the same time, we will also gain a measure of technical insight into how a number of V-Ray tools are working. This will, in turn, help us produce work of a higher standard than would have been possible without such knowledge. If we can accomplish these things by the conclusion of this chapter, then we will be well on our way to not only being a skilled render artist, but also one who understands how our tools work and how to get the best out of them.

As noted, also keep in mind the fact that most, if not all, of the material covered in this chapter can be transferred over to working with any 3D application and/or render engine that we may be called on to use. This fact makes the material we cover in this chapter even more valuable in terms of helping us improve our professional skill set.

How light behaves

The need and desire to understand just what light really is and how it works has been the motivation behind questions and research that have been going on for many centuries now. It wasn't until the late seventeenth century, however, that these questions and the research work they fuelled started to yield results. They brought to the forefront theories and experiments that have since come to form the foundation of our current understanding regarding the nature and workings of light.

In 1690, Dutch mathematician and astronomer *Christiaan Huygens* put forward the proposal that light was made up of undulating waves that stimulated vision upon reaching the eye. His idea was that light behaved in pretty much the same manner as sound waves, which stimulate hearing upon reaching the ear.

English physicist *Sir Isaac Newton*, however, had been applying his own thinking to the questions surrounding the workings of light and didn't agree with Huygens. So, Newton proposed a different theory, one that described light as particles or rays that travel in straight lines, bouncing or reflecting as they come into contact with solid matter. Indeed, research had already proven that light can be seen to travel in straight lines; the simple example of reflections in a mirror had demonstrated that fact.

Learning about light – exercise one

To see just what Newton was basing his theory on, stand directly in front of a mirror and take a look over your shoulder. What you see is the product of light travelling in a straight line, giving you the ability to see whatever is directly behind you. Now, take one step to your right. You will see that the reflection in the mirror is no longer of the objects that are behind you, but rather ones that are away to the left-hand side of the mirror itself. This trick of light is seen because the angle of light reflection is always equal to and the opposite of the angle of incidence, often referred to as the viewing angle.

See the following diagram:

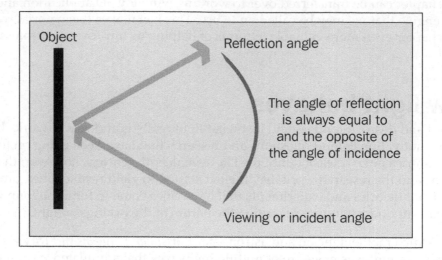

Learning about light – exercise two

To help visualize the angle of incidence versus the angle of reflection phenomenon a little more clearly, you could also take a very low wattage laser pen (preferably less than 1 milliwatt for the sake of safety) and shine it at an angle onto a mirror. The bounce or reflection of the laser that you will see instantly demonstrates the law of incidence angle versus reflection angle at work.

By the time the early nineteenth century came around, English physician and mathematician Thomas Young had come up with an experiment that seemed to prove once and for all that light was indeed made up of wave forms and not rays or particles as Newton had proposed. His now-famous **Double Slit** experiment passed monochromatic light through a thin plate with two slits cut into it. That light was then captured on a screen placed behind the plate and the visual result that it produced (see image) only really made sense if the viewer accepted that light does indeed travel as a wave.

 For an overview of the setup involved in Young's experiment, take a look at the article on the studyphysics.ca website at www.studyphysics.ca/newnotes/20/unit04_light/chp1719_light/lesson58.htm.

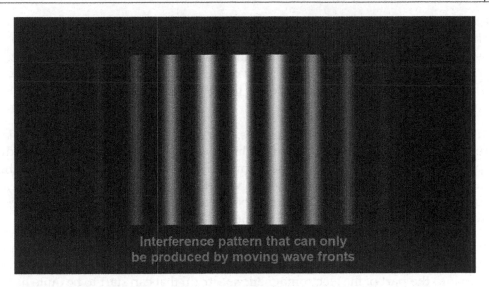

Interference pattern that can only
be produced by moving wave fronts

The interference pattern generated, which has the intensities decreasing to the left and right, could only be caused by wave forms that were being generated at the mouth of each slit. The wave fronts themselves would then intersect with one another and create new waves that would ultimately create this interference pattern. Young's simple piece of science seemed to have proven, on this occasion at least, that Sir Isaac Newton was wrong and that light did indeed travel in waves.

In the 1860s, Scottish physicist James Clerk Maxwell built on Young's work and put forward his theory of electromagnetism. In his theory, he described light as a unique kind of wave, one made up of both electric and magnetic fields. Hence, it was also referred to as electromagnetic radiation.

Maxwell's work itself was, in turn, enlarged upon with a system of dual measurement for both wavelengths and the frequencies being created. Wavelength was used to describe the measurement of the peaks and troughs in a light wave, with values ranging between 0.1 nanometers at one end of the scale and climbing up to the centimeter and even meter ranges at the other end.

[Both ends of this scale are, of course, outside the visual perception range of humans.]

The second aspect of this measuring system was frequency, and it was used to check how many times in a given second the peak of an electromagnetic wave passed a fixed point. The measurement value given to this movement was hertz. The range can be measured from 50-60 Hz on the low end, which is the frequency of AC electricity, all the way up to greater than 10^{19} Hz, which would take us into gamma ray territory.

Sitting right in between these two extremes, however, is a range of wave types that we refer to as the visible light spectrum, which occupies only about one thousandth of a percent of the entire electromagnetic range. At one end of this visible spectrum, we have red light that has both the longest wavelength and the lowest frequency, making it the least dangerous radiation type for humans. This is why we are able to use infrared signals to control devices such as TV remote controls.

At the other end of the scale comes violet light that has both the shortest wavelength and the highest frequency. Once you get just a little higher on the scale, into ultraviolet, you dip into the part of the electromagnetic spectrum that can start to be quite harmful to humans should they have intense or prolonged exposure to it.

Although all of this work seemed to indicate that light had ultimately been accepted to travel as a wave form, the debate over its nature wasn't quite done yet. Just as everything seemed to be settled, along came some guy named Einstein in 1905 and put the cat among the pigeons by embracing the idea of wave-particle duality in light.

Einstein's unusual approach was to accept the model of light behavior that best fit the work he was currently doing. He basically concluded that as light was clearly an immensely complex phenomenon in terms of its behavior, he was quite happy to accept that it could (as the evidence seemed to suggest) behave in a dual wave-particle manner. It seemed then that Newton wasn't, strictly speaking, wrong after all.

Current scientific thinking also readily accepts this dual nature in the behavior of light. When it is travelling away from a source, light is accepted to be working as an electromagnetic wave; if it passes through a gap, as in Young's experiment, then new wave fronts are assumed to form at the point of exit.

When light impacts a surface, however, the wave field is assumed to disappear or collapse to an infinitely small point from which a photon is then generated. These photons or packets of energy then bounce around an environment in unquantifiable numbers, eventually making their way into our eyes, striking the rods and cones inside, and thereby making it possible for us to actually see the world around us.

It must be noted that these statements are a hugely simplified overview of the whole amazing process regarding the way light works and its interaction with the equally amazing human eye. Go to `http://science.howstuffworks.com/life/human-biology/eye.htm` for more.

Understanding light decay

When working with lights in a computer graphics application, typically speaking, there are two options available to help us control the distance that light is allowed to travel in a scene. One is attenuation, which is generally a forced cut off point beyond which light isn't allowed to travel. A typical set of controls for attenuation would involve values that can be set for both near and far cut off points or distances in the scene.

One important thing we need to keep in mind regarding attenuation, however, is that it is not a naturally occurring phenomenon. In the real world, light has no built-in mechanism whereby we can just tell it to stop travelling beyond a fixed point in space. If you have ever tried to create a completely blacked out environment, you will no doubt have wished that such a control was available, as light seems to find a way to travel in an environment no matter how hard you work to block it.

Decay or falloff, in contrast to attenuation, is a natural phenomenon and refers to something that decreases or declines gradually in size, quantity, activity, or force. In the real world, light follows a very specific decay or falloff pattern; this is often referred to as **Quadratic or Inverse Square** falloff and is governed by the **Inverse Square Law**.

Not that the Inverse Square law applies only to the way that light works. It is actually at work in quite a number of areas including gravity, electricity, and sound to name just a few. This law states that a physical quantity or strength is inversely proportional to the square of the distance from the source of that physical quantity or strength.

Let us put this in a practical example: at 2 meters from its source, a travelling sound has already lost one quarter of the energy or volume that was present at the 1 meter point, and so, it is already only one quarter as loud as it was at its original source. By the 3 meter point, it has lost one-ninth of its intensity, and so on.

Light decay – exercise one

Now, while our sound example may help us understand the technical aspect of how the Inverse Square law works, it doesn't really give us an easy-to-use and real world method for testing it. This is because, our ability to evaluate sound levels or volume in an environment depends on quite a number of shifting variables that includes both physical (our own hearing ability) and environmental (acoustics of the area) factors.

Because Inverse Square decay affects all types of radiation, we can in fact use heat as a much more measurable example of this law in action. All we need to do is stand at a reasonable distance from a decent heat source such as a fire, oven, or radiator, and then slowly walk towards it. Initially, we will cover a large percentage of the distance between ourselves and the heat source without feeling an equally strong increase in the heat coming from it. It is only once we get really close to the heat source that those levels start to climb quite dramatically, with the final quarter of the travel distance yielding the biggest change of all.

This is the Inverse Square law at work, and this is how light decay works. As light travels away from its source, it essentially spreads itself over a wider and wider area, and so the level of illumination it can provide in the environment decreases, becoming less and less powerful.

Light decay – exercise two

At nighttime, take a candle into the smallest room of your home and with all other light sources turned off, take note of how much detail in the room you can see (in other words, note how much of the surrounding environment is illuminated).

Then take that same candle into the largest room in your house and compare the level of illumination or amount of the surrounding environment that you can now see. Even with only a reasonable increase in room size, the change in illumination levels will usually be quite obvious. The bigger the difference in room size of course, the bigger the difference in the candle's ability to illuminate it. Again, this is the Inverse Square law at work.

Of course, the only drawback with this experiment is that our eyes are superb at detecting light and so adjust very quickly whenever they need to compensate for changes in illumination levels.

To see how this can be illustrated using V-Ray in SketchUp, let's open up the `Room_Sizes.skp` file from the downloaded exercise files.

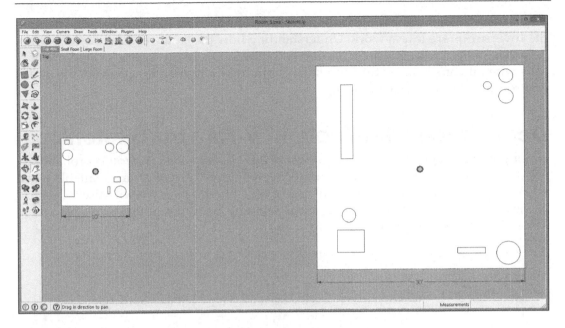

Light decay – exercise three

What we have here is a simple SketchUp scene set up with two pseudo rooms, each with a completely different amount of floor space and each with its own scene tab or camera view that looks directly down into it. The smaller room measures 10 x 10 square feet, while the larger one is 30 x 30. At the center of each room is V-Ray Omni Light that has been set up to behave in a physically accurate manner regarding decay and then copied into each room.

A quick set of test renders (see the following image) reveals the different levels of illumination that these identical lights bring to their respective environments. In the small room, the walls themselves receive a fair amount of light; in the larger room, the walls are left pretty much in complete darkness.

The difference in illumination levels seen here demonstrates in a very visible way the Inverse Square law at work. Understanding how this law works and affects the behavior of light in any given situation will certainly help us make good judgment calls when it comes to creating and balancing proper illumination levels in the digital environments that we are building.

Decay types available in V-Ray for SketchUp

Having gotten to grips with how real-world light decay works, it would probably be good if we now spent some time considering the decay types that are available when working with V-Ray lights in SketchUp. For ease of reference, we will discuss each of the available decay types themselves as separate headings, noting as we go which V-Ray light object makes use of them.

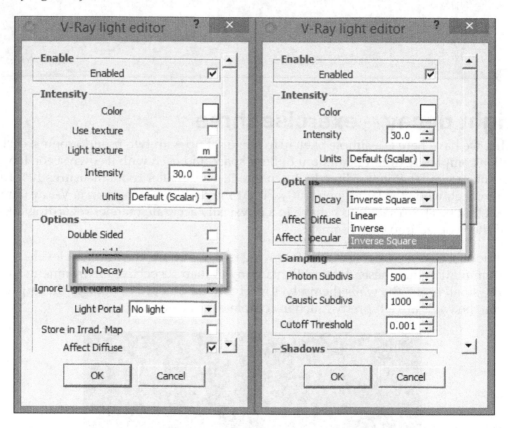

The None and Linear decay options

The logical starting place would be to highlight which V-Ray for SketchUp light types give us the ability to turn decay off altogether. Now unfortunately, this is an area of V-Ray lighting where terminology can get a little bit confusing, especially for the user who is somewhat new to CG lighting in general. I say this because, strictly speaking, the only light types in V-Ray that have an explicit option that says "no decay" would be the rectangle and sphere area lights.

Confusingly, both the Omni and Spot lights also have the ability to enable a no decay option, it is just called something different. Here, we would need to make use of the Linear Decay type in order to have no decay applied to these direct light sources. This of course is not especially helpful given that the term linear is generally applied to something that happens in a straight or constant manner. This would naturally lead us to expect a constant or straight falloff when using this decay type, rather than the option referring to the constant or unchanging nature of the direct light itself.

Be that as it may, having a no (or linear) decay option can prove to be extremely useful if we need to add a constant or unchanging light source to our scene. Here, we see a render of our 30 x 30 feet square room with the light source set to use Linear decay. The light never loses energy now, no matter how far it is required to travel.

Understanding Inverse decay

The next option we can look at is Inverse decay. This particular decay type can be thought of as a half-and-half solution that allows us to add some decay to our scene lights, but without having to use the kind of rapid falloff that we would normally associate with physically accurate light sources. This particular option can only be found on the Omni and Spot light types. This means that if we find ourselves working with a scene that has some very specific lighting requirements, one or both of these light types could become our new best friends.

Again, there is plenty of potential for confusion here, especially among users coming from other rendering packages, as the functionality provided by the Inverse decay option is what some people would correctly describe as Linear Rate falloff. Again, the decay is described as linear because it is constant or straight.

We could illustrate the way this works by considering a 100-pixel greyscale gradient that makes a strictly linear transition from black to white. Only the first pixel in that scale will be 100 percent black and only the last pixel will be 100 percent white. All the other pixels in the gradient will be precisely 1/100th brighter than the previous as we travel from left to right, with pixel number 50 sitting at exactly 50 percent grey.

The term Inverse, however, can also rightly be used to describe this decay type as this refers to the Inverse relationship between distance travelled and illumination levels. At the source, the light's brightness can be said to be 100 percent. However, as soon as a unit of distance is covered, a decrease in the level of illumination starts to take place; the level of decrease is the inverse of the measurement of distance travelled.

By the time our light has covered half of the distance that it is capable of travelling in the scene (which is determined by the initial energy output from the light source itself), it will have lost half of its brightness levels.

Again, we have a render of our 30 x 30 feet room, this time with the Omni lights decay option set to Inverse.

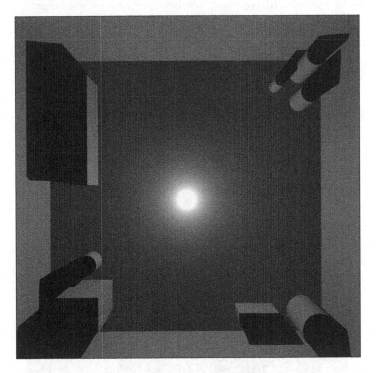

Due to the fact that we have introduced a measure of decay onto our light, we now see changing greyscale values in the image produced by the falloff of the lights energy.

The Inverse Square decay

The final decay option available to us is the only one that is common to all of the V-Ray light types, and indeed it is the one that we have already discussed in some technical detail: Inverse Square decay.

Given that we have already discussed the fact that this is the way light behaves in the real world, it isn't surprising that the V-Ray IES light, which has been designed specifically to mimic the real world energy and distribution patterns of light fixtures, makes exclusive use of the Inverse Square decay type. In fact, there is no facility at all for altering the decay type on an IES light.

The V-Ray Rectangle and Sphere area lights also of course make exclusive use of the Inverse Square decay type.

Although we have already seen a render of our 30 x 30 feet square room with the Omni light set to use Inverse Square decay, for the sake of completeness, we can again include the image here.

Using color temperature

In the nineteenth century, Glasgow born physicist Lord William Kelvin produced what is now known as the Kelvin color temperature scale, which was based on his experiments using a black body emitter (a block of carbon). On heating, the black body produced a range of colors that he noted followed a definite progression.

The Kelvin scale assigns a numeric value in degrees Kelvin to each step of that progression, from black through red, orange, white, and then beyond that into the blue area of the color spectrum. Over the years, this scale has become so much a part of the standards and terminology used in disciplines such as photography, stage and film lighting, and now the creation of digital imagery, that anyone who wants to work in these industries really needs to understand at least the basics of the Kelvin scale and how it is used.

Often, you will hear a particular light type or maybe a lighting setup being referred to as being warm or cool in nature. This temperature reference is taken from the Kelvin scale itself. Of course, using the scale can on occasion become much more specific and technical than simply using covering terms such as warm or cool. For instance, light fixtures and bulb types will often have a Kelvin temperature or equivalent **Correlated Color Temperature (CCT)** associated with them, and as visualization artists, our clients may at times request that the lighting we use on a particular project match these exact specifications.

To help give you a quick idea of how the scale works, the overview table below lists a number of Kelvin temperature ranges and matches a number of possible light sources or types that would produce light at roughly those temperatures. This is by no means an exhaustive list, but it will hopefully prove useful as a quick start reference guide. As V-Ray lights don't currently make use of the Kelvin scale in order to set color values, we have also included the closest equivalents in RGB color space.

| 1700k | 2500k | 4500k | 5500k | 6500k | 7500k | 8500k | 10,000k |

The following table shows approximate light source colors using both degrees Kelvin and RGB values:

Light sources	Degrees Kelvin	RGB values
Match flame	1,700 to 1,800	255, 121, 0 to 255, 126, 0
Candle flame	1,850 to 1,930	255, 128, 0 to 255, 132, 5
Sun at sunrise and/or sunset	2,000 to 3,000	255, 137, 18 to 255, 180, 107
Household Tungsten bulb	2,500 to 2,900	255, 161, 72 to 255, 177, 101
500- to 1k-watt Tungsten lamp	3,000	255, 180, 107
Quartz lights	3,200 to 3,500	255, 187, 120 to 255, 196, 137
Fluorescent lights	3,200 to 7,500	255, 187, 120 to 235, 238, 255
2k Tungsten lamp	3,275	255, 189, 125
5 to 10k Tungsten lamp	3,380	255, 192, 131
Noon sun	5,000 to 5,400	255, 228, 206 to 255, 235, 220
General daylight (sun and sky)	5,500 to 6,500	255, 236, 224 to 255, 249, 253
Daylight with clouds/haze	5,500 to 6,500	255, 236, 224 to 255, 249, 253

Light sources	Degrees Kelvin	RGB values
RGB monitor white point	6,000 to 7,500	255, 243, 239 to 235, 238, 255
Overcast sky	6,500	255, 249, 253
Shaded outdoors	7,000 to 8,000	245, 243, 255 to 227, 233, 255
Partly cloudy sky	8,000 to 10,000	227, 233, 255 to 204, 219, 255

Color temperature – exercise one

To work through this particular exercise, you will need to have access to a digital camera that that allows you to set a fixed white balance point. (As even camera apps for smart phones provide such functionality these days, that shouldn't hopefully be a problem.) The first step in the exercise is to set that white balance option to what is typically referred to in preset terminology as "daylight balanced". If you are dialing in the Kelvin values manually, that would be somewhere between 5,500- and 6,500-degree Kelvin. My personal preference is to use a setting of 6,500k.

Now, armed with a white piece of card or paper, spend some time at a variety of points in wandering around and taking shots under as many varied light sources as possible, especially those that are used indoors at night time. Be sure to place your piece of card or paper at the center of each shot before taking it. As long as you keep the autoexposure option enabled, you should be able to get a decent level of illumination in most, if not all, of your shots.

The next step in the exercise would be to review the images that we have captured. Examining the images with the naked eye will reveal the shifts in color cast that each distinct light source produces. If we then take those same images to an image editing application such as Photoshop and use the color picker to grab the color from the white object that we were using in our shots, we will be able to measure in much more precise detail the color shift that each of the lighting scenarios produced.

Now, although you may be tempted to skip time-consuming exercises such as this, you do so at your own peril. Becoming familiar with how real-world light sources affect the color balance in a photographic image can become an invaluable tool in the hands of a CG render artist who is trying to create photographic looking images.

Color temperature – exercise two

As seen in the `Color_Temperature.skp` file, another way that we can program our brain to understand color temperature settings would be to mimic the temperature of specific light sources using the HSV values found in our quick reference table. We apply these to the color swatch in the Intensity section of the light editor options. Then, once each image is rendered, save it to disk and again use the color picker in Photoshop or a similar image editor to compare the coloration values being picked up by the white walls that the light is shining onto.

This particular example shows the coloration we get when we set our light color to HSV 20, 255, 255. This is equivalent to a temperature setting of 1,850 degrees on the Kelvin scale.

 It is worth noting that this particular version of our scene file has the Omni light set to use Inverse and not Inverse Square decay.

The cause of color bleeding

Color bleed, as discussed in the context of architectural visualization renders, is not the product of colored lights in a scene as per our previous exercise. Rather, it is a phenomenon caused by the interaction of physically accurate lights, V-Ray's Global Illumination systems, and also physically accurate materials in the scene.

In the real world, color bleed (also known as indirect diffuse illumination) is an effect that occurs as light is bounced from one surface to another. As the light leaves one surface, it takes a little bit of the object's diffuse coloration along with it. This is then mixed with or added to the color of the next surface the light interacts with, and it goes on with the travelling light essentially creating a color reflection or bounce effect.

Color bleed – exercise one

To see color bleed in action, take a piece of white, non-reflective cloth or paper and place a strongly-colored object on it. Better still, coat a shallow box with the white material, and place the strongly-colored object inside it. Even under average daylight conditions, the transmission of color from the object to the white material will be instantly noticeable. This is color bleed in action.

The strange thing is that color bleeding goes on all around us without our paying too much attention to it at all. This is because the brain does a superb job of auto white-balancing or filtering out the bounced colors, letting us see the colors that we think we should be seeing. This is especially the case with objects that we perceive as supposedly being white.

The problem with this phenomenon going largely unnoticed is that it can lead clients who look at renders containing physically correct color bounce to ask why the coloration in their beautifully crafted environment looks all wrong.

Fortunately for us, reducing or even removing the effects of color bleed in a scene is really not that difficult a thing to do if we make good use of the tools that V-Ray gives us. In fact, there are actually quite a few ways that we could go about reducing color bleed. Some are handled from inside our scene materials, others make use of the features available in the controls for V-Rays GI engines.

To demonstrate just how simple this operation can be, we are going to make use of the saturation control found in the postprocessing section of V-Ray's Indirect illumination controls.

To take a look at the kind of result we can get when using that control, open up the `Color_Bleed.skp` scene file from your downloaded exercise files.

Bringing color bleed under control

This scene is a variation of the room we worked with in our opening chapter, but this time around it has been set up with a couple of very specific requirements in mind. First of all, it has been optimized to be pretty much neutral with respect to the color of light being bounced around the environment (as seen in the rendered image).

Secondly, as a consequence of that neutrality, the Global Illumination system is now extremely sensitive to any kind of coloration that may be introduced into the room. This, of course, is exactly what we are going to do in this exercise. To do that, we will need to perform the following steps:

1. Double-click on the floor geometry in the scene to open up the group.

2. Then, click to select the floors facing the polygon (we could of course triple-click straight away if we prefer).

3. From the V-Ray toolbar, click on the Material editor icon to open that up.

4. In the material list on the left, locate the **Colored Floor Over Ride** material, right-click on it, and use the **Apply Material to Selection** option.

5. Close the **Material** editor.

6. Click on the **Edit** menu and click on the **Close Group/Component** option.

If we now hit the render button up on the V-Ray toolbar, what we get from the completed render should match the rendered image that we can see in the following screenshot:

As you can see, the amount of color now being carried around this environment by means of the three elements mentioned earlier has altered the look of the render quite dramatically. For a client who wanted to keep their nice and neutral looking walls intact, this particular final result would be totally unacceptable. To make an effort to control the color bounce, let's perform the following steps:

1. Open up the V-Ray options dialog box by clicking the toolbar icon.
2. Click to open the **Indirect illumination** rollout.
3. In the **Post Processing** section, reduce the **Saturation** value from **1.0** to **0.15**.
4. Close the options dialog box.
5. Click on the render button up on the V-Ray toolbar.

Now when the render starts up, you may be tempted to just hit the *Esc* key and cancel the render as nothing appears to have changed, and the GI precalculation looks every bit as saturated as before. However, be patient; we have to keep in mind the fact that the saturation control is housed in the **Post Processing** section of the GI options, which means it will work its magic at render time and not before.

What we get shows quite a dramatic reduction in the amount of color bounce in the environment. Of course, now there is a difference in the color found in the carpet, but in reality that should be expected as the carpet itself is no longer receiving the fully saturated bounced light that it was receiving before.

As a compromise, we could of course work with less drastic values in the saturation field, which would have the effect of reducing rather than eliminating the color bleed in the scene. This can often be an acceptable compromise as it balances realism with artistic expectations. Our final render of the room uses a saturation value of 0.35.

As already noted, there are a number of options available for controlling color bleed in V-Ray, but being aware that this often overlooked quick fix control exists, can come in very handy at times.

Summary

Let's summarize a few of the things that we have covered in this chapter.

Well, for one thing, we have taken a look at how the Inverse Square law works and in particular seen how this affects lighting in the real world. We also noted that besides making this physically accurate decay type available to artists, V-Ray lights also offer a number of nonphysical decay options, whose behavior we demonstrated.

We also looked briefly at the color of light sources, noting that real-world lighting artists make use of the Kelvin color temperature scale to accurately describe or define their color. Since, mimicking real-world lighting setups and making use of real-world lighting data is something that we may be required to do when rendering with V-Ray, getting to understand the Kelvin color temperature scale should be considered an important part of our technical rendering education.

Color bleed, we noted, is a product of bounced light and surface material coloration that can present quite a problem for newer rendering artists. Given that fact, we discussed just one of the control options available for dealing with this in the form of the saturation option that can be found in V-Ray's GI controls.

Because color bleed is in part a product of materials in the scene, it seems appropriate that in our next chapter, *Creating Believable Materials*, we will be taking a look at using V-Ray's extremely powerful material creation tools to start enhancing our gallery's interior.

6

Creating Believable Materials

With our lighting setups firmly in place, it's now time to move on to adding some life to our rendered images using V-Ray's extremely powerful material creation tools. Of course, typically speaking, when phrases such as *adding life to a shot* are used in connection with 3D rendering, people may tend to think of adding motion to the shot—possibly in the form of animated characters. To a visualization artist, however, the life and vitality of an image will oftentimes be found (or lost) in the creation of the scene materials themselves.

For this and other reasons, we will, over the next couple of chapters, discuss the creation and set up of scene materials and their surface properties.

In this chapter, we will look at the following topics:

- Using existing SketchUp materials in V-Ray
- The V-Ray Standard material
- The new VRayBRDF layer / V-Ray material
- Bitmap textures in materials
- The .vrmat and .vismat preset formats

Getting started with our materials

In this chapter, we are going to work with our existing Daylight Interior scene and pick up where we left off at the conclusion of *Chapter 2, Lighting an Interior Daytime Scene*. To follow along, open up the `Daylight_Interior_with_Materials_01.skp` file found in your `Exercise_Files | Model_Files | Chapter 6` folder.

 In order for the scene files in this chapter to function correctly we will need to have worked through the exercises found in *Chapter 2, Lighting an Interior Daytime Scene*.

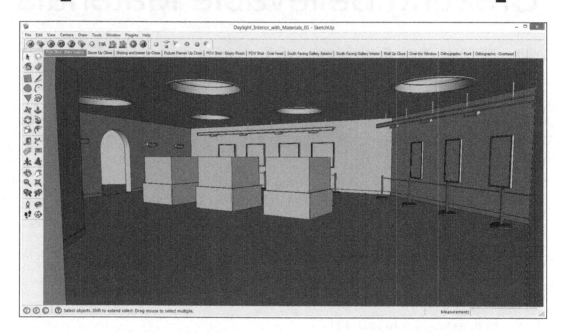

Defining our goals

We will, of course, once again want to define our goals for this chapter. In this instance, there are actually two ways that we could possibly go about this. One would be to give ourselves a general idea of what we feel our scene materials need to accomplish, perhaps describing in brief what the texture and feel of the materials ought to be.

Another possible approach would be to go for something more in depth, breaking down the objects in the scene into as many individual material components as possible. This would involve writing down (in as much detail as possible) the types of materials to be used for each object. A description of the mood or feel that each material needs to evoke and, where possible, photographic or drawn reference material that would help clarify the written description.

While this may sound like an awful lot of work to go through before we even get started on the real work of material creation, in this instance, you are going to have to trust me when I say that time spent on this particular aspect of the texturing process at this stage of the production, can and will save hours of head scratching and test renders further down the line.

Which of these two approaches we decide to take on any given project will probably depend on quite a number of external factors.

For instance, we may ask what is the type of project on which we are working? Is it a personal skill building exercise or is it a show piece being created for one of our most important clients? What is the situation regarding available time? Do we only have a few days before deadline, or have we budgeted well and so still have a reasonable amount of time in which to get the required work not only done but done well?

Whichever approach we do settle on, one absolutely critical aspect of the initial texturing phase is that we must budget time for our research. We will need to gather as much reference material and real-world experience with our subject materials as we possibly can. If we are, as is the case here, adding materials to an architectural space that has a number of objects inhabiting it, then we again need to find some real-world examples of both the space and objects and go visit them. We need to walk around and more importantly, wherever possible, photograph every relevant aspect of the environment. At the very least, we should be taking down lots of notes and supplementing them with simple sketches or diagrams wherever that will help clarify a concept or point.

Now, you are probably thinking that you have heard all of this advice already. Didn't we cover all of these thoughts in connection with our lighting work? Well, yes we did. However, while lighting and materials in a scene are hugely interdependent, I would very strongly recommend that, whenever possible, the reference gathering phases for each of these unique aspects of an environment should be done in separate passes. They could even be completed on different days so as to keep them both separate and fresh in our minds.

If time constraints mean that we do have to do them on the same day, be sure to take a break between each of the reference gathering passes, perhaps taking the opportunity to go grab some refreshments as a means of separating them out in our minds. By deliberately giving our brain an information gathering focus, we will typically find that we start to notice all kinds of subtle details and nuances that would otherwise have passed us by had we tried to gather information on both lighting and materials at the same time. When trying to create photorealism, of course, such nuances and details can turn out to be very important indeed.

[
Of course, the point of this exercise isn't to avoid any mention
of lighting while gathering material reference nor vice versa.
Instead, the idea would be to keep in mind that any mention of
light during the material phase should be focused specifically
on questions regarding how and why the surface material is
reacting to light in the way that it does.
]

As you probably want to go ahead and just get on with creating some V-Ray
materials at this point, I am going to keep my definition of our goals in the scene
to a minimum. I will adopt an approach that assumes we have been given very
little time in which to get our material work done, and so can only afford to create
a general overview regarding what we want to do with our scene materials.

Defining the materials

Given the type of space we are working with here and keeping in mind that this
scene has been designed in many respects to function as a training environment,
we will attempt to create as many hard surface material types as possible. However,
we will keep everything within the confines of surfaces that we would expect to
find in this kind of setting, focusing on working with the parameters and features
that will give the materials a realistic (and therefore photographic) look and feel.

At the same time, we also need to make certain that the materials we create are
adding a definite feel or mood to the space. Clean, light, and airy are all terms that
come to my mind as I think about the kind of look that would go with the lighting
scheme we already have in place. It would also be nice if we could possibly add just
a hint of individualism to the space, breaking away from uniformity wherever we
have the option.

Using a SketchUp material to create our diffuse floor coloring

One thing that we will probably want to get straight as we begin the material
creation process would be the question of what workflow or workflows we can
or should use as we create materials in V-Ray for SketchUp.

On the one hand, it could be that we are an experienced V-Ray user who has
been asked to produce some work inside the SketchUp application, and so we
will naturally prefer to approach the texturing process from a V-Ray workflow
or pipeline perspective.

On the other hand, it could be that we are a long-time SketchUp user who has become completely comfortable with the basic material workflow in SketchUp, and have possibly built up a comprehensive library of our own SketchUp materials over a number of years. For this reason, we would probably feel much more comfortable if we could approach the texturing process from a SketchUp-oriented perspective. Alternatively, it may be that we are new to both pieces of software and would like to see all of the approaches available and then choose one that simply works well for us.

Well, seeing that there are aspects of how materials work in SketchUp that will be important for us understand no matter which render engine or approach to material work we decide to adopt, let's make a start here by first looking at a more SketchUp-centric approach. We will look at how we can go about using materials from a SketchUp material library while getting them to render correctly in V-Ray.

Using SketchUp materials with V-Ray

In fact, what we can do is go ahead and imagine that we are a long-time SketchUp user who wants to use a material from a library of our own. (I say *imagine* because we will in fact only work with a default SketchUp material here. However, as the steps we use would be identical even if the material were one of our own, a little imagination won't hurt.)

Before we do anything with SketchUp materials, however, we need to go to the main V-Ray toolbar and click on the big **M** button to open up the V-Ray material editor for ourselves. We need to take notice of the fact that we currently have only two materials listed, **Grey Exterior - 35 % reflectance** and **Grey Interior - 70 % reflectance**. This will be significant when we come back here in a moment or two and make a comparison.

To pull up the SketchUp Material browser, all that we need to do is to close the **V-Ray material editor** window and then click to select the Paint Bucket tool on the SketchUp toolbar (we could also select the **Materials** option from the **Window** menu).

Creating the diffuse component for our floor

To demonstrate how easy it is to work with already existing SketchUp materials when rendering with V-Ray, let's add a diffuse color element to our floor by performing the following steps:

1. First of all, activate SketchUp's **Select** tool by pressing the Space bar and then double-click and single-click on the floor geometry in the scene to select it from inside the group (it should turn blue).

>
> Triple-clicking to open the group and selecting all in one go would unfortunately also select the walls in this instance; hence, the double and then single-click approach is recommended.

2. In the SketchUp material browser, access the library dropdown and click on **Tile** in the tile material section.

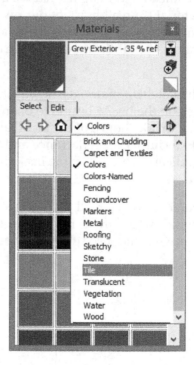

3. From the material choices in the **Tile** section, select the **Tile_Hexagon_White** option.

4. Click on the floor to apply the material to it (the cursor should change to a paint bucket icon as you do).

So far, the steps we have followed here are utilizing a pretty standard SketchUp workflow and would be used each and every time we apply an already existing SketchUp material to the scene geometry.

What isn't standard, though, is what has just happened behind the scenes. To see just what that is, let's once again come up to the V-Ray toolbar and open up the material editor. What we now see is that we have a new material entry in the list titled **Tile_Hexagon_White**. If we left-click to select it (assuming it isn't already selected), we can tell from the options available that this is indeed a V-Ray Standard material. In fact, just to prove that this new material will render with V-Ray, we can come up to the V-Ray toolbar and click on the render button.

This is almost an automatic way of creating materials for use in V-Ray, which means that we can not only continue to use our existing SketchUp material libraries, but we also have an exceptionally quick and easy way of applying materials that have the diffuse (or color) component already set up in them.

Perhaps even more importantly though this approach automatically applies a UV Mapping scale that V-Ray can now use when rendering any bitmap image that we may be using inside the material, such as diffuse, bump, or displacement. This map scale value is determining how many times the diffuse bitmap seen in the following screenshot is tiling or repeating at render time:

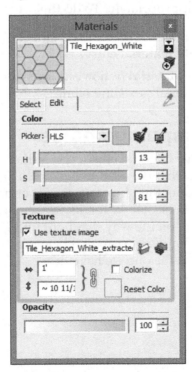

In fact, let's quickly demonstrate how we can make use of these map scale values by performing the following steps:

1. In the **SketchUp Materials** dialog box, with the **White_Tile_Hexagon** material selected, click on the **Edit** tab.

2. In the horizontal field, increase the size value to something like 4 foot 2 inches (we could also just type a value of 50 in here and let SketchUp convert to feet and inches for us).

When we do this, because the two axes are linked together, the vertical value updates automatically, giving us a bigger, more prominent floor pattern.

If, on the other hand, we drop this value all the way down to something like 10 inches, we obviously get a much smaller and busier pattern going on. Do keep in mind that small patterns such as this can cause a ray trace renderer such as V-Ray a lot of extra work in terms of image sampling, which will naturally convert into longer render times. Let's settle for a horizontal scale value of 18 inches (1 foot 6 inches) for the diffuse map and then close the **SketchUp Material editor** window. We can also close our geometry group by using the **Close Group/Component** command from the **Edit** menu.

It would also be a good idea at this point to organize the materials we are adding to the scene by naming them appropriately. To do this, perform the following steps:

1. Open up the V-Ray material editor and right-click on the **Tile_Hexagon_White** material entry.

2. Choose the **Rename Material** option and add Floor_ at the beginning of the material's existing name.

Making a color-mapping choice

Having made a start with our material creation in V-Ray, before we proceed further, we have a fairly big decision that we need to make. Up to this point, our scene has been set up and rendered using the Linear workflow option discussed in *Chapter 4, Lighting an Exterior Daytime Scene*. However, as we demonstrated in that exercise, this option has a huge impact on the way that light interacts with the surfaces it comes into contact with, and nowhere can that be more clearly demonstrated than with an interior setup such as the one we have here.

If we were to render our scene as it currently stands, we would produce what we see on the left-hand side of the following image:

With the Linear workflow option disabled, however, you can see on the right-hand side of the image the incredible difference that we get in terms of light bounce and overall brightness in the scene.

This difference occurs because with the Linear workflow option disabled, V-Ray is now interpreting light interaction with the current material settings in roughly the same manner as real camera would if we were photographing a physical environment under the same lighting conditions, with the same surface reflectance values as our scene materials and using the same exposure settings on our camera.

The question we need to answer then, is do we proceed with the Linear workflow option on or off? Both approaches have their good and bad points, and so neither one can be said to be better or worse than the other. Of course, most artists will either have or will develop a personal preference for a workflow that works for them, but this shouldn't be confused with one approach being intrinsically better than another.

What can be said, however, is that the choice we make here will most definitely impact the workflow that we use from this point forward, particularly with regard to post-production operations. Now, my personal preference is to render 16- or 32-bit floating point images out of V-Ray and then take care of both gamma correction and color grading in post-production.

16- and 32-bit images belong to a category of image file formats known as floating point. These files, which include the HDR and EXR formats, store their pixel information in floating point values.

Now, the term floating point refers to the fact that the decimal point in a group of numbers can float, meaning it can be placed anywhere relative to the significant digit(s) of the number. For instance, a number with a significant digit such as 1 can be used to represent differing values such as 1.1, 1.01, and 1.001.

This in turn means that these file types are capable of holding significantly more pixel information than their 8-bit cousins, indeed significantly more than what our current crop of computer display devices are capable of showing.

This again in turn means that when working in a post-processing environment, 16- and 32-bit images give a compositing artist greater latitude regarding the types and strength of edits that can be made.

This means I have a fairly specific setup to work with and one that I will share with you now. In the V-Ray option editor, in the **Color mapping** rollout, we need to make a number of changes by performing the following steps:

1. Disable the **Linear workflow** option.
2. Uncheck the **Affect background** control.
3. Then, as a final tweak in this rollout, enable the **Don't affect colors (adaption only)** feature.

Unchecking **Affect background** does exactly as the name suggests and stops anything we do in the color mapping controls from affecting the image being rendered in the background, which means we can exercise separate control over that as we want or need.

Enabling the **Don't affect colors** control means that while our light bounces in the scene will be calculated in a properly gamma-corrected color space, the colors seen in the render itself will remain linearized. This, for me at least, gives a best of both worlds approach as the lighting illuminates the environment in a much more natural way, while the colors on the materials are rendered much more in line with the values chosen inside the material editor.

As we ideally still need to be able to see our renders in a final gamma-corrected form, we have to perform the following steps:

1. On the V-Ray toolbar, click on the **F** icon for the Frame buffer.

2. In the controls found along the bottom of the **V-Ray frame buffer** window, click to enable the sRGB option.

3. We also want to open up the **Camera** rollout and dial back our exposure a little by setting the **F-number** to **8**, the **Shutter speed** to **150**, and the **Film speed (ISO)** to **200**.

With the **Srgb** button enabled, the V-Ray frame buffer is now giving us a pretty accurate representation of what our render will look like with a 2.2 gamma correction applied to it. I say pretty accurate because despite advice to the contrary sometimes be found on Internet forums, an sRGB color curve is not actually identical to a gamma 2.2 correction (although it is very close in terms of the final look).

Do be aware that this correction is only seen in the V-Ray frame buffer itself. If we save an image to disc either by means of the frame buffer window or through V-Ray's output controls, we get (as seen in our render) a linear, non-corrected image that is ideal for working with in a post-production application.

The final exposure tweak will help make our image look a little more palatable in terms of brightness as we examine the test renders that we will be taking.

Using the V-Ray Standard material

With the alterations in place and having already examined how we can take an existing SketchUp material and easily make use of it in V-Ray, let's spend a little more time to examine the workings of the V-Ray Standard material that we created just a while ago.

In V-Ray for SketchUp, the Standard material has typically been the best option available for creating realistic looking surface types. And even though with the Version 2.0 release we have some very welcome material additions, this strongly held position hasn't really changed at all.

In terms of how the material works, if we just take a look at the options for our floor material in the V-Ray material editor, you can see that it comes by default with three rollouts—each housing a number of options. These are only the defaults and not the complete set of controls available for this material. There are in fact a wealth of options and parameters that can be added to this material as and when they are needed. To do that, we need to perform the following steps:

1. Right-click on a material in the editor list, in this instance, the **Floor_Tile_Hexagon_White** material.

2. If we hover our mouse cursor over the **Create Layer** entry in the menu, we get an add layer flyout.

The idea here is to select the type of controls that we want to add to the material and then apply them as a new layer. A few of the choices available are as follows:

- **Emissive**: This control allows us to add lighting capabilities to the material.

- **Reflection**: This control brings a whole host of reflectivity controls into play.

- **Diffuse**: This control means that we can have more than one diffuse layer contributing to the properties of a material.

VRayBRDF is the new kid on the block for V-Ray 2.0. This multi-function layer adds Diffuse, Reflection, Refraction, Translucency, and Bidirectional Reflectance Distribution Function (BRDF) controls and is pretty much a material in and of itself.

The final layer type that can be added to the Standard material would be **Refraction**. This allows us to create a wide range of Transmissive materials such as glass and water.

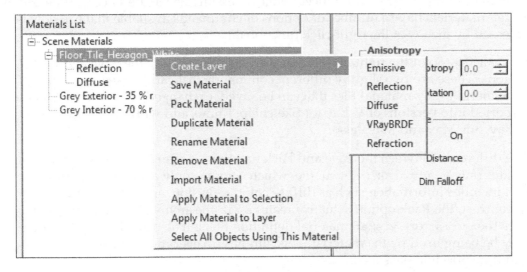

The same set of options found in the VRayBRDF layer can also be added at the material level by using the aptly named V-Ray Material. I say aptly because the controls found in both the VRayBRDF layer and in the V-Ray Material are identical to one another and almost identical to the V-Ray Material found in both 3ds Max and Maya. This uniformity across applications makes it much easier for users coming from those packages and dive into material creation with SketchUp.

There are, however, two potential problems worth noting when we use the V-Ray Material in SketchUp as opposed to adding a VRayBRDF layer to the Standard material. The first is that the V-Ray Material has no current connection to SketchUp's UV scale system, and so it is unable to effectively make use of bitmaps in its controls. The second problem, which is a consequence of the first, is that it currently has no available options or slots for adding bump or displacement maps to a material.

As our floor material will need some reflection properties, let's click on the **Reflection** entry in the flyout menu so as to add a Reflection layer to the material.

Knowing your right-click menu commands

One thing that you will have noticed while accessing the **Create Layer** option is that V-Ray materials have a number of options or commands available that can only be accessed by means of the right-click functionality.

Up near the top of the right-click menu for instance, we have the **Save** and **Pack** options. These are two slightly different commands that can be used to create standalone V-Ray material files that can be saved, exchanged, transported, and then imported into versions of V-Ray for SketchUp, Rhino, and with the 3.0 release of V-Ray, 3ds Max and Maya also.

The difference between the Save and Pack functions is seen in that the Save option creates only a `.vrmat` or `.vismat` file, which contains only a material definition that includes information such as diffuse color, reflection, and refraction values. In contrast, the **Pack** option actually creates a ZIP file archive that can contain not only the `.vrmat` or `.vismat` material definition file, but also any bitmap files that may be being used by the material. This bundles up everything into one neat, tidy, and transportable package for us.

Beside these options, the right-click menu gives us access to important material controls such as the mechanism by which we apply and remove them from objects in the scene, as well as giving us the ability to organize them properly using options such as the Rename command. The important thing here isn't to try and memorize everything found in the right-click menu, but rather to remember that the menu is there and available for use whenever we work with V-Ray materials in our scene.

Let's move things forward with our floor material and work with some of the parameters that have been added by using our new Reflection layer.

Adding reflections to our floor material

Perhaps the first thing we should point out is just how the reflection controls work in both the Standard material and the newer V-Ray Material. Essentially, V-Ray makes use of greyscale values as a means of controlling the level or strength of reflections found in a material. Black equals no reflectivity, while white adds full reflectivity to the object, creating mirror like surfaces.

If we take a look in the **General** section of the **Reflection** rollout, we can see that the **Reflection** parameter already has a map placed into the map slot by default. If we click on the button to open up the V-Ray texture editor window, we can see that this is in fact a **TexFresnel** map as seen in the following screenshot:

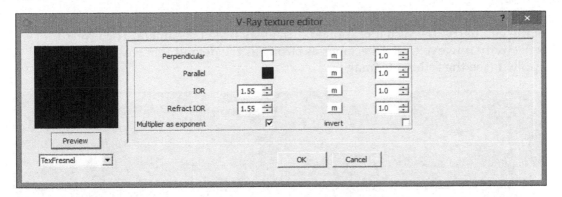

This map, just like the main reflection control, uses greyscale values as a means of determining the reflection levels. In this instance, though, there are two color swatches, one (the top one) for controlling the **Perpendicular** or glancing angle levels, while the other, **Parallel**, handles reflectivity on areas of the geometry that are facing directly toward the camera.

We also need to note that the reflection levels set by the greyscale values here will in turn be affected or modified by the **IOR** and **Refract IOR** settings that the **TexFresnel** map also uses.

> Although called Index of Refraction, this value has an equally strong impact on reflectivity levels in a material. If you are uncertain about just what an Index of Refraction value does, please refer to both the reflection and refraction sections that can be found in *Chapter 7, Important Materials Theory*.

When we use the default settings, the reflectivity we get from our floor material will lack realism, appearing far too reflective for a floor of this type. We can improve things by tweaking the controls for our **TexFresnel** map a little by performing the following steps:

1. With both **IOR** (**Index of Refraction**) options set to a value of **1.55** (default), set the **Perpendicular** color swatch to use HSV values of 0, 0, and 75.

2. Then, set the **Parallel** swatch colors to HSV 0, 0, and 3.

3. Click on **OK** to exit the texture editor and then render the material preview inside the material editor window.

What we have now is a material that has reflections that get stronger as the faces of the geometry to which it is applied turn away from the camera. The level of reflectivity however never becomes as strong as the default that was initially applied (see the following image):

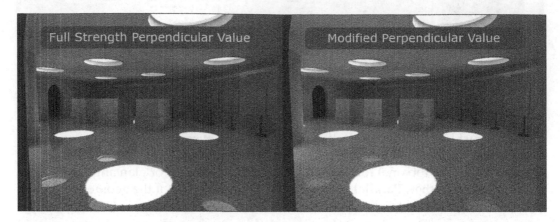

While we still see very clear and obvious reflections in the adjusted version of our test render, it is clear that our altering the **Perpendicular** value in the **TexFresnel** map has significantly reduced the level of reflectivity we are seeing, particularly from our glancing angles, which in a long shot such as this are very apparent and obvious.

> Do remember that what we are seeing in the image here is the scene as V-Ray see's it and so will save to disc.
>
> In order to evaluate how renders saved to disc will really look, we need to disable the sRGB button that we earlier enabled on the V-Ray frame buffer.

Obviously, not all changes in material properties made from this point on are going to produce differences as noticeable as this. So, it will probably be a good idea for us to start working straight away in an iterative manner, comparing and evaluating our material alterations as we go. To do that, we will again need to make use of the new to V-Ray 2.0 frame buffer history tool, so let's perform the following steps:

1. First of all, come up to the V-Ray toolbar and hit the render button to capture our already altered reflections.

2. Once the render is completed, we can click on the **H** icon on the bottom row of tools.

3. In the **Render history** window that pops up, click on the save icon to write the current render to a `.vrimg` file on our hard drive.

We can now load our renders back into the V-Ray frame buffer anytime we want and make A/B comparisons between both previous and current renders, testing whether or not our latest material changes are taking us in the right direction. Once we have saved our changes, we can close the **Render history** window by clicking on the **H** icon once again.

As we evaluate our render, it is clear that there is still a fair amount of work to be done on our reflections before we can claim that they are adding a nice level of realism to the material. One option that should always be given consideration as a part of the reflection setup process would be the choice of which bump map, if any, we can use to improve on the level of realism we have. It is after all the bumpiness or roughness found on the surface of real-world objects that determines how sharp or how blurry their reflections will be. With that in mind, let's go ahead and apply a bump map to our floor material.

As the diffuse map we have used here is almost a greyscale image, it is perfectly suited to create a tile and grout effect for us, as the darker outlines of the hexagon shapes will be rendered in the bump effect as sitting lower in height than the bright central sections.

The only slight problem we have is that the bitmap used in this default SketchUp material is actually embedded inside the materials, definition file, and so cannot be navigated to and selected in the way that we would a regular image file. The good news is that V-Ray has already given us a way to work around this limitation. As soon as we created the V-Ray material, this bitmap was extracted from the material definition and added to a texture cache folder that V-Ray uses on the hard drive.

The bad news is that the cache folder, as is typically the case with all such folders, is hidden by the operating system. So, without going through the process of unhiding, we cannot easily navigate to it. The other good news is that as long as we know what we are looking for, we should be able to get the folder to show up in a general search operation.

The folder that we need to locate is the `ChaosGroupTextureCache` folder. On Microsoft Windows Versions 7 and 8, for instance, this folder is located at `C:\Users\YOURUSERNAME HERE\AppData\Local\Temp\ChaosGroupTextureCache`. However, as we say, the actual path isn't really an issue as a quick system search should reveal its location to us.

To show how we can use this information to create our bump map, we need to perform the following steps in the V-Ray material editor:

1. Select our **Floor_Tile_Hexagon_White** material and open up the **Maps** rollout at the bottom of the material controls.

2. In the **Maps** rollout, put a check in the **Bump** map option and click on the map button.

3. In the V-Ray texture editor that appears, access the map type dropdown located beneath the **Preview** button and select the **TexBitmap** option.

4. In the **Open Bitmap File** browser window, if you are not automatically taken there, browse to and open the ChaosGroupTextureCache folder.

5. From the ChaosGroupTextureCache folder, select the Tile_Hexagon_White_ extractedTex.jpg file and click on **Open**.

6. Finally, click on **OK** to exit the texture editor.

Before we take another render and compare it with our previous effort, let's speed up our test renders a little by making use of the V-Ray frame buffer's region render tool. From the tool icons along the top of the frame buffer window, simply click to enable the tool as shown in the following screenshot:

What we can do now (inside the frame buffer window) is left-click and drag to draw a render region around only the portion of the image that we wish to re-render: in this case, just the floor. Once ready, we can click on the render icon on the V-Ray toolbar.

Once rendering is completed, we can once again open up the **Render history** window, and to make a simple A/B comparison, all we need to do is simply left-click to select our previously saved render in the history list, click on the **A** channel button on the history window toolbar, and instantly our **V-Ray frame buffer** window is divided into two halves with our previous render sitting on the left and our current render on the right. (I would recommend that you first save your newly created render to the history list, just so you know it is saved should anything untoward happen.)

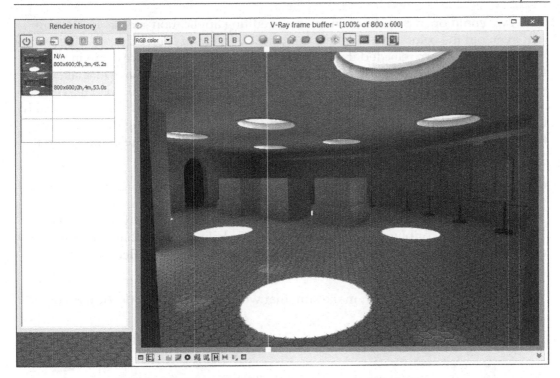

If we grab the divider bar in the middle of the window, we can slide left and right, switch between the two renders, and easily compare the differences between them. As we can clearly see, the bump map that we added has created quite a bit of breakup in the reflections, which is exactly the direction we want to go. It is this type of real-world detail in a material that will, in the end, add up in order to help make a render feel photographic.

> You may need to toggle the sRGB option off in order to see more clearly how much effect the bump map is having on the reflections.

At this moment in time though, the effect we are getting from our bump map is just a little too strong in my opinion. While we are expecting that the outline or grout areas in the render will sit a little lower than the center of the tiles, the difference we are seeing here is just a little too pronounced.

Now, we could open the bitmap in an image editing application such as Photoshop and even out the color values in the image, which would of course decrease the overall bump effect once we reloaded it into our material and rendered once again in V-Ray. However, if you look carefully at the reflections in the render you have just taken, you should be able to see that there is a subtle bit of extra reflection breakup in the center of each tile (particularly noticeable in the skylight reflections) that we would probably lose if we dial all of the values in the image down. Rather than doing that, let's play things safe in this instance and dial down the **Bump** multiplier value in the material editor, going from the default value of 1.0 to 0.5.

Before re-rendering, I think we could also add a little bit of extra breakup to the reflections. Each of the small tiles represented in the diffuse color image would probably have a measure of surface roughness that would naturally add another level of distortion or blurring to the reflections. To help simulate that, we can make use of the glossiness controls found in the Standard material's **Reflection** rollout. To do that, perform the following steps:

1. In the material editor, make sure that we are inside the **Reflection** rollout for the floor material.

2. In the **Glossiness** section, set the **Hilight** and **Reflect** values to **0.95**.

 For physical accuracy, it is oftentimes a good idea to keep these two values in step or tied together. Make certain also that you are not altering the map multiplier to the right of the map buttons.

3. In the **Render history** window, click on the save button to keep our current render for comparison (if you haven't already).

One thing we may want to do with our reflections is to have them diffused or spread out on the surface, giving something of a satin finish to them. To achieve this, we could switch the **Shader Type** from **Blinn** to **Ward** in the **Glossiness** section of our **Reflection** rollout. The difference this can make to the spread of reflections will oftentimes be quite significant, so I would strongly recommend doing specific testing to see which algorithm you prefer. As I have tested and know that I like the diffused reflections that come from using **Ward**, I am going to leave it set as shown in the following screenshot:

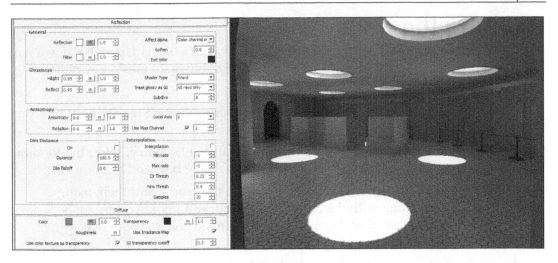

With these tweaks applied, we have probably taken our floor material about as far as we can for the moment, until we are ready to start working with the actual quality settings in our scene. This means we need to decide which element (or elements) of our scene we want to tackle next. Well, perhaps one thing we can keep in mind is the fact that, generally speaking, the larger the surface area of an object in the scene, the bigger its potential impact on the overall look of our rendered images.

For this reason, we will probably want to tackle those parts of the scene as early in the texturing process as we possibly can. This narrows down the choice quite a bit, suggesting that either the ceiling or walls in the scene should be our next port of call.

Indeed, as the reference material gathered for this phase of the project showed that adding some color to the walls of a room can oftentimes also add a little bit of a unique feel to the space, we will work first of all with the wall geometry.

As ceilings can generally be kept pretty neutral in terms of color, it is obvious that the walls are more likely to change the feel of our interior. Therefore, tackling the colored wall material before moving on to the ceiling seems like a sensible way to proceed. Again, the choices made here are very much scene dependent and may need to be quite different when you work on your own scenes.

Painting the walls

This time, rather than starting the texturing process with a SketchUp material, we will approach things from more of a V-Ray-oriented perspective. In our V-Ray material editor, let's perform the following steps:

1. Right-click on the **Scene Materials** label and select the **Standard** option from the **Create Material** flyout.

2. Right-click on the newly added **DefaultMaterial** list entry, select the **Rename Material** option, type `Walls` in the pop-up dialog box, and click on **Ok**.

3. Double-click on the wall geometry to open the group, and then, using the *Ctrl* key along with the Select, Pan, Orbit, and Look Around tools, left-click to select all of the wall geometry in the gallery room that we are currently viewing.

4. In the V-Ray material editor, right-click on the **Walls** material and use the **Apply Material to Selection** option.

5. From the **Edit** menu, use the **Close Group/Component** command.

6. Finally, click on the **POV Shot - Main Gallery** scene tab in order to reset the camera view.

If you are uncertain as to whether or not a particular material assignment operation has worked, simply select the diffuse color swatch in the new material and switch it to something very obvious such as a bright green. This should instantly show up in the SketchUp viewport. If it doesn't, then clearly the material assignment needs to be re-done.

The material we want to create for our walls is in most respects fairly simple and straightforward in that it will consist of just three basic elements: a diffuse color, some slight levels of reflectivity, and finally a bump map that will add some texture and also help diffuse the reflections. However, things are not going to be quite as straightforward as we would like. You can see that we again need to use a bitmap in the bump slot. Of course, without a bitmap applied in the diffuse slot, SketchUp doesn't assign any kind of UV scaling to the geometry. This leaves us with no obvious means of controlling the scale or size of our bump effect.

Now, in previous versions of V-Ray for SketchUp, we would have had to perform a convoluted workaround in order to fool SketchUp into giving us what we need, namely a UV map scale.

In V-Ray 2.0, however, we can simply make use of the new VRayBRDF layer.

To show how we can use this new tool to give us what we need here, let's perform the following steps:

1. In the **Diffuse** rollout of our **Walls** material, click on the map button to bring up the V-Ray texture editor.

2. From the map dropdown on the left, select the **TexBitmap** node.

3. In the **Open Bitmap File** pop up, navigate to your Exercise Files | Textures folder and select the Wall_Stucco_Bump.bmp file, click on open, and then click on **Ok** to exit the V-Ray texture editor.

In order to easily see the map that we have just added, follow the next steps:

1. Click on the paint bucket tool to bring up the SketchUp material editor.

2. With the **Walls** material selected, enter a value of 200 (16 feet 8 inches) in the horizontal parameter of the map scale controls in the **Edit** tab.

   This scales up the map to quite an extent, which means that we can easily see it in the SketchUp viewport. This tells us that it has definitely been applied to the wall geometry.

3. Set the map to a usable scale for our bump map by typing in a value of 15 (1 foot 3 inches) and closing the SketchUp material editor window.

The good thing about the way the Standard material will now work is that although the diffuse map is the color we see displayed in the SketchUp viewport, we can go ahead and add a VRayBRDF layer to the material, effectively giving us a diffuse override option. To set that up and apply a color of our choice to the walls, let's perform the following steps:

1. Right-click on the **Walls** material and choose the **VRayBRDF** option from the **Create Layer** flyout.

2. In the **Diffuse** controls at the top of the VrayBRDF rollout, click on the color swatch and set HSV values of 53, 136, and 203, respectively.

These settings will push the light reflecting (reflectance) capabilities of this material to about 80 percent, which means that we are able to bounce quite a bit of light around the environment. Of course, color choice for an interior space such as this will always be something that people have strong opinions on, so please feel free to work with whatever color hues you prefer here. Just keep in mind that a higher *value* setting in the materials color will push the light bounce to unnaturally high levels that can introduce very obvious color bleed problems, especially so if added in tandem with an increase in color saturation.

3. Down in the **Maps** rollout, put a check in the **Bump** option and then click on the map button.

4. In the map dropdown, select the **TexBitmap** option. Then, from the browse window, select the same `Wall_Stucco_Bump.bmp` file that we used in the diffuse slot a moment or two ago and click on **Open**.

5. Click on **OK** to exit the **V-Ray texture editor** window.

With our Diffuse color and bump map now in place, if we click on the **Wall Up Close** scene tab and then (making certain that we disable region render first) hit the render button up on the toolbar, we get a nice close up view of the subtle Bump effect that we have created. Of course, the bump value could be pushed further if we wanted to create a somewhat stronger effect, but what we have seems to be working just fine for now.

[Again, we may need to toggle the sRGB button in order to get a better view of how the Bump effect is working.]

The last thing that we need to add to this particular material would be a small measure of reflectivity. Rather than having to add a new Reflection layer as we did with our floor material, however, we can simply take advantage of the functionality that is already sat waiting in the new VRayBRDF layer. To do that, let's perform the following steps:

1. In the **Reflection** section of the VRayBRDF layer, click on the map button found to the right of the **Reflect** color swatch.

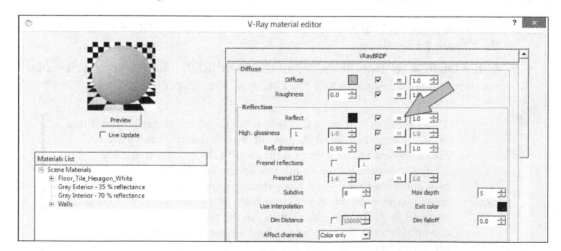

2. From the map type dropdown, select the **TexFresnel** option.

3. Set HSV values on the **Perpendicular** color swatch to 0, 0, and 10.

4. Set HSV values on the **Parallel** color swatch to 0, 0, 0.

5. Set the IOR value to **1.1** and then click on **Ok**.

6. Set the **Refl. glossiness** value to **0.95** (by default, the Reflect and Hilight values in the VRayBRDF layer are already locked together, as they are in versions of V-Ray in other applications such as 3ds Max and Maya).

7. Scroll down to the **BRDF** section of the rollout and set the **Type** in the dropdown to **Ward**.

 Many artists have different opinions regarding the best way to set up and test reflections in a material. Some would argue that doing so with the correct diffuse color in place, as we have done here, is the best way to do it, while others (myself included) find that testing reflections using a dark or medium grey color in the diffuse property makes it much easier to see and evaluate the level of reflections being produced by current settings. In order to come up with reflection values that I wanted to use in this material, I temporarily replaced the diffuse color with a medium grey while testing and then replaced the color once I was done.

To take a look at what those tweaks give us, let's click on the **POV Shot - Main Gallery** scene tab and then hit the render button on the V-Ray toolbar once again.

The finished render shows that there is some life in our scene now. Of course, we are seeing a measure of color bleed in the scene, especially on the display cases, but as we have already noted, color bleed is a naturally occurring phenomenon that is also automatically generated in V-Ray by its Global Illumination systems. We may want to evaluate and tweak the amount of color bleed we are getting during the later stages of production, but for now I am reasonably happy with what we are seeing.

As the ceiling is the final piece of large area geometry in our scene that still needs a material applying, let's quickly move ahead and deal with that next.

Playing it safe with the ceiling

Now, we can be as adventurous as we like when it comes to creating the color scheme for our room, but we do need to keep in mind that anything we add to the ceiling by way of color will show up in the reflections on both the floor and other objects in the scene as well as contributing to color bleed in the scene. For these reasons, I feel that taking a neutral approach for the ceiling material will probably work best.

As I also want to create a similar textured feel to the ceiling as with the walls, now seems like a good time to make use of another feature made available by means of the right-click menu inside the V-Ray material editor. To go ahead and do that, we can perform the following steps:

1. Right-click on the **Walls** entry in the material editor list and choose **Duplicate Material** from the menu options.

2. Right-click on the newly created **Walls1** material and select the **Rename Material** option.

3. In the **Rename Material** dialog box, call the material `Ceiling` and then click on **Ok**.

4. Click on the **Diffuse** color swatch on the ceiling material's **VRayBRDF** layer and set the color to HSV values of `60`, `3`, and `210`.

These settings will push the light reflecting (reflectance) capabilities of this material to about 82 percent, again improving the movement of light around the environment. Of course, we do need to be careful with reflectance values here as once we take the properties beyond those of realistic material behavior, we will end up detracting from rather than adding to the potential for photorealism in the render.

5. From the SketchUp toolbar, grab the Select tool and then double-click on the ceiling geometry to open the group and then single-click to select just the ceiling plane itself.

6. Back in the materials list, right-click on the **Ceiling** entry and use the **Apply Material to Selection** option.

To add a little extra variety to the texturing at this point, I want to add a slightly different bump effect to the ceiling by using a V-Ray noise map. To do that, we can perform the following steps:

1. With the **Ceiling** material still selected, scroll down to the **Maps** rollout and click on the map button for the **Bump** option.

2. In the V-Ray texture editor, click on the map type dropdown under the **Preview** button and select **TexSpeckle** from the list.

3. In the **Size** parameter, found in the right-hand column of the map's controls, set the value to **4** and click on **Ok**.

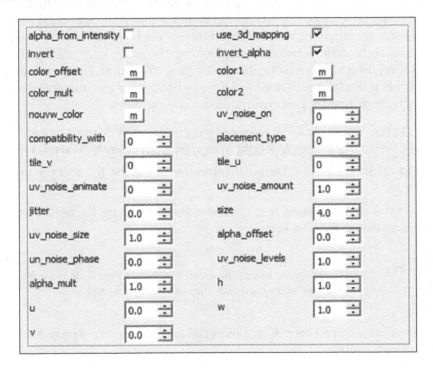

With the walls and ceiling looking good, let's move on and work with yet another scene element. Now, although our doorway isn't currently seen in the rendered frame nor indeed are the doors even present in the scene at this moment in time, they will at some point be very clearly seen, and because the material we want to apply is a little bit more complex than those created so far, now seems like as good a time as any to tackle it.

Door materials – the frosted glass

The first thing we will need to do is make our door geometry visible in the scene. To do that, you can either use the Layers dialog box in SketchUp to unhide **SouthEast_ Door** and continue working with this scene, or for convenience, you may want to go ahead and open the `Daylight_Interior_with_Materials_02.skp` file from your `Exercise_Files` folder.

If we straight away switch views by clicking on the **Doors Up Close** scene tab, we can then click to select the geometry making up the door and see that this isn't just a single, selectable object or group, but rather a series of individual pieces that combine to form the appearance of a door system. We have two frames (one each for the left and right doors), two central glass panels (again one each for the left and right doors), and also two sets of handles (one interior and one exterior). As the glass panels will obviously need to allow light to enter into our interior space, let's deal with those first by performing the following steps:

1. Inside the V-Ray material editor, right-click on the **Scene Materials** heading and choose the **V-Ray Material** option from the **Create Material** flyout.

2. Right-click on the new **DefaultMaterial** entry in the list and rename it `Door_Glass`.

3. Select the central panels in each of the doors by using the Select tool and holding down the *Ctrl* key.

 You may need to use the Orbit tool here to get a clear view of the geometry elements that are being selected.

4. Right-click on the **Door_Glass** material and choose the **Apply Material to Selection** option.

If you aren't sure whether a material has actually taken on its new assignment, just deselect everything in the scene by coming up to the **Edit** menu and apply the **Select None** command (shortcut *Ctrl + T*). Then, right-click on the material name in the editor list and choose the **Select All Objects Using This Material** command. If the assignment has taken, your objects will again become selected.

Unlike with the Standard material, the Reflection and Refraction properties of the V-Ray Material are built in and so do not require additional layers to be added, but of course they are controlled by means of the same greyscale values to determine the intensity with which each of these properties will be seen in the material. Black, the default here, gives no reflections and/or refractions at all, while white takes things in the opposite direction, producing reflections and/or refractions at full strength.

As glass is a material that has both reflective and refractive properties, let's perform the following steps:

1. In the **Reflection** section of the **Basic Parameters** rollout, click on the color swatch and set HSV values of 0, 0, and 250.

When working to create realistic materials, I have developed a habit of staying away from using full intensity values such as 255 due to the fact that very few finishes in reality can be called 100 percent. Dialing the values in a material property back from full, even just a little, can oftentimes help add to its potential realism.

2. In the **Refraction** controls, we need to perform exactly the same steps.

If we just hit the **Preview** button in the material editor at this point, we quickly see that things are not really looking as we want. Rather than a reflective/refractive material, we are getting only reflections with no transmittance (or passing through of light) taking place at all.

This is probably not surprising as we currently have a material that is using one control (reflection) telling it that most of the light striking the geometry is to be bounced or reflected, while at the same time using another control (refraction) which says that most of the light striking the material should be passing through it. Clearly, both sets of instructions cannot be applied at the same time.

Fortunately, the V-Ray Material has a switch that when enabled lets V-Ray regulate the level of reflection versus the level of refraction based (as it is in real life) on the angle from which the material (or object) is being viewed.

To enable this option, all we need to do is perform the following step:

1. In the **Reflection** section of the **Door_Glass** material, put a check in the **Fresnel reflections** checkbox.

Now when we use the **Preview** option, we can see a definite change; the material is now both reflective and refractive, letting light pass easily through it. Well almost, in order to get physically accurate direct light and shadow interaction from a glass material, we also need to check the **Affect shadows** box down at the bottom of the **Refraction** section.

Fresnel equations (or Fresnel conditions), as written down by French engineer and physicist Augustin-Jean Fresnel, describe that light moves between surfaces that have a different index of refraction.

When such a transition happens, both reflection and refraction of the light can occur. The Fresnel equations describe what fraction of the light is reflected and what fraction is refracted (that is, transmitted). The equations assume the interface is flat, planar, and homogeneous.

Taking a render now from the **Doors Up Close** scene view shows that we have a fairly decent, basic glass material in place.

Currently, the **IOR** value inside the **Refraction** controls for this material is set at **1.6**, which should work very nicely. If, however, we wanted to give the impression of a somewhat denser/thicker glass, we could increase the **IOR** value to give us a somewhat stronger refraction effect. I would, however, strongly recommend that you perform quick test renders with your chosen IOR settings, especially rendering the glass from different angles before committing to it and then rendering at higher quality settings.

 IOR values for glass typically range between 1.5 (standard) to around 1.7 (dense flint glass).

Of course, we haven't quite finished with our material yet. Having such a clear view of what is going on in the outside dining area is a little too distracting for my tastes, and not necessarily something that would be welcome in an exhibition or gallery type space such as this.

To do something a little more appropriate, let's give our glass more of a frosted look. As we will need a clear glass material for other objects in the scene, however, rather than starting from scratch, we can keep what we have created so far and use it as the base for a new material. To set that up, let's perform the following step:

1. Right-click on the **Door_Glass** material entry and choose **Duplicate Material**, and then select the duplicate and rename it Glass.

When it comes to creating a frosted effect for glass, the method or methods we use will depend very much on the type of effect we are trying to recreate. Some frosted effects are created by manufacturing the glass in such a way that the surface becomes one giant collection of bubbles or divots, thereby giving a completely distorted and unclear (frosted) view of anything sitting on the opposite side of the glass.

More common production methods, ones that produce the kind of frosted look we are perhaps more familiar with, would include acid etching and sandblasting. Sometimes, the imperfections or frosting is created on the surface of the glass, causing it to be rough to the touch. At other times, however, the frosting is sandwiched between two thin pieces of clear smooth glass, creating what appears to be an internal frosting effect.

As we have said, which of these effects we want to create will determine which approach we take with our material. Generating the effect on the geometry itself would perhaps be one way to go. This can be done either by using the modeling tools available in SketchUp, or we could use V-Ray's displacement/bump mapping capabilities to create surface distortions at render time (that would mean using the Standard material as opposed to the V-Ray Material being used here).

We could also take the simplest approach available and work with the material's Glossiness controls to create something that looks more like an internal frosting effect. To show how we can do just that, let's perform the following step:

1. In the **Refraction** controls, for the **Door_Glass** material, set a **Glossiness** value of 0.8.

This option essentially tells V-Ray to simulate lots of tiny imperfections inside the geometry volume, imperfections that would cause the refracted light to be bounced or scattered around quite a bit before it is finally able to exit the geometry. This in fact is exactly what happens with frosted glass in real life. To test our effect, let's perform the following steps:

1. On the **V-Ray frame buffer** window, enable the **Region Render** tool and draw a region around the doorway in the previous render.

2. Then, click on the render button found on the far right of the frame buffer's upper toolbar.

Naturally, all of the extra refraction calculations we have added here will cause quite a slowdown in render time. However, once done, we will be able to clearly see the effect working very nicely.

The big problem is that as we are simulating an internal frosting effect, the reflections on the surface of the glass are still perfectly smooth. This may or may not be the look we are after. If we wanted to give the glass the appearance of a slightly rough surface, we need to perform the following step:

1. Go into the material's **Reflection** controls and set its **Refl. glossiness** to a value of around about **0.98**.

 Although we may be tempted to, simply copying the refraction glossiness value here would only give us reflections so blurry that they would pretty much disappear.

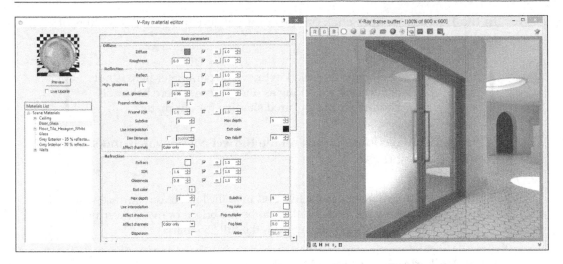

A quick render shows that although the change is very subtle, it does make the reflections look a little more natural. As what we have here seems to be working fairly well for the moment, and will of course clean up nicely as we improve image sampling quality in a later chapter, let's move on to creating a material for the frames and handles of the door system.

Giving the doors an aluminum look

Because what we are looking to create here is something along the lines of an aluminum / brushed metal material, we should be able to move along quite quickly as most of the material properties that we will need to make use of are ones that we are by now already familiar with.

To create the material we want for the doors, let's perform the following steps:

1. Right-click on the **Scene Materials** list header and choose **Standard** from the **Create Material** flyout.

2. We want to rename the new material and call it Doors_Blurred_Metal.

3. Using the Select tool while holding down the *Ctrl* key, select the outer frame, both door frames, and the interior handle group (again, we may need to use the Orbit and Zoom tools to situate our view more appropriately for these operations).

4. Next, right-click on the **Doors_Blurred_Meta**l material and use the **Apply Material to Selection** command.

5. Right-click on the material again, and this time, add a new **VRayBRDF** layer from the **Create Layers** flyout.

6. In the **Diffuse** section, click on the color swatch and set HSV values of 0, 0, and 10.

> The exact number used in the value parameter here is not overly critical, so as long as it is set somewhere below 50, we should get the required shading for our metal.

7. In the **Reflection** controls, click on the **Reflect** color swatch and set HSV values of 0, 0, and 230.

> Again, we want a reflective and metallic look to our surface, but we don't want the reflections to be too bright or overpowering. This means staying away from the full 255 mark.

8. In the **Refl. glossiness** control, set the value to **0.8**.

9. Just below the **Refl. glossiness** parameter, put a check in the **Fresnel** option box, click on the **L** (lock button) next to it to unlock the parameter field, and enter a **Fresnel IOR** value of 15.

10. In the BRDF section, set the **Anisotropy** value to 0.5 and switch the **UV vector derivation** option to **Local axis** with the **Local axis** option set to **Z**.

> The term Anisotropic often refers to an object's ability to exhibit different physical properties along different axes. Wood, for instance, is much easier to cut along the grain as opposed to cutting across it.
>
> The **Anisotropy** option in the reflection controls lets us stretch the reflection highlights a given direction, hence the UV vector and local axis options. This means we can quickly and easily create a fake brushed metal kind of effect.

With the door material taken care of then, let's go to the **Doors Up Close** scene view and then hit the render button on the V-Ray toolbar to see what we have.

Although the metal looks ok, as we move forward with the project, we may decide that it is a little too bright, or maybe a touch too reflective. Rather than getting into any serious tweaking at this stage, however, it is generally best to wait until we have all of the scene materials in place. In this way, we won't waste time fine tuning a component on a material that will change anyway due to other factors at work in the scene. Typically, a first pass (as we have here) that gets us most of the way towards the desired end result can be considered good enough at this point in the process.

Adding chrome to the barriers

Like glass, another extremely common material found in the kind of space we are working with here would be chrome, or at least something that is chrome like in appearance. The lightweight barriers that have been set up to deter the public from touching the wall exhibits in this space are the perfect candidates for such a material. To create that, let's perform the following steps:

1. Right-click on the **Scene Materials** header in the editor, and from the **Create Material** flyout, choose the **V-Ray Material** option.

 I have chosen to use the V-Ray Material in this instance as it is highly unlikely that we will want to add any kind of bump or displacement map to our chrome-like finish.

2. Right-click on the new material and rename it `Barrier_Chrome`.

3. In the **Diffuse** controls, click on the color swatch and set HSV values of 0, 0, and 0.

4. In the **Reflection** controls, click on the reflection color swatch and set HSV values of 0, 0, and 225, and then in the **Refl. glossiness** controls, set the value to **0.98**.

 While we tend to think of chrome as a totally reflective material, only the most expensively manufactured versions could claim to come anything close to being completely reflective. Most of what we think of as highly reflective chrome (if you look carefully that is) has a noticeable blur in the reflections. This is what we are simulating here by lowering the reflection value and adding a slightly lowered level of glossiness to add just a touch of breakup.

5. In the **Skirting and Barrier Up Close** scene tab, double-click on one of the barrier groups to open it up and then use either the *Ctrl + A* keys or the **Select All** command from the **Edit** menu to select all of the pieces in the group.

6. Next, right-click on the **Barrier_Chrome** material in the editor and choose the **Apply Material to Selection** option from the list.

7. Finally, repeat the process for the second barrier group.

Painting the skirting board

While in this view, let's add a little bit of a non-standard or individual feel to our interior by adding a color to our skirting or kickboards that will stand very much in contrast with the pale yellow applied to our walls. We can do this by performing the following steps:

1. Create a new **Standard** material in the material editor and then rename it Skirting.

2. In the **Diffuse** rollout, click on the color swatch and set HSV values of 219, 215, and 127.

3. Add a new **Reflection** layer from the **Create Layer** flyout, which automatically adds a TexFresnel map for us.

4. Set the **Hilight** and **Reflect Glossiness** values for the reflections to **0.93**.

5. Using the Select tool, click on the skirting geometry. Then, right-click on the **Skirting** material entry in the editor and use the **Apply Material to Selection** command.

Using the Standard material here means that we can easily add a bump map to simulate brush strokes at a later date, should we decide that the material really could do with it.

Now, as we clearly cannot cover the creation of every material we need for this scene in this chapter, seeing as we have covered many of the basics regarding realistic material creation in V-Ray, now would be a good time to start getting a little selective and cover some of the more unusual materials that we may need to make use of on a project. The first such process involves the application of some bitmaps to our wall-mounted exhibits.

Creating the wall paintings using bitmaps

To get our paintings in place, we are going to have to do a little bit of work with SketchUp's Texture Position tool as we are (quite deliberately I should add) going to make use of bitmaps that don't accurately fit the aspect ratios of the geometry to which we are applying them. To show how this will work, let's perform the following steps:

1. In the editor **Materials** list, create a new Standard material and call it `Painting_01`.

2. In the **Diffuse** rollout, click on the map button, add a **TexBitmap** node, browse to your `Exercise Files | Textures` folder, and select the `Painting_01.png` file.

3. Click on **Ok** to exit the texture editor and then click to select the **Picture Frames Up Close** scene tab (feel free to adjust the view to suit as you work here).

 It is worth noting here that our bitmap textures are being gamma corrected or linearized on import when we use the **Gamma Corrected** option in **Color space** with the **Gamma** value set to **1.0** as we see in the following screenshot. This avoids the oft-bemoaned situation where bitmap textures used in a render look overly desaturated or washed out.

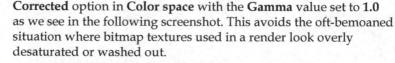
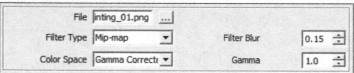

4. Using SketchUp's Select tool, double-click and then single-click on the right-most frame to select the single plane picture panel that is part of this group.

 Be sure to move your mouse a little before the final single-click, otherwise SketchUp will assume it is a triple-click and select all geometry inside the group.

5. Select the paint bucket tool from the SketchUp toolbar, and after making sure that you have your **Painting 01** material selected in the SketchUp material editor (you may have to click on the In Model button in order to access this material), click on the selected geometry to apply the material to it.

6. To set a usable map scale, in the SketchUp material editor's **Edit** tab, set the horizontal and vertical values for the **Painting 01** material to **60** inches (5 feet).

7. To reposition the bitmap, right-click on the geometry and choose the **Position** option from the **Texture** flyout.

8. By default, we are in the Move mode (Scale/Shear, Distort, and Rotate are the other options available), so we can just left-click and drag to reposition our bitmap (be careful not to introduce any obvious tiling by pulling the repeat seam into view, unless of course that is your deliberate intent).

9. Once placed, simply left-click on the bitmap display and choose **Done**.

10. To finish, we can go up to the **Edit** menu and choose the **Close Group/ Component** option.

As we have textured only one of our wall exhibits here, we will need to repeat this same process for each of the other seven by performing the following process:

1. Duplicate the last created Painting material (sequential numbering should automatically be applied in the V-Ray material editor, so next up will be Painting_02).

2. Apply the supplied and sequentially named bitmap image from the Textures folder.

3. Apply the material to the selected geometry.

4. Then finally, adjust the bitmap positioning for each material.

Once we are done, we can return to the **POV Shot - Main Gallery** scene tab and take a render. What we get should look pretty close to the following render. I say pretty close because slight differences will probably be seen regarding the placement of the bitmap images inside each frame.

If you prefer, you can skip the repetition of texturing all of the paintings by simply loading the `Daylight_Interior_with_Materials_03.skp` file found in your `Exercise_Files | Model_Files | Chapter_06` folder, as this version of the scene file has them all in place.

Art sculpts – import vismat

A very useful option when texturing with V-Ray and one that can speed up the texturing process quite a bit is the ability to use, or maybe we should say reuse, the already existing V-Ray materials in the form of V-Ray's own `.vrmat` and `.vismat` application agnostic material types.

As Chaos Group have announced that the `.vrmat` format will be included in both 3ds Max and Maya with the release of V-Ray 3.0, the possibilities of acquiring readymade, high-quality materials in this manner will only grow.

One brilliant thing about this format is that regardless of where it came from, the process of loading a vismat material is always the same. All we need to do is perform the following steps:

1. Create a new **Standard** material in the editor and call it `Sculpts`.
2. Right-click on the **Sculpts** material entry, and from the menu, choose the **Import Material** command.
3. In the dialog box, browse to the `Exercise Files | Textures | Vismat | Sculpts` folder and select the `Ceramic_Sculpts.vismat` file.
4. From the **Window** menu, select the **Layers** command, and in the Layer's dialog box, turn off or hide the **Display_Glass** layer and turn on the **Sculpts** layer.
5. Select all five sculpt objects in the scene and then right-click on the **Sculpts** material and use the **Apply Material to Selection** command.

And that's all there is when it comes to using a saved `.vrmat` or `.vismat` material. In this instance, the `Sculpts` folder was created from the extracted Vismat Zip archive. So, it contains both the `.vismat` material definition file along with its saved bitmap preview. The Zip archive itself was created by using the **Pack Material** function, which can be accessed by right-clicking on the material in the editor list.

As the `.vismat` file contains all of the relevant material settings, there really is nothing else for us to do other than checking out what our new material looks like.

As you can see, the vismat material import works perfectly and can be yet another time saver, especially if we have taken the time to build and collect an organized library of vismat materials. These can be especially useful if we make certain that they can be accessed by any workstations available on our business network.

 If we sometimes work on the go, we may want to make such a library available to ourselves at all times by using online storage options such as Dropbox, Google Drive, or Microsoft's Onedrive.

One thing that we will need to give attention to in our render is the amount of color bleed that our supposedly white ceramic sculpts(and floor) are clearly picking up from the yellow wall material. Although, this is an issue that we will look at addressing as we approach our final render, we could (if we wanted to get a clearer idea of what the materials are looking like without color bleed) use the saturation option in our GI controls as we did in *Chapter 5, Understanding the Principles of Light Behavior*.

Your challenge

Although we now have a number of the major materials in place, there are still quite a few items left in the scene that need some attention—including some that are currently still on hidden layers. To finish things here, we have a challenge for you. Open up the `Daylight_Interior_with_Materials_04.skp` file found in your `Exercise_Files` | `Model_Files` | `Chapter_06` folder and finish applying the completed and named materials to their corresponding geometry.

If you prefer, you can just jump ahead and examine the materials in the completed scene by opening up the `Daylight_Interior_with_Materials_Final.skp` file that is found in the `Exercise_Files` | `Model_Files` | `Chapter_06` folder.

Feel free to play around with the materials, save out your own version of the final scene file, and then compare what you create with my final render as seen in the following screenshot:

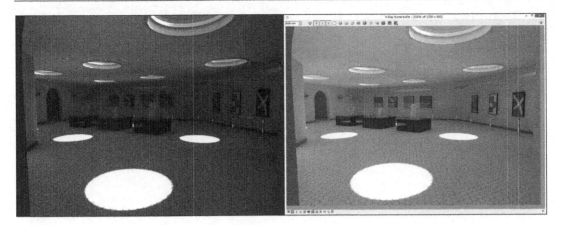

Of course, we are still a long way from being ready to create any kind of final renders. Material tweaks, camera and composition setup, GI, and image sampling quality, all of these elements and possibly more will need to be dealt with before we can say we are ready for that. Again, for the time being, we have come far enough to be able to call this phase finished for now.

Summary

Let's recap some of the material we have covered in this chapter.

The workhorse material in V-Ray for SketchUp has always been the Standard material, and even though in the 2.0 release we get some very welcome additions to the materials and maps options, the Standard material remains the most versatile option available for recreating most surface types.

Having said that, one of the welcome additions to the material system in V-Ray has been the inclusion of the new VRayBRDF layer, which of course also doubles as the standalone V-Ray Material. For V-Ray users coming from the likes of 3ds Max and Maya, this option adds a much more familiar working environment as well as avoiding the need to add extra reflection and refraction layers to a material in order to work those properties.

Although we have tried to create materials that behave in a physically plausible manner, taking the time to understand why it is that real world surfaces look the way they do can go a long way towards helping us produce photographic looking final renders.

Because of this, we are going to spend some time in the next chapter taking a look at some of the aspects of light and object interaction that affect our current project. We will, at the same time, garner some important insights into the material process that will help us advance our skill as a V-Ray render artist.

7
Important Materials Theory

While in the final analysis, the truly important consideration regarding material creation is that, things look the way we want or need them to. There is still no denying the fact that being able to understand how real-world physics causes object surfaces to look the way they do, can go a long way towards helping us produce more realistic-looking materials and so in the end more photographic-looking final renders. One nice side effect of such insight is that we will find ourselves able (generally speaking) to create materials in a much shorter time frame than would otherwise be the case.

Because of this, we are going to spend some time in this chapter taking a look, albeit in a fairly brief manner, at some of the more applicable aspects of light and object interaction that have a bearing on our current project and hopefully in the process garner some important insights that will help us advance our skills as V-Ray render artists.

Defining our goals

As the introduction of the chapter has to a large extent already set out what we want to accomplish here, we can very quickly define our goals for this stage of the project, noting really that they are twofold at this point.

First, we want to increase our personal understanding of just why it is that objects we see in the real world look the way they do. And secondly, we want to stir up in ourselves a desire, a thirst if you like, for gaining ever deeper insights into the workings of the world around us. This will then hopefully stimulate and cause us to make further investigation and experimentation a part of the typical approach we take to all of our lighting- and material-based projects. In fact, this secondary objective should really be considered a critical element in the ongoing development of any 3D artist.

Light and material interaction – why objects in the real world have color

The amazing ability that we have been given as humans to see the world in glorious color is controlled by two interdependent mechanisms or systems. The first is the physical interaction of light itself with the solid matter that exists in the world around us. By this, I mean the walls, chairs, plants, fabrics, and in fact everything solid that makes up the environment in which we live. This *physical* interaction is something that we will explore quite a bit throughout the course of this chapter as it is both observable and measurable. Being able to gain even just a little understanding on this particular subject will most definitely impact (in a positive way) our ability to create believable V-Ray Materials in SketchUp.

The second mechanism is, in essence, you and I ourselves. In a truly amazing way, our eyes, when combined with the workings of our brains, give us the ability to actually see (in many ways *perceive* would probably be a better word), the interaction of light and matter that is continuously occurring all around us.

Light is where it all starts

When dealing with lighting and rendering inside a 3D application, we are using, in essence, a simplified version of the basic laws of physics that are at work, not just in the world but in the entire universe around us.

As briefly noted in *Chapter 5, Understanding the Principles of Light Behavior*, in the late 1800s and early 1900s, physicists realized that light was just one tiny part of a much greater wave spectrum that came to be classified as electromagnetic radiation. In an attempt to more readily understand and explain the workings of these waves, a classification or measurement system was devised, which assigned both a wavelength and a frequency to them. Visible light, which occupies only about one-thousandth of the total spectrum, was found to sit at wavelengths ranging from about 400 (violet) to 700 (red) nanometers.

In the case of frequency, the colors are reversed as red has the lowest frequency while violet has the highest. In fact, the terms infrared and ultraviolet are based on the frequency and not wavelength values of the visible spectrum. Infra being a Latin word that carries the thought of something *below*, while ultra, also of Latin origin, means *beyond* or *on the far side of.*

In *Chapter 5, Understanding the Principles of Light Behavior,* we also highlighted how in the 1800s, physicist Lord William Kelvin produced what is now known as the Kelvin color temperature scale. This was based on his observations of how a black body emitter (a block of carbon) when heated, produced a range of colors that followed a definite, measurable progression.

The scale assigns a numeric value in degrees Kelvin to each step of the progression, ranging from black through red, onto orange and then up to white, and beyond that into the blue part of the spectrum. In other words, the carbon emitted varying wavelengths of light according to the amount of heat it was generating.

1700k	2500k	4500k	5500k	6500k	7500k	8500k	10,000k

Exactly the same thing happens with stars: they emit varying wavelengths of light according to the heat being generated at their core. Our own sun very helpfully generates light that comes from the white part of the light emission spectrum although we of course perceive it as leaning towards yellow due to its complex interaction with our atmosphere.

For the purpose of keeping our discussion as simple as possible though (given that our eyes and brains also do a lot of perceptual filtering behind the scenes), we will work here with the assumption that light coming from our sun is for all intents and purposes white. This gives us a nice base point from which to understand how we see colored objects in the world around us. To help open up our understanding, we will essentially step through some aspects of the process regarding what happens when white light falls on or strikes the surface of a real-world object.

How absorption, reflectance, and transmittance work

In fact, for the purpose of this simplified discussion, we could say that one of three things, will occur at that point. Our light (or parts of it at least) will either be absorbed, reflected, or transmitted (that is, pass through) the object it is falling on. To use the technical parlance, we will see absorption, reflectance, and transmittance or maybe a combination of two or more of these occur. Exactly how these combinations work will depend entirely upon the physical properties of the material/object that the white light is striking.

- **Absorption**: This is what happens when the substance from which an object is made holds onto or absorbs certain component wavelengths of the light striking it. In the case of a black or nearly black object for instance, pretty much all of the light wavelengths are being absorbed, and so what we are left with is (quite literally) an absence of diffuse light reflection. You will have probably noticed that many black objects only have a recognizable shape or a defined outline because the materials from which they are made also have what we call reflective properties.

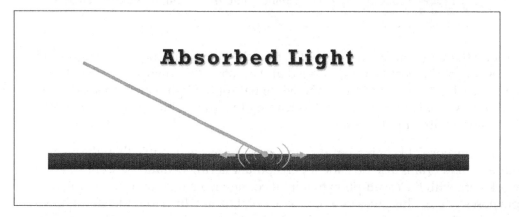

- **Diffuse Reflection (Reflectance)**: This is really the exact opposite of absorption in that it profiles the light wavelengths that are being reflected off a surface and so producing a visible surface color. The reflectance value for a given surface is used to describe the energy or strength with which various wavelengths are being reflected. A reflectance value typically equates to what we would call the brightness of an object's surface color.

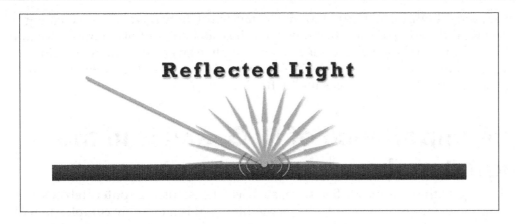

- **Transmittance**: This measures the ability of real-world materials such as glass to let light pass through rather than bounce off their surface. Where a high level of transmittance occurs, we typically find a complete absence of surface color information due to the fact that no reflection of any of the component wavelengths of light has occurred. This is why clear glass is only visible due to its specular reflection as well as its refractive properties.

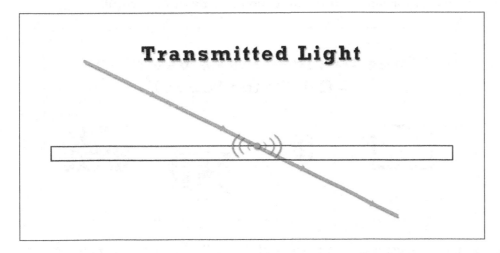

When we start to consider the possible number of variations that exist in just these three basic interactions of light, combine those possibilities with the enormous variety of materials or surface types that are available in the physical universe, and then combine those facts with the variety of lighting and indeed visual systems (eyes, cameras, and so on) through or on which color images can potentially be seen, then we should start to realize that there are a staggering number of color shades that can potentially exist.

In fact, armed with that thought, we may start to ask how (given that recreating reality would perhaps be a little bit beyond the capabilities of our humble desktop PC) we can possibly represent color in anything like an accurate manner using computer hardware and software. Well, this is where we start to understand the importance of what is known as the RGB color model.

The importance of R, G, and B in the digital realm

Technologies that use the RGB system, such as televisions, computer/tablet screens, and digital cameras are in fact taking something that is incredibly complex in real-world terms (visible light) and breaking it down into a much simpler model that can then be used to approximate and so simplify the complexity of the original.

Ray trace render engines such as V-Ray are perfect examples of this particular approach to problem solving. Pretty much everything they do simplifies an extremely complex real-world process, which in turn gives us the ability to compute and produce single-frame renders in minutes and hours instead of the much, much longer time frames that a completely accurate simulation of reality would require.

This can be done, especially in the case of the RGB system, for the most part because of the amazing way that our eyes and brains work together to decipher information regarding light intensity and color values. By simply mixing varying levels of these three primary colors as they have come to be known, most of the visible light spectrum can be quite satisfactorily represented even though the actual wavelengths being mixed to recreate the colors aren't technically correct from a physics point of view. In other words, the amazing ability that our brain has to interpolate or fill in missing information allows the RGB system to cheat in a convincing manner.

The RGB Spectrum

Red, green, and blue are designated as primary colors of light due to the fact that they are unique. While these three colors can be mixed together to create a *representation* of all other colors found in the visible light spectrum, they themselves cannot be created by means of the same mixing process.

Because the display technologies that digital artists would work with were already making use of this simplified yet extremely functional color model, it seemed only sensible that computer graphics applications, such as editing software and render engines, would adopt this same approach to color reproduction for their internal calculations.

What this means for the digital artist working inside a 3D render engine is that, rather than worry about reproducing complex physics interactions in order to reproduce color, we can simply choose the color we want in our materials by means of numeric RGB values. Because this model contains a comparatively simple set of computational instructions, we can both quickly and easily create and edit colors as much as we want or need to.

With the huge increase in computing power that has taken place over the past decade or so, unbiased render engines such as Maxwell Render have been able to replace RGB with what is known as a spectral model for internal calculations, the idea being that this allows them to more accurately recreate lighting and material effects. In truth though, taking this approach (up until the time this book was being written, at least) only makes a noticeable difference to a very small set of material types such as those needing to make use of dispersion effects.

Why are we using the HSV color model?

Given the obvious importance of the RGB color model then, you may be wondering why all of the color values used in the book up to this point have been given in the HSV (that is Hue, Saturation, and Value) color model rather than RGB?

Well, the reason I personally tend to work with the HSV model is that I find it describes color in a more familiar manner than does the somewhat abstract sounding RGB system.

To illustrate this point, if you were having a conversation with your decorator about the kind of color scheme that you have in mind for your lounge refurbishment, it is highly unlikely that either of you would be describing the colors to be used in RGB values. Rather than saying you wanted a color to be 255, 255, and 105 R, G, and B respectively, it is much more likely that you would discuss the pale yellow that you really liked. This is the strength of the HSV system, it presents color values in a manner that much more closely matches how we both think and talk about color.

Ultimately though, even when using the HSV system inside our graphics applications, we are still typically working with the RGB model for internal color calculations. The HSV controls are typically nothing more than an interface overlay that can help make working with color a little more intuitive.

The importance of realistic color values

As interesting as the facts regarding the way things work may be, the points we have been discussing here are far from just academic in nature. The creation of realistic materials in a believable and consistent manner inside our render engine will depend greatly upon our ability to put all of this interesting information to some kind of practical use.

For instance, when we look more closely at the wavelengths of light seen in the world around us, the insights we gain can help us avoid the kind of mistakes that newer render artists may be prone to, a typical example of which would be the tendency towards using colors in materials that just do not (or at least very rarely) exist in the real world. What I mean by that are fully saturated (255) color values that, for obvious reasons, look unnatural in a finished render. The extra vibrancy and saturation they give can often cause a surface to almost look as if it is glowing.

 Such over-saturation has for decades been associated with artificial imaging processes such as technicolor, a film process used in a very obvious manner to create the hyper-real Oz sequences in the 1939 film, *The Wizard of Oz.*

To avoid creating unnatural colors in a material, we typically need to keep saturation levels below 85 percent. When using the HSV model, this is as simple as keeping the saturation value at 218 or lower.

Another common mistake is to create materials that have unnaturally high reflectance or diffuse light bounce properties. Once reflectance (determined by the brightness of the diffuse color) passes the 80 percent mark in a material, we will typically find ourselves suffering from troublesome hotspot and color-bleed problems in our renders. Once introduced, these issues can be extremely problematic to deal with, especially if we are not aware of the reasons why the problems have started to occur in the first place.

The best way to deal with such issues of course is to avoid introducing them in the first place. This can be done by taking time to carefully consider the brightness or value of the colors we are using and the effect that this will have once lights and global illumination start to interact with the material properties in the scene. Keeping a material's reflectance property below the recommended 80 percent mark can be accomplished by making certain that the Value parameter (as in Hue, Saturation, and Value) is always set at 204 or below.

 In the case of certain special material types, this can climb to a value of around about 218, which would give us a reflectance value of about 85 percent.

The end result of all this care and attention will of course be the creation of materials in our scenes having color components that look and behave in a very realistic manner, thus making it that much more likely that we will be able to create a genuinely photographic final render.

Light and material interaction – what is reflectivity?

In discussing only the color or diffuse aspect of light reflection (reflectance) in our materials, we have so far neglected to mention that surfaces often have physical properties that can cause light to reflect off them in a very different manner. This change in light behavior causes it of course to produce a very different visual result.

In computer graphics, the Lambertian model for diffuse reflection (reflectance) of light describes a perfectly uniform micro-faceted (or rough) surface that diffuses or scatters light equally in all directions. Whenever we discuss a surface in terms of its color alone, (what we might call a matte surface, for example) it is generally this kind of reflectance model that we have in mind.

Lambertian reflectance is named after Johann Heinrich Lambert, who introduced the concept of perfect diffusion in his 1760 book *Photometria*, a publication that is in fact still available in paperback even today.

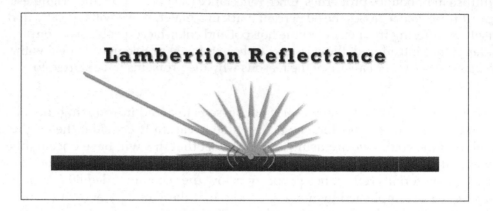

However, as a surface gets smoother at the microscopic level, the way that light reflects from it alters. Instead of continuing to be scattered in a multitude of directions as in our illustration here, the reflection angles narrow, become fewer in number, and so introduce blurred reflections.

Eventually, on a completely smooth surface, the light can essentially be described as bouncing only in a single direction. This, to our eyes, makes a surface look highly, if not completely, reflective.

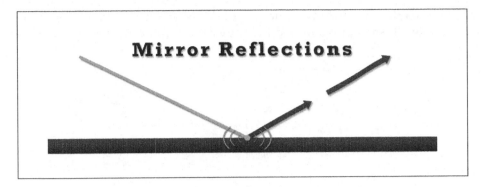

To be able to both differentiate between and describe the very different look that these changes give us, we give this type of light reflection a unique name, referring to it as specular rather than diffuse light reflection. Specular reflection is what we are typically referring to when we talk about an object as being shiny or reflective.

Just to be clear, we need to restate that reflectance and reflectivity are not different aspects of light; they are simply different visual results created by altering the direction(s) in which light bounces. This directional change is caused by the unique properties of the surface with which the light interacts.

To be able to set realistic and believable levels of specular reflection in our materials, we would again need to take time out to carefully research the physical makeup of the surface we are recreating in order to understand how it would interact with the light striking it. Having done that, we will then be in a position to make informed changes to our materials rather than simply punching in arbitrary values based only on guesswork.

How glossiness controls work

While creating the two extremes of either a completely diffuse or completely reflective surface is a fairly simple and straightforward process when using either the Standard or V-Ray Material types, getting the correct look for a surface that lies somewhere in between will require a little bit of extra work and the use of an extra set of parameters in the form of the material's glossiness controls.

Although, in reality, the controls found in each of these two materials work identically, the defaults have been set up a little differently as seen in the following screenshot:

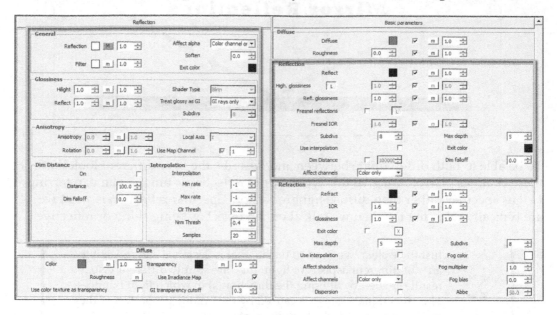

Whereas the Standard Material's Reflection layer has two glossiness parameters, one for the reflections themselves and another that controls the highlights, the V-Ray Material by contrast (and of course, by extension the V-RayBRDF layer) gives us just a single reflection glossiness control with which to work.

 If we need to, we can unlock the glossiness highlight control on the V-Ray Material, in which case things will work exactly in the same manner as the Reflection layer.

The purpose of these glossiness controls is to help us simulate the various levels of roughness that can occur at the microscopic level on an object's surface and so cause the reflections created there to become broken or blurred as the bouncing light is scattered in numerous directions. Now, although this effect could theoretically be achieved by means of geometry displacement, the resulting load on both CPU and memory resources would be intense, and in a 32-bit application such as SketchUp, running into out of memory crashes would also become a very real possibility.

Not that using the glossiness controls themselves come without penalty. When we enter a value of less than 1 in any of these options, the simulation of light scattering that we enable will require more in the way of sample rays in order to produce an acceptable final result. And extra samples in a ray trace renderer of course, always translate into longer render times. If we decide not to add the extra samples, then we will find that we get a lot of noise showing up in the blurry reflections we are creating.

Perhaps the best way to demonstrate the difference this can make to the quality of our finished material would be to take our highly reflective barrier chrome material, apply it to one of our sculpts, and then lower its glossiness value to 0.75 to introduce a fairly high level of scattering to the reflections. The three comparison renders we can see here demonstrate the difference between the default sample or subdiv value setting of 8 as compared to the subsequent doubling up of 16 and then 32 glossiness subdivs. Note also the difference in render times on a pretty low-powered quad-core Intel i5 laptop.

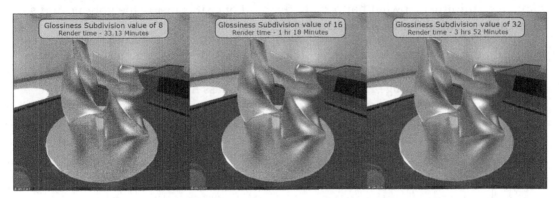

The reason for the big increase in render times that we will experience as we double each of these numbers also comes in part from the fact that the subdivs values found anywhere in the V-Ray UI does not report the actual sample or ray numbers being used, instead giving us the square of them.

With a subdiv value of 8 set in the **Glossiness** controls of our material for instance, we are in fact making use of 64 samples or rays per pixel (8 multiplied by 8) to create the scattered reflections. At a subdiv value of 16, we are using 256 samples per pixel, and at 32 subdivs, we are using a whopping 1024 samples for every single pixel in the rendered image, which is a lot of samples.

Remember also to factor in the fact that lots of other sample types are being used by V-Ray to create other aspects of the rendered image, and it shouldn't be surprising to us that we see our render times escalating.

Light and material interaction – the transmittance effects

While the diffuse and specular reflections we see on the surface of objects are two different visual results that come from the same basic operation of light, transmittance by contrast, is an effect created by pretty much the opposite process. Here, rather than bouncing off the surface of an object, light is allowed to pass into its volume. As with light bounce, this process can also produce a variety of material looks.

Understanding refraction

Describing an object as being transmissive, though, only tells us that it is allowing at least some of the light energy striking it to pass into the object's volume. From that point onwards, other properties of the object's physical makeup will come into play, determining just what happens to the light once it is inside the volume and so ultimately creating the final visual appearance of the object.

For instance, with glass, which in most situations is a highly transmissive substance, the light rays passing into it are caused to slow down due to the change in density produced by their passage from air into the solid glass material. This slow down causes the light rays to bend or alter course, which in turn produces the visual phenomenon known as refraction. The effect of refraction can easily be demonstrated by simply holding a clear glass object such as a drink tumbler to your eye and observing how objects on the opposite side appear distorted and offset.

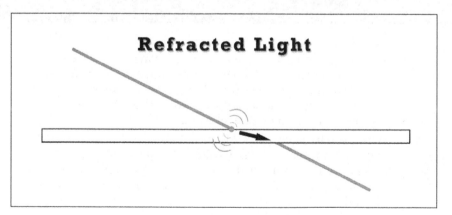

Refracted Light

Making use of IOR values

Just how much distortion or bending takes place will depend very much on the amount of directional change that is forced on the light rays as they enter into the glass object's volume. Again, this will be determined by the physical properties of the object, density being one of the big contributing factors here.

Does this mean that in order to recreate realistic glass for our scene materials, we would need to know and include all of the complex molecular information contained in every type of glass known? Fortunately, the answer to that question is no. Instead, we can make use of a piece of measured data that is made readily available to us in the form of an index or table. This is known as the index of refraction, and it contains numeric values that describe the slowdown and so directional change of light as it passes into and through all transmissive objects.

The following table includes a number of averaged IOR values that can be used to describe the refractive properties of a number of fairly typical transmissive materials:

Material	IOR value
Air	1.000293
Carbon dioxide	1.00045
Ice	1.31
Alcohol	1.329
Water	1.333
Ethanol	1.36
Glycerin	1.473
Glass	1.5
Emerald	1.570
Heavy Flint Glass	1.65
Ruby	1.770
Sapphire	1.770
Crystal	2.0
Diamond	2.419

By making use of these values, we can, in a very predictable manner, mimic the bending of light inside the volume of an object and so with relative ease, re-recreate complex transmissive materials such as glass, water, diamond, and others.

A bit more on Fresnel equations

Now there is a potential problem that we could find ourselves running into when creating materials such as glass and water in that as well as being highly transmissive, these materials are also under certain circumstances, highly reflective. In truth, they exhibit a very specific behavior in that the ratio of transmittance to reflectivity is very much dependent upon the angle from which they are viewed.

Now, the Standard and V-Ray Materials aren't actually set up to automatically take this unique aspect of light and substance interaction into account. To successfully mimic this particular behavior, we would first of all need to create a material that is both reflective and refractive, make certain that we have set an accurate IOR value in the refraction controls, and then as a final element, add Fresnel equations into the mix. We could accomplish this final step in either of the following ways:

- In the V-Ray Material/V-RayBRDF layer, put a check in the Fresnel box
- In the Reflection layer of a Standard Material, add a TexFresnel map to the reflection map slot (this is now added by default in V-Ray 2.0 as soon as a new Reflection layer is created)

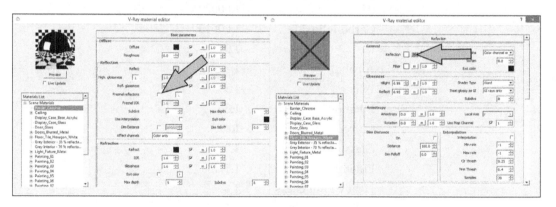

Understanding translucency

Of course, not all transmissive surface types allow so much light through that they can rightly be called transparent or see-through. Some, while clearly allowing light to pass into the volume, retain (to a greater or lesser degree) a measure of opaqueness to them.

For instance, if we were to hang thin cotton curtains at a window that has bright sunlight pouring through, as well as being able to see any color or pattern information found on the interior surface of the fabric, we would also be able to clearly see the outline or shape of any solid object on the opposite side of the curtains. We see the same effect at work when we hold a sheet of paper or a very thin plastic object up to a bright light. We tend to refer to these particular transmissive effects as translucency.

What we are seeing at work of course is a combination of both reflectance and transmittance, whereby light is being transmitted into the volume of the object, but then rather than being allowed to pass straight through as with glass, the physical makeup of the substance causes a measure of diffuse reflection or light bounce to take place inside the volume before at least some of the light wavelengths are allowed to exit.

How subsurface scattering is different

Now you may well wonder given that description, what the difference is between translucency and another light interaction phenomenon commonly referred to as subsurface scattering? Well, the honest answer is, there really isn't any difference, as both terms are in reality describing the same basic process.

The different terms are typically used to describe the same effect at work in objects of differing volumes or thickness. Translucency, for instance, is a term that is typically applied to thin objects found exhibiting this scattering behavior. In such objects, we will often see a big percentage of the light being transmitted into them still make its way out of the opposite side of the volume, which is why we are able to see shadows and shapes through the given examples of thin cotton curtains and piece of paper.

Subsurface scattering (SSS) on the other hand is a term generally applied to objects with more volume to them, such as candles, blocks of soap, or fruits such as grapes and tomatoes. Typically, these objects scatter the light in lots of directions, with some of the thicker substances often bouncing much of the light back the way it came.

SSS can sometimes give objects the appearance of having a glowing interior as in the example of our grapes in the following photograph:

The importance of energy-conserving materials

Fortunately for us (given all of these complex processes taking place), the one thing that we don't have to worry about when using either the Standard or V-Ray Materials is the need to balance out the various reflectance, transmittance, and reflectivity properties as both of these materials handle incoming and outgoing light energy in a physically accurate manner, which means that they can correctly be referred to as energy-conserving materials.

In the bad old days of computer graphics, before render engines like V-Ray came along, materials relied on the good judgment of the artist in order to create a good looking balance between diffuse and specular components, which unfortunately (without a decent grounding in the physics of light) is not quite as easy to do as it may at first sound. This is why many renders produced in the 1990s suffered from what came to be referred to as the CG look.

It does need to be said that unrealistic materials were not the sole contributors to this particular look. A lack of usable global illumination tools, inaccurate lighting setups, and other elements certainly contributed greatly to the unrealistic look of many 3D renders at the time.

The problem that shader or material writers were wrestling with back then was the fact that light only strikes a surface with a finite amount of energy, which then of course has to be accurately disposed of in accordance with the type of surface it is supposed to be. So a material cannot realistically be set up so that it has 50 percent diffuse reflectance, 50 percent specular reflectivity, and at the same also be 50 percent transmissive or see-through. This would mean that from apparently nowhere, our light had suddenly gained an extra 50 percent of incoming energy (3 x 50 equaling 150), which of course breaks the laws of thermodynamics and so cannot, if a material is to be realistic looking, be allowed to happen.

In general, physically correct energy distribution dictates the following points:

- Transmission or transparency takes energy away from a material's diffuse coloration, and so at 100 percent transparency, a material can have no diffuse color coming from its surface at all.

- Reflectivity can take energy away from both the diffuse and transparent components, and so if a material has 100 percent specular reflectivity, then there typically should be neither diffuse color nor transparency present.

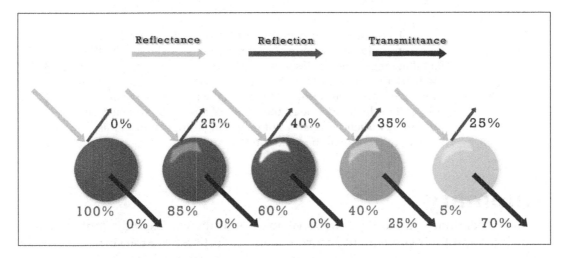

What we have accomplished?

Now you may be asking: is all of this physics information really important in the final analysis of material creation? And the answer, beyond a shadow of a doubt, is yes. The adage *he who does not know where he has come from, cannot know where he is going* would apply perfectly here.

You see whenever we take a photograph, all of these complex interactions between light and matter are already at work and so produce the scene that we see before us. In order to create a photographic-looking render of an environment, we will of course need to recreate, at least to a reasonable degree, the manner in which these light and solid matter interactions take place.

Of course, the programmers at Chaos Group have taken care of huge chunks of this by creating lighting and material tools that do most of this work for us. We can, however, enhance the work they have done (and so of course, improve the final results of our own rendered images) by taking the time to understand the workings not only of the tools found in V-Ray, but also the workings of the world around us that those tools help us recreate.

 Certainly, the importance of understanding and so accurately recreating color and other material properties can be seen in the fact that many interior designers and architects are going to want the work they have put into their designs correctly represented in the renders and marketing materials that we produce for them. If we don't understand at least the basics of the theory touched on in this chapter, then the chances of us getting things right in this area are naturally going to be greatly reduced.

Summary

We have seen that without light, we have no color as the wavelengths contained in white light and their subsequent absorption and reflection from the surface of objects in the real world is the mechanism that brings color to the world around us.

We also noted the importance of the RGB color model as regards color reproduction given that trying to recreate the entire light spectrum inside both hardware and software applications would be problematic and costly to say the least.

And very importantly, we considered some of the typical behaviors seen in real-world surfaces that need to be recreated inside our V-Ray Materials, including:

- The use of realistic color values to create believable reflectance
- Reflectivity and the scattering of light to produce blurred reflections
- Transmissive effects, such as refraction, SSS, and translucency
- Finally, the importance of energy conservation in materials so that they behave in a physically accurate manner, thus enhancing their photographic quality

In *Chapter 8, Composition and Cameras*, we will return to the subjects of composition and camera setup so that we can better understand how issues such as *shot type, aspect ratios, output resolution*, and *focal length* can all massively affect the quality of any final renders we create.

8
Composition and Cameras

Although we have already discussed the subject of composition a little in our introductory chapter, there is quite a bit more to the subject that we need to both understand and apply to the photographic renders that we want to produce. For instance, one thing that we haven't touched on up to this point is the fact that there are quite a few technical considerations that will, to one extent or another, impact the way we compose the shots that we will use for our final deliverables.

Defining our goals

Our goals for this chapter will be as follows:

- Finalize the technical requirements for the finished renders.
- By making use of our artistic sensibilities (generally, in conjunction with guidance from the client in the form of their original brief), lockdown the type of shot or shots that we are going to produce.
- And finally, using the controls offered by both the V-Ray physical camera and SketchUp's own viewport, create final camera views for our scene that have a strong and pleasing compositional element to them. This final step of course will need to take into account the basic principles or guidelines of composition, and apply them to our scene or camera views as we go further.

One thing to note here is that the material we will be covering in this chapter hasn't really been arranged in any kind of specific progression that must be adhered to on your particular project. Rather, it is in this order simply because I typically find that getting the technical considerations (covered in the first part of the chapter) out of the way before moving onto the more artistic aspects of shot composition, more often than not provides the most efficient and problem-free approach to the process. This is typically due to the fact that with technical details decided and settings dialed in, we find ourselves free to focus entirely on getting the shot we want, confident in the knowledge that the framing and aspect ratios we are using will not be altered later in the production process.

Deciding the shot type

Interestingly though, the first point of the final shot setup that we will tackle here can in many ways be described as both technical and creative in that both elements have to be factored into the final decisions that we make. The point in question would be a consideration regarding the type of shot or shots that we are trying to create. To understand what I mean by the phrase *type of shot*, let's make use of SketchUp's **Susan** character as our subject matter and look at some very basic examples of the more frequent or commonly used shot types.

Although V-Ray and SketchUp will most probably be used by CG artists as a toolset to create environment and product renders, we are making use of a character in these definitions due to the visual familiarity with the shot types discussed that mediums such as film and TV have naturally given us. When making renders of our own, we will of course have to take the principles highlighted here and then apply them to the environment or products that are the focus of our shots.

To experiment with your own variations of these shot types, open up the `Shot_Type_Examples.skp` scene by navigating to the `Exercise Files | Model_Files | Chapter_08` folder.

The long or wide shot

The idea behind the use of a long or wide shot (often called an establishing shot in cinematic terms) is to give the viewer a broad overview or picture of the environment or locations layout and setup. With this shot, we are trying to give the viewer a more complete sense of the scene as a whole as opposed to only showing them fragmented and very often randomized sections of it, which places the burden of piecing together a more complete picture solely on the viewer's imagination.

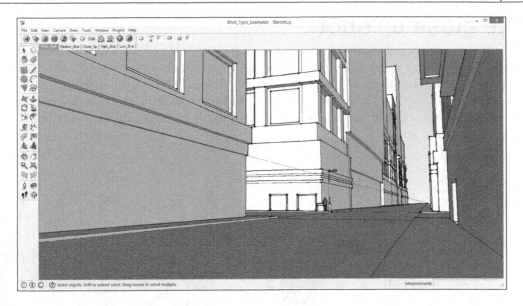

The medium shot

The medium shot, is, as its very name suggests, designed to sit somewhere between the long and close up shot that comes next, and looks to give us a little bit of the best of both of them but without of course the extremes of either. The medium shot can still reveal a reasonable amount of space found in the environment while at the same time (with good use of framing and composition of course) being able to focus our attention more closely on one or two specific elements inside the scene.

The close up shot

The close up shot on the other hand puts us up close and personal in the frame with generally speaking one, but on the odd occasion maybe two very specific elements in the scene, making them the very obvious focal point of the shot. This shot type lets us bring out or highlight details (in the focal point or subject), as well as make use of artistic effects such as depth of field to defocus background elements in a very naturalistic way.

Of course, lots of variations can be built around these three basic setups or shot types by adding other descriptive words to them such as ultra, medium, or extreme. So for example, we may decide that we want to make use of a medium wide or medium close up shot, both of which would obviously add either a little bit more or a little bit less to the original shot types framing.

The danger, however, with using only these somewhat straightforward shot types is the fact that they tend to present a somewhat ordinary view of the scene to us. This mainly comes down to the fact that we see these types of views all the time as we tend to focus our attention and examine our surroundings in these three general ways.

When out and about, especially when visiting somewhere new, we tend to take in our surroundings in a broad way, seeing how the environment connects together as it were. When in our homes or at work, we tend to navigate the enclosed space by focusing on or being aware of elements and objects that are in our more immediate vicinity. Finally, of course, when we are occupied with much more specific tasks such as preparing a meal or working on a computer, our vision becomes very much focused on just one or two very specific elements in our environment.

Besides, the distance type shots that we have already mentioned, which obviously deal (for the most part) with moving the camera into and/or out of a scene, we could also make use of the camera's height or Z axis position.

The high shot

The high shot is a situation in which the viewing camera is deliberately placed above, sometimes high above the subject that is the focal point of the shot. In motion pictures, this type of shot is often employed to create a sense of smallness or vulnerability in the character(s) that we are viewing. Another way of looking at the same setup would be to see it as emphasizing the scale, possibly the grandeur, or maybe even the intimidating nature of the environment itself.

This type of shot can be very effectively used to give the viewer an overview or bird's eye view of a location and add drama, of course, as shown in the following screenshot:

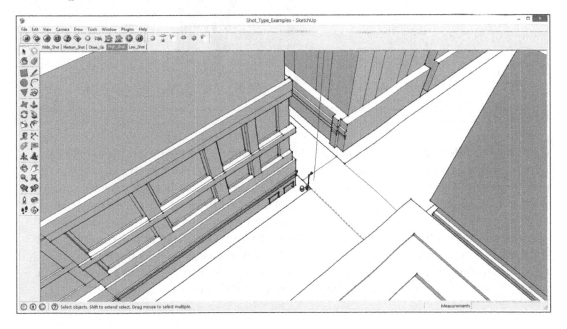

The low shot

The low shot on the other hand is something we typically see used in motion pictures to create in many ways the opposite of a high shot. When a character or object looms large in the frame, occupying a large portion or possibly even most of our field of view, then a feeling of strength, power, and on occasion menace, can be imparted to the viewer.

In a purely environmental sense, similar feelings can be evoked in the viewer especially when looking at a structure of large proportions such as a castle or fortress. These can be made to feel strong and impenetrable. A cathedral can be made to feel grand and majestic, and when the shot is handled carefully, the looming skyscrapers in a city setting can be made to feel menacing and oppressive.

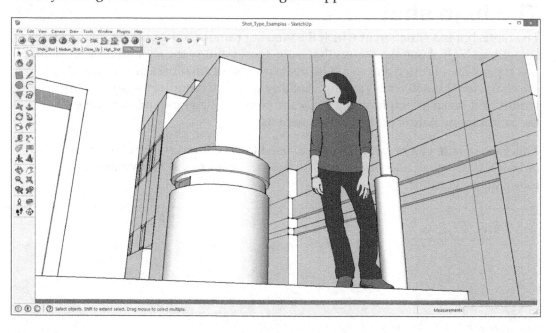

One final or alternative shot type that could be used is the **Point Of View (POV)** shot, designed to give the viewer a human or first person perspective of a scene or environment. Typically, the camera is placed at average eye height, which in many places around the world is around the 5 feet 5 inches to 5 feet 10 inches mark or approximately 1.65 to 1.77 meters. An alternative would be to place it at average shoulder height which is somewhere around 4 feet 8 inches (so approximately 1.42 meters). It also typically makes use of a 45 to 55 mm lens, which is the focal range that closely equates to normal human vision. This of course is based on the assumption that either a 35 mm film or a full frame sensor digital camera is being used.

In our gallery scene file for this chapter, `DT_Interior_Composition_Start.skp`, we have a single default camera view set up (the same one that we have been working with for most of our projects so far) that can be used as the basis or starting point from which we can create a number of other render views.

 As this basic POV shot from inside the archway is a somewhat bland looking view, from this point forward we will only be keeping hold of it as a base or reference point from which we will be creating our new scene views.

Aspect ratios

Before we go ahead and start creating any new camera views in our scene, however, there are a few critical pieces of information that really need to be input into both SketchUp and V-Ray before we can attempt to set up any kind of final composition for our render views. One such critical piece of information would be the choice of aspect ratio at which we want our final images to be produced.

For those of you who are a little unfamiliar with this particular term, aspect ratio is a numerical value that describes the proportional relationship between the width and height of either an image or video frame. More often than not this relationship is described by two colon separated numbers such as 16:9 and 4:3, which are themselves two common ratios used in video and broadcast production.

Perhaps in a slightly confusing manner, this exact same relationship can also be correctly represented in a slightly different format, this time using the values 1.777:1 and 1.333:1, respectively. These numbers represent the smallest values at which the ratio can be described while using a value of 1 for the height setting and are derived from dividing the width of an image by its height. So for instance, if we divide 1024 by a value of 768 we get 1.33 recurring. When expressed using the smallest whole number possible, this becomes a ratio of 4:3.

It is important to be clear on the fact that these numbers describe a relationship and not a fixed size or measurement. The actual size of a 16:9 image could be measured in inches, meters, pixels, picas, or any other valid form of image measurement. What makes it a 16:9 image is the fact that its width and height measurements always maintain a ratio of 16:9 across the width and height.

This means, for instance, that a printed image could be the output at either 48 x 27 inches or 4 x 2.25 inches, and both, despite their being completely different in terms of size, would correctly be described as sharing an aspect ratio of 16:9 (or 1.777 to 1).

Which aspect ratio we need to use will most likely be determined by our client, based on the output devices that they are going to be targeting with your images. Some common ratios you may be asked to render would be as follows:

- **1.333:1 (4:3)**: This aspect ratio was used commonly in the past for broadcast and video but is now more readily associated with still image photography and print. Common resolutions include 768 x 576, 1024 x 768, and 1600 x 1200. At the time of writing, the current generations of Apple iPad screens use a 4:3 ratio.

- **1.500:1 (3:2)**: This is the aspect ratio of a 35mm film and is also a typical ratio used in photographic printing, a resolution such as 6 x 4 inches (or 10 x 15cm) being a fairly typical or common print size.

- **1.777:1 (16:9)**: This is the current standard for High-Definition (HD) video playback and broadcast TV. Common resolutions include 1280 x 720 (720p) and 1920 x 1080 (1080p).

- **1.85:1 and 2.35:1**: These are two typical widescreen ratios used in the production and presentation of big screen movies. Typical resolutions include 1828 x 988 and 3656 x 1976 for the 1.85:1 ratio and 2048 x 872 and 4096 x 1744 for 2.35:1.

Refer to the following diagram for classification of different aspect ratios:

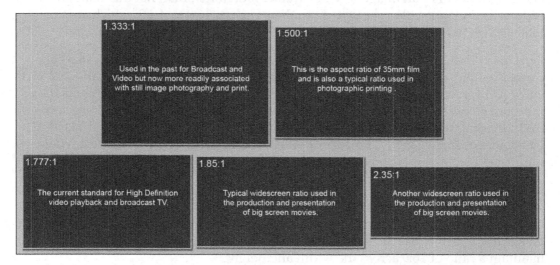

The important thing that we need to note here is that the aspect ratio we set for our final renders will naturally have a massive impact on the composition and staging that we set up in our render views, hence the need to discuss the subject here first. If we fail to set up our render views using the required ratio, then chances are that our renders will not turn out as well composed as we had perhaps hoped or even expected.

For instance, the following two renders were both taken from the POV camera view in our DT_Interior_Composition_Start.skp start scene. Clearly though, each scene has been rendered using very different aspect ratio settings in V-Ray. The one on the left was completed using the current 1.333:1 (or 4:3) ratio and a pixel resolution of 1000 x 750, while the one on the right uses a 1.77:1 (or 16:9) ratio and a pixel resolution of 1000 x 562. The difference this automatically makes to both the composition and staging of the images is strikingly obvious.

The 1.77 (or 16:9) version feels more balanced and focused on the scene content because it matches the SketchUp scene view that it was set up with much more closely. Whereas, the 1.33 (or 4:3) version feels a little bit unfocused and unfinished compositionally speaking.

Choosing our ratio

Obviously, the question of which ratio to use as we move forward with a project will depend upon a number of factors, not least of which is the medium on which our final renders will be used. For the purpose of our composition exercises here, let's assume that our client has indicated that they want to place these renders inside an HD Blu-ray presentation they are putting together. This means of course that we will need to stick with the current HD aspect ratio setting of 1.777:1.

 If we find ourselves needing a little help calculating our aspect ratios, lots of online aspect ratio calculators exist; one easy to use version that I particularly prefer can be found at www.digitalrebellion.com/webapps/ aspect_calc.html.

Beware of the difference between the viewport and render

One gotcha with regard to aspect ratio that we need to take note of here is the fact that we will often see a discrepancy between what is displayed in the SketchUp viewport and what actually renders inside the V-Ray frame buffer window. In the following screenshots you can see (on the right-hand side) the 16:9 render that we have just taken in comparison (on the left-hand side) to the SketchUp view from which that render was taken.

Note that while the left and right edges of the frames are fixed at identical points, the height dimensions are noticeably different with the V-Ray render showing more of the ceiling than can be seen in the SketchUp viewport.

This discrepancy occurs because even though we are viewing the SketchUp application on a 16:9 monitor (specifically I am working with the SketchUp application window set at a 16:9 resolution of 1600 x 900), the SketchUp viewport itself, due to space being taken up by the applications toolbars and other UI elements, is not set at a 16:9 ratio.

To see that this is indeed the case, we can make use of some existing V-Ray functionality to give us an exact readout of the SketchUp viewport's current aspect ratio. To follow along, you will need to open up the `chapter 8 DT_Interior_Composition_Start.skp` file and then perform the following steps:

1. Open up the **Output** rollout in the V-Ray options editor.
2. At the bottom of the **Output size** section, click on the **Get view aspect** button.

What you will see is that V-Ray now alters its current **Height** dimension read out so as to accurately match the aspect ratio of the SketchUp viewport, which in my particular case happens to be 2.0105:1, the specific pixel resolution now being 1000 x 497.

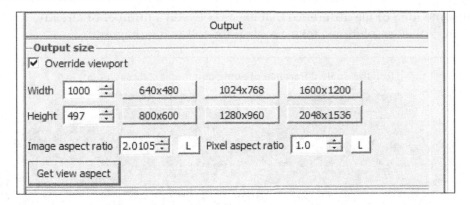

 As V-Ray will always assume that the edges of the SketchUp viewport are the fixed points around which we want our aspect ratio to be created, this behavior is obviously something we need to be very much aware of when it comes time to creating our final composition, because if we for some reason end up resizing our SketchUp application window, we will also be altering the final framing and composition of the image that we are rendering.

The requisite maximum resolution

Before we can go ahead and set up the final aspect at which we will produce our renders however, there is yet another important piece of information that needs to be decided upon, this being the maximum pixel size (specifically the maximum width value) that will be required for the final rendered images.

As well as, being a needed piece of information for setting up the final aspect ratio, the maximum pixel resolution at which we render is, in its own right, a setting that will affect both the composition and staging of our image.

Of course, the maximum resolution used in final renders can and will vary from project to project and will to some extent be determined by the type of output media that either the client or we ourselves are targeting. Typically speaking, projects that are going to print tend to require higher resolution renders than those being used for onscreen presentations simply because of the need to pack extra image detail into each printed inch of paper. Without that extra detail, a printed render could potentially look extremely blocky and low quality.

To get some idea of the difference that exists between a number of already mentioned pixel resolutions, take a look at the following diagram:

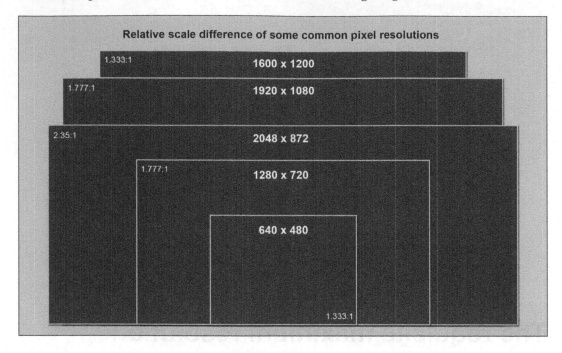

With that thought in mind, let's say that along with being included in an HD Blue ray presentation, that our renders will also be used for both a web-based presentation and included in printed marketing materials, with the printed material showing the images at a maximum width on the page of about six inches.

Taking all of these requirements into account, we can settle on a maximum rendering resolution that uses full HD framing of 1920 x 1080 pixels, giving us the ability to output an image from Photoshop with a **Pixels Per inch** (**PPI**) setting of 300 giving us a clear high quality print at 6.4 x 3.6 inches. This setting also of course maintains our requirement for a 1.777:1 (or 16:9) aspect ratio in the images.

To set that up in V-Ray, let's perform the following steps:

1. In the V-Ray options dialogue, open the **Output** rollout.

2. For the **Width** parameter, enter a value of 1920 and in the **Height** field enter a value of 1080.

3. Next to the **Image aspect ratio** spinner, click on the **L** (for Lock) button that will hopefully fix our image aspect at 1.777:1 no matter what value we enter for the **Width** parameter.

 This can be handy if we need to quickly drop down our resolution for even quicker test renders but don't want to lose the aspect ratio that we have composed for.

How focal length affects composition

The final important piece of information that we need to put into place here is again both technical and creative and can potentially affect our final composition in quite a drastic manner. This would be the choice of the focal or lens' length that we decide to use for the rendering camera(s).

 Focal length can also be described in terms of a camera's **Field Of View (FOV)**. This setting describes the area of an environment that can be seen by our camera and is expressed as an angle, measured of course using degrees.

The following simplified diagram gives us an idea of what happens whenever we extend the focal length on a real world camera lens:

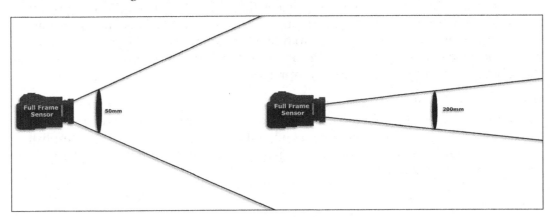

Using a focal length of around 50 mm, the lens stays reasonably close to the body of the camera and so produces a fairly broad FOV. As we dial in longer focal lengths however, jumping all the way up to 2000 mm here, we physically move the lens away from the body of the camera, creating a much narrower FOV that will of course dramatically alter the overall feel and composition of our shot(s).

To demonstrate just how much this will affect our images, let's use SketchUp's viewport **Zoom** tool to see for ourselves the different look we get when making use of the two focal lengths seen in the diagram.

To do that, let's perform the following steps:

1. Click to select the **Zoom** tool from the SketchUp toolbar and notice the feedback that you get from the readout down in the bottom-right corner of the interface.

 Depending on how you have SketchUp set up, this will be showing you either an FOV read out set at 39.60 degrees or a focal length value of 50mm.

2. To see how the two focal lengths alter composition and framing, simply type in a value of 200 using your keyboard followed by mm to ensure that you are getting a read out in millimeters and then hit the *Enter* or *return* key.

What we see now is a drastically altered view of the environment that has a completely different compositional feel to it. It seems as though our camera has moved forward in the scene and pushed right up close to the display case on the right. We know, however, that the camera has remained in exactly the same position while using both of these very different focal length values.

The important thing to note here of course is the fact that focal length changes can dramatically alter the perception of depth or space in a scene. At 50 mm, our space feels fairly open with plenty of room to move around, whereas the 200 mm setting closes the space down quite dramatically, making the distance between objects in the room look and feel much more compressed.

Unlike our choice of pixel resolution though, the focal lengths we use for our different renders will more than likely vary even between renders taken inside the same environment. The question of just what it is that we are trying to accomplish with a given shot will always need to be given serious consideration in order to make such choices wisely.

Of course, one of the brilliant things about using V-Ray as our render engine of choice is that we can fairly easily set things up so that we are able to quickly render out a number of focal length tests and then compare them side by side using the history function **H** in the V-Ray frame buffer. At this moment in time, full frame test renders would take much longer than we can afford on a commercial project so let's go ahead and make a quick change to our settings so that we can get some test renders here:

1. In the V-Ray options dialogue, open up the **Global switches** rollout.

2. And in the **Materials** section, check the **Override Materials** box.

3. Finally, uncheck the **Reflection/refraction**, **Maps**, and **Glossy effects** options.

Rendering will now proceed much faster as we have essentially cut out all of the computationally expensive material properties in the scene.

Setting up scene views for final shot rendering

Time to keep things moving by going ahead and nailing down some of the hard choices we need to make regarding the final camera views that we will be rendering from, including the choice of which compositional guidelines we will be applying as we set them up.

First up – the wide shot

The first type of shot that we will set up here is a wide or establishing shot that can be used to give the viewer a pretty good sense of the space in its entirety. Leaving the viewer to have to mentally stitch the general layout of the room together by means of separate and visually disconnected renders can often lead them to some wrong conclusions regarding the environments' general makeup. As this is not a desired effect here, an establishing shot that sets up the scene for them will probably be a good idea.

To set up the required **Scenes** tab, we can perform the following steps:

1. Right-click on the existing **POV Shot - Main Gallery** scenes tab and click on the **Add** button in the menu.

2. As the new scene view that we have just created is instantly set as the active one, we can go ahead and use the **Orbit** tool to level out our view a little and then right-click on the **Scenes** tab and choose the **Update** option.

3. We can also keep things tidy here by right-clicking on the **Tab** option again and this time selecting the scene manager option.

4. In the **Name** field, for this view, let's type `Wide Shot  35mm` and then hit the *Enter* or *return* key.

5. Next, we need to set our focal length to match what is stated in the **Name** field. So, let's click on the SketchUp toolbar and select the **Zoom** tool, enter `35mm`, and then hit the *Enter* key again.

   We will need to reposition our view/camera so as to take advantage of the wider FOV that we now have available so let's continue further.

6. From the SketchUp toolbar select the **Walk** tool and then left-click on the viewport to gently push forward until the edges of the archway can no longer be seen.

7. Now, we can use the **Orbit, Pan**, and **Walk** tools to reposition our view to match the following screenshot:

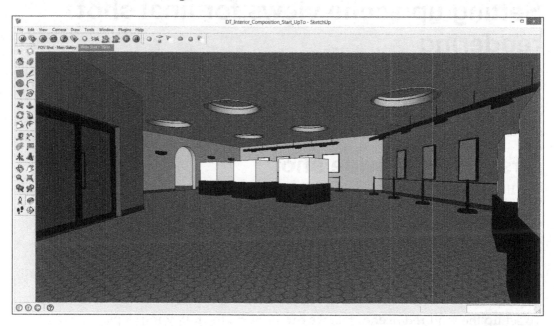

8. We will need to right-click on the **Scenes** tab and choose the **Update** option to lock those changes into place.

9. And finally, we can hit the **Render** button on the V-Ray toolbar to see how things are looking.

If you want to speed up your test renders a little more, you may want to go back into the **Output** rollout in the V-Ray options editor and lower the **Width** parameter down to something like 1000 or maybe even 800 pixels. As soon as you hit the *Enter* or *return* key, your height parameter will automatically update so as to keep the locked 1.777:1 ratio intact.

Take a look at the following screenshot:

Exercise – review

If you prefer to skip creating your own test renders for now, you can go ahead and open up the the full sized Chap08_WideShot.bmp version of this render (found in your Exercise_Files | Final_Renders | Chapter_08 folder) and see if you can identify which of the basic rules of composition listed in *Chapter 1, Diving Straight into Photographic Rendering*, you can see at work there.

You should be able to spot the following parameters:

- Leading lines
- Positive and negative space
- Symmetry
- Thirds
- Depth
- Balance

Scene two – close up

For our next shot, let's go to the opposite end of the spectrum so to speak and create a fairly extreme close up of some of the exhibits found inside our glass display cases. This will give us the opportunity to try out some **Depth of Field** effects in our renders should we have a mind to. Setting up this shot will be a bit of a challenge, however, as we are working here in a very fixed environment that doesn't really offer much in the way of staging opportunities to us.

Staging refers to the way that we arrange characters and objects within the frame in order to create a composition that we like. Often photographers and cinematographers will repeatedly restage a scene until they find something that works just right for them. In an environment such as our gallery space, however, where objects have a fixed place that they need to be in, staging the scene in any meaningful way is typically not an option and so finding well-composed shots can become a bit more of a challenge.

To get started, we will of course need to make a bit of a change to the scene, hiding the glass cover geometry so as to be able to see the exhibits or sculpts in the SketchUp viewport, meaning we will be able to see the framing we are getting on them. Before we create the scene view, let's go ahead and perform the following steps:

1. Right-click on our recently created **Wide Shot – 35mm** scene tab and choose the **Add Scene** option. This ensures that we keep our wide shot view intact.

2. Next, we can hide the display cases by clicking on the **Window** menu at the top of the SketchUp UI and choosing the **Layers** option from the drop-down menu.

3. In here, we want to uncheck the **Visible** option for the **Display_Glass** layer and then dismiss the layers dialogue.

4. Next, we can set our **Focal Length** for the shot to something a little more appropriate for the extreme closeness that we may want to create. With the **Zoom** tool selected over on the toolbar, we can enter a value of 80mm and then hit *Enter*.

5. To make sure we don't accidentally lose what we have created in the scene view so far, let's right-click again on the **Scenes** tab and then on the **Update** option.

6. Now we can move our camera into position as it were by using the **Orbit**, **Pan**, and **Walk** tools to set up a view that looks as similar as possible to the one seen in the following screenshot:

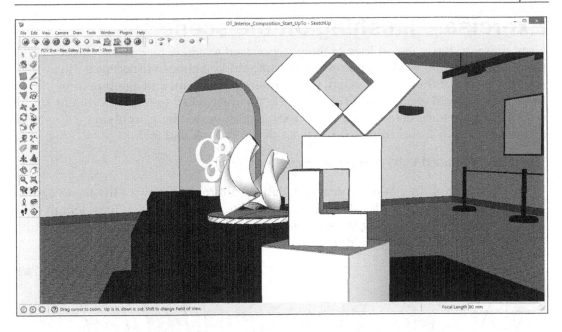

7. Now, we need to turn our view into an extreme close up by really pushing the telephoto aspect of our lens. This can be done by again selecting the **Zoom** tool and this time setting a focal length of 225mm.

8. Once that is done, right-click on the **Scenes** tab again to open up the scene manager and rename the **Scene Close Up** value as 225mm, remembering of course to click on the **Update** button on the far left of the **Scene** manager toolbar.

Exercise – review

Again, open up the full sized Chap08_CloseUpShot.bmp version of this render (found in your Exercise_Files | Final_Renders | Chapter_08 folder) and see if you can identify which of the basic rules of composition that we have already discussed you can see at work.

You should be able to spot the following rules:

- Point of view
- Subject and background
- Framing
- Cropping
- Focal point

Exercise – finishing off the scene

Now that you have a good idea of the process used to create new scene views from which we can render, your challenge, should you choose to accept it, is to set up the rest of the views needed, take renders from them, and again review the compositional elements that are at work. As always feel free to experiment with your own variations on the views we have suggested here, applying different compositional rules so as to get a different look and feel.

Shots that still need to be created are as follows:

- **High shot**: In this shot, create a balanced alternative view of the scene by making use of an elevated camera position. Use a suggested focal length of around 40mm, naming the scene tab **High Shot** as 40mm and remembering to click on the **Update** button on the **Scene** manager toolbar.

- **Low shot**: In this shot, create a balanced view of the scene as it is perhaps the trickiest of all to pull off given the nature of the environment that we are working with. Still, keeping in mind the fact that we are able to knock out reasonably fast test renders, a measure of experimentation should be a part of the way we are working here. For this shot, I would suggest using a final **Focal Length** of 70mm, and in the scene manager dialogue, name the scene view as Low Shot-70mm.

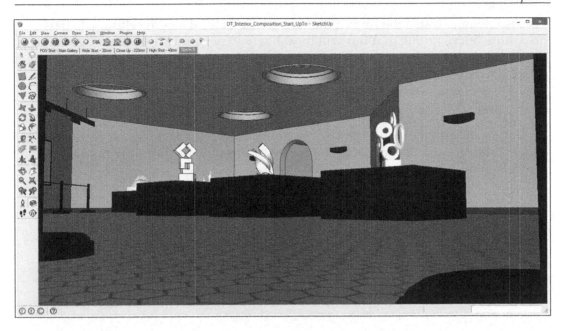

Of course, if you want to skip all of this scene setup completely, you are welcome to open up the `DT_Interior_Composition_Final.skp` file and take your renders from there, or if you prefer to skip rendering altogether and just do the compositional reviews, you can simply open up and use the full size renders that can be found in your `Exercise_Files | Final_Renders | Chapter_08` folder and make use of those.

Summary

Now, what we have covered in this chapter is by no means an in-depth look at the subject of camera setup and composition. We have nevertheless managed to cover a number of extremely important aspects of the topic.

Firstly, we identified a number of standard shot types that we can make use of such as wide, medium, and close up. We also considered the impact of our output aspect ratio setting for composition and highlighted some of the more commonly used ones. Closely tied to the aspect ratio setting is the pixel resolution at which our final renders will be made. Here, we settled on a full HD, 16:9 ratio output of 1920 x 1080 pixels.

We also demonstrated the impact that our choice of focal length setting will have on composition, noting that this will most likely vary greatly from shot to shot on a project, even when we are rendering inside the same space. And finally, we have set up a number of render views for ourselves, each employing a number of the basic rules of composition that we discussed in *Chapter 1, Diving Straight into Photographic Rendering*.

Having dealt with a number of important output settings then, we are ready to take a look at improving our rendered output by means of V-Rays' numerous quality controls in our next chapter.

9

Quality Control

Up until this point in our project we have been working pretty much exclusively with V-Ray's default quality settings. Given that we are now closing in on creating our final output renders, the time has come to take a look at making improvements to the quality settings in a number of key areas. Specifically in this chapter, we will take a look at improving lighting, global illumination, image sampling, and scene materials. Taking the time to make even tiny improvements in each of these areas will ultimately lead to the production of much cleaner looking, higher-quality final renders.

To help us examine each of these key areas, we will need to make a series of high-quality test renders that we can take into our image viewer or editor of choice and then scrutinize closely.

While you can certainly take renders of your own as we work through this chapter, given the time required to complete many of these high resolution renders, you may wish to simply refer to the printed images seen in this chapter.

Of course, while some of the changes made will be clear and obvious in the printed graphics, others may be too subtle to be easily picked out at the sizes seen here. To be able to access and then scrutinize the final high resolution renders up close, please go to the `Chapter_09` folder under `Exercise_Files | Final_Renders` and open them up.

Whichever version of the renders you use, just be sure that once you have them open in your viewer or editing application, you zoom in close, examine them carefully, and then make copious notes on what you think may be missing or could be improved inside the scene. If we really want to push the quality of our work at this stage of the process, we will need to be as critical as possible, preferably getting one or two outside critiques on the renders so as to help us compile as objective a set of notes as possible. Good Internet forums can be especially helpful in this regard.

If you are the kind of person who gets easily offended or disheartened when others pick holes in your work, it may be best to forego the extra help. In truth though, listening to and evaluating the validity of all criticism can be an essential **Quality Control** tool that a good artist should learn to use.

Defining our goals

To get started, as in our previous chapters, we do want to set ourselves some definite goals for this phase of the project. In this instance, these could be very simply stated as wanting to evaluate and then improve the key areas of lighting, global illumination, image sampling, and materials so as to ultimately improve the technical and artistic quality of the final renders we will be taking.

We do need to note that in V-Ray there are a number of different ways in which we could approach improving our final image quality, each of them having their own merits and drawbacks. Some approaches, while quick and easy to set up, pay a heavy penalty in terms of final render times.

Others, although producing quicker final renders, are much more technical in their set up and require a deeper level of understanding of how the parameters being tweaked interconnect and so affect one another. In this chapter, we will focus on creating a setup that uses a little of both so as to balance both speed and quality.

Fine-tuning scene lighting

As a starting point, let's go back to pretty much where we started on this project and once more take a look at the lighting that we have set up in the scene. In order to make an honest evaluation of just what each direct light source in the scene is contributing to the illumination, we really need to render them one at a time with all scene materials enabled.

To set this up in V-Ray, let's perform the following steps:

1. Open up the `DT_Interior_QualityControl_Start.skp` scene.
2. Then, go into the V-Ray option editor's **Indirect illumination** rollout and turn off GI in the scene.

Now, any renders we take will only show us the contribution of direct light sources in the scene. Also, as we are going to be taking these images into either a viewer or editing application for close examination, we will really need to view them in their gamma corrected form.

To do that, perform the following step:

1. In the **Color mapping** rollout of the option editor, uncheck the **Don't affect colors** option for now.

[We will need to keep in mind that this option has to be re-enabled before our final renders are taken.]

Tuning up the sunlight

Of course, for a careful evaluation we need to narrow things down a little further. So, first of all, let's focus on the sun or spotlight in the scene. To be able to take a sunlight-only render we need to perform the following steps:

1. Click on the **Orthographic Front** scene tab so as to switch to that view, and then we can right-click on the Dome light to open up the light editor for ourselves.
2. From here, we can disable the Dome light and then click on **OK** to exit the editor.
3. To take our render, we now need to click on the **Wide Shot – 35mm** scene tab and then hit the render button on the V-Ray toolbar.

Again, we will need to keep in mind that as we are rendering at **full HD** resolution with all material effects enabled, the renders we take in this chapter (depending upon our hardware capabilities) may take a considerable and ever increasing amount of time to complete. As we are making serious quality evaluations, however, we should try to avoid reducing resolution for the sake of speed here if at all possible.

The *direct light only* render we see here is also an excellent way to review how both reflections and bump mapping are working in the scene without any extra distracting details.

Reviewing our sunlight render

Because we already made certain in *Chapter 2, Lighting an Interior Daytime Scene* that the positioning of our spotlight was just right, there are only two things that stand out here as obviously problematic. The first would be the noise that is clearly present in the shadow edges or penumbra in the pools of light coming through the ceiling openings, and the second problem would be the over bright or blown out centers of those same light circles.

If we want to see just how bright those pools are, we can right-click in the **V-ray frame buffer** window and check the floating point values in the readout that pops up. At the center of the front-most circle, I am getting values of around about 1.7, 1.7, and 1.6.

Now, there are a couple of ways in which we could approach solving both of these problems. For the noise in the shadow penumbra, we could for instance go to the spotlights control parameters found in the light editor and increase the number of subdivs used in the shadow controls to smooth things out. Or, we could improve matters by means of the global image sampling controls themselves. This approach, besides improving the quality of shadows for the spotlight, would also improve every other noise-based effect in the scene, such as blurry reflections and refractions in our materials.

Ideally, we want to strike a balance between the two so as to give V-Ray as little extra work to do as possible. This will of course mean that our renders' times are kept as low as possible. For this reason then, let's perform the following steps:

1. Click on the **Orthographic Front** scene tab and right-click on the spotlight to open up the light editor.

2. Down in the **Shadows** section of the spotlight controls, set the Shadow **Subdivs** value to 12 and click on **OK** to exit the editor.

The super bright areas in the light pools that we are seeing here could also be handled in a number of ways. We could, for instance, make use of V-Ray's **Color mapping** controls to essentially clamp our white values at around about the **1.0** mark, which would of course make any later required post-production adjustments much more minor in nature.

As we want to keep our images in linear color space and so give ourselves as much freedom as possible to make alterations to our renders during post-production, this is an approach that I tend to save for projects where time is of the essence and post-production work needs to be kept as minimal as possible.

In this instance then, we will leave things as they are for now and see what we can do with these hotspots in post-production.

Adjusting the skylight

Next, we need to make the switch and turn our Dome light *on* and at the same time turn our spotlight *off*. To do that, let's perform the following steps:

1. Click on the **Orthographic Front** scene tab and right-click on the Dome light to open up the light editor. Then, enable the Dome light in the controls.

2. Click on **OK** to lock the Dome options in place and then right-click on the spotlight to open up the light editor controls for it.

3. From here, we want to turn our spotlight off and again click on **OK** to lock the change in place.

4. Now, we can return to the **Wide Shot – 35mm** scene tab and once again hit the render button on the V-Ray toolbar.

Reviewing our skylight render

With the Dome light, the only major problem we see from the initial render is one of noise, a lot of which is being introduced by the shadow sampling settings. Now, we could wait and see if the addition of global illumination and an increase in the quality of image sampling in the scene will help the problem—which they inevitably will, but that will only happen to a limited extent.

On interior shots, cleaning up shadow artifact from the Dome light can be notoriously difficult, especially when the direct light entry points are quite limited as we have them in this scene. So, in this case, it would probably be wise for us to make use of the Dome light's shadow sampling controls and give V-Ray a helping hand with improving the noise levels we are getting here. The aim is to balance out the load between local shadow samples and the main image sampler options. To do this, we need to perform the following steps:

1. Click on the **Orthographic Front** scene tab and then right-click on the Dome light to open up the light editor.

2. In the **Shadow** section of the Dome light controls, we can then set the **Subdivs** value to 24, allowing V-Ray to use a possible 576 samples per pixel for shadow creation.

3. Finally, click on **OK** to lock the settings in place and then return to the **Wide Shot – 35mm** scene tab and hit the render button.

While what this gives us still looks a little rough, the addition of GI and improved image sampling settings to the scene later on should be enough to clean things up nicely without our render times climbing unnecessarily high.

Cleaning up our GI solution

Now that we have reviewed the quality of direct lighting and shadows in the scene, let's move on to cleaning up our GI solution so that we can call the final lighting for the scene done. In this instance though, we will want to take our review renders without materials enabled, leaving us free to focus solely on the GI. The last thing we want is to be unnecessarily increasing GI parameters if what we are seeing are in fact noise problems coming from elsewhere in the scene.

To do that, we need to turn our material override function on, so let's perform the following steps:

1. Open up the option editor and jump into the **Global switches** rollout.

2. In the **Materials** section, we need to enable the **Override materials** option, while disabling the **Glossy effects** option at the same time.

3. Once we are done, we can close the option editor, return to the **Wide Shot – 35mm** scene tab, and again hit the render button.

The reflection/refraction option can stay on so that we can see if any of the GI rays passing through our glass material are causing any problems. The "Maps" option needs to remain enabled so that the HDRI being used by the Dome light still works.

Reviewing our GI render

In this instance, what we get from our initial render looks pretty good. In fact, the only immediately noticeable problem would be the large splotches that are most clearly visible on the ceiling and the wall just above our glass door. Now, we could easily get carried away here, turning the GI settings up to high values that will completely eliminate this noise. However, to be honest, in order to bring what we have here up to acceptable quality for final renders, we only need to make use of some mid-range quality settings. To apply these quality tweaks to the global illumination controls, let's perform the following steps:

1. Open up the **Irradiance map** rollout in the options editor, and in the left-hand column of the **Basic parameters** section, we can set the **Min rate** value to -3, **Max rate** to -1, **HSph. subdivs** to 125, and **Interp. samples** to 35.

2. Now, jump into the **Light cache** rollout and set the **Subdivs** value to 1250 in the **Calculation parameters** section.

Obviously, with each increment that we make in our V-Ray settings, we are bumping up the render times quite noticeably. What we do get from the render now, however, is a clean and very usable GI solution with good contact shadows added in for good measure. What little splotching there may still be will easily be hidden by the ceiling material, given the fact that we have a bump map applied.

Before moving on, one thing that we may want to do, in order to speed up the image sampling and material tests that we will be doing in just a moment or two, is save the current GI solutions to the disk so that they can be reused. This eliminates the need for the GI to be recalculated each time we hit the render button. To see how we go about doing that let's reopen the Irradiance map rollout in the options editor, where down at the bottom of the parameters rollout we see an On render end section. By default the Don't delete option here is enabled which essentially tells V-Ray to hold the last calculated Irradiance map in memory, making it available for us to save to disk at any point, should we desire to do so.

Of course the instant that we start a new render the current map is discarded and a new one created, so it is important that we save these high quality GI maps now, before we go and hit the render button again. To do that, perform the following steps:

1. In the **Current map** section, click on the **Save** button to place the map on any storage device and/or folder that you like.

2. In my case, I will save it in the Chapter_09 folder under Exercise_Files | Model_Files as High_Quality_with_Override_material.vrmap.

3. Next, we need to repeat these steps in the **Light cache** rollout. This makes exactly the same UI controls available to us, so let's save the **Light cache** as High_Quality_with_Override_material.vrlmap.

Saving these GI solutions to disk is a trick that we can use to eliminate color bleed completely from our render, given that the GI solutions have been calculated for the most part using the light grey override material. Be aware though, that due to both **Irradiance mapping** and **Light cache** being solutions calculated from the camera's point of view, these maps will only work for the view in which they were created.

You may have noticed that we haven't turned on the **Ambient occlusion** option in the **Indirect illumination** rollout. This is because baking the AO effect into the final renders means surrendering any kind of control over it, and generally speaking that is not a good idea. Should we or the client decide a little later that the AO effect is either too weak or too strong, we may find that we have to do our high-quality renders all over again.

Working with the Image sampler controls

Although we have saved our GI solutions to disk, we haven't yet set them up to be used at render time. As we are now moving on to tweaking controls that can have quite a significant impact on overall render times, now would probably be a good time to go ahead and do that. This will help reduce the time it takes to produce our test renders. To do so, let's perform the following steps:

1. In our **Irradiance map** rollout, go to the **Mode** section, which is just above the **On render end** controls, and set the **Mode** dropdown to **From File**.

2. Next, we need to click on the **File** browse button to the right and select the Irradiance map that we saved to the disk in the previous steps.

3. Repeat these same steps in the **Light cache** rollout.

Whenever we hit render now, rather than starting with GI calculations, V-Ray will jump straight to the final image sampling phase. Before rendering though, we also need to disable the override material. So, let's perform the following steps:

1. In the **Global switches** rollout of the option editor, uncheck the **Override materials** option and also enable the **Glossy effects** control.

Before we go ahead and make any alterations to our image sampling settings , we do need to understand that the image sampling settings we use here will play a major role in both the final quality and speed at which our rendered frames are produced.

To cover a variety of render situations, V-Ray offers three image sampling modes with which we can work: Fixed, Adaptive DMC, and Adaptive Subdivision. In the majority of cases, and certainly wherever we are making use of noisy effects such as blurry reflections, refractions, and soft-edged shadows, Adaptive DMC (the default) will be both faster and yield higher quality final results. So, for those reasons, this is the mode that we will be working with here.

In fact, with our GI maps set up, let's go ahead and take a test render so that we can make use of it in our evaluation of the current settings.

Reviewing the image sampling render

As things are looking good at this point, the only real problem that needs to be solved by image sampling would the same one that we have identified on a number of occasions already: noise. We do though have a choice as to how we go about solving the noise problems we see here, as most of the issues that can be spotted on close inspection are material based.

This means we can either increase the number of subdivs being used for effects such as the frosted glass at the material level, or we could force a global cleanup of the scene using the image sampling controls themselves. As doing this would also clean up any noisy soft shadows in the scene, this is the initial approach we will take. This will still leave us with the option of going in and giving any problematic materials in the scene a final tweak should we need to do so. To do that, let's perform the following steps:

1. In the **Image sampler (Antialiasing)** rollout of the option editor, ensure that the **Type** in the **Image Sampler** section is set to **Adaptive DMC**.

2. Then, in the controls immediately below it, set the **Min subdivs** value to 1 and **Max subdivs** to 16.

These settings give V-Ray the option of using a maximum of 256 samples per pixel wherever it deems them necessary, while at the same time allowing it to drop all the way down to a minimum of 1 sample per pixel whenever it can. This can save on a lot of unnecessary render time as V-Ray now has the option of *only* using extra samples whenever it becomes really necessary. The control that will make the determination as to when extra samples are applied can be found in the rollout just below, this being the **DMC sampler** control.

You can see in the **Image sampling** rollout that, by default, the **Use DMC sampler thresh** control is enabled. This tells V-Ray to make use of the threshold controls found in the **DMC sampler** rollout in order to determine when more samples need to be used.

In our case, the only parameter that we need to change here is the noise threshold value; we will set it to 0.007.

> The lower this number, the more sensitive V-Ray will be to the use of samples, making it more likely to use of the **Max subdiv** setting. If we leave this setting too high, then it wouldn't matter how high we set our **Max subdiv** values because V-Ray would never actually get around to making use of the extra samples available. Conversely, if we go too low, we can increase our render times dramatically without ever seeing a corresponding increase in image quality.

Finally, let's set our **Antialiasing filter** type to **Box** from the dropdown (this is a slightly soft yet good all round AA filter, as it doesn't sharpen like **Lanczos** nor over-soften like **Area**), and then take another render.

Improving our materials

The final quality control tweaks to be made in our scene will be on the materials themselves. This, for now, is our last opportunity to evaluate and adjust any aspect of the materials in the scene that we are not completely happy with.

Now, ideally, we would want to make this final set of evaluations from each of the render views we have set up in the scene. However, as these renders have become quite time consuming to create, we will make use of only the **Wide Shot** scene in this instance.

In order to correctly evaluate how our materials are looking and behaving, we will need to render without using our saved GI solutions. This will allow us to gauge how much color bleed the materials are throwing into the scene, and so subsequently, how much (if any) in-scene adjustments will need to be made. To set that up, we will perform the following steps:

1. In the **Irradiance map** rollout of the option editor, come down to the **Mode** section and choose the **Single frame** option from the dropdown.

2. Then, we need to repeat these same steps in the **Light cache** rollout.

We would also do well to make use of some of the diagnostic tools that V-Ray 2.0 makes available to us, such as the Sample Rate VFB channel. This can help us understand which parts of our scene are making the **Image sampler** controls work overly hard. Now, although V-Ray for 3ds Max and Maya's render elements system is more complete than the extra VFB channels that we have access to in SketchUp, the workflow here couldn't be simpler. So, to add our diagnostic channel, let's perform the following steps:

1. Open up the **VFB channels** rollout in the option editor and then left-click on the channel lists scroll bar to make it active.

2. When we click, we should see the **RGB color** and **Alpha** options become highlighted. This tells us that they are going to be included as channels in the final render. To add others from the list, all we need to do is scroll down the list and then left-click to add channels as we go.

3. In this instance, let's click to add the **Sample Rate** channel, and then finally, we can come up to the V-Ray toolbar and hit the render button.

As soon as our render has finished, let's go ahead and save the new GI maps that we have just calculated, as these can now quite happily be used for the final render that we will take in just a little while. To do that, let's go back into the **Irradiance map** rollout and perform the following step:

1. In the **Current map** section, click on the **Save** button to save the newly calculated **Irradiance map** to disk.

   In my case, I will save it in the `Chapter_09` folder under `Exercise_Files | Model_Files` as `High_Quality_with_Materials.vrmap`.

2. Next, we need to repeat these steps in the **Light cache** rollout that makes exactly the same UI controls available to us, saving the light cache as `High_ Quality_with_Materials.vrlmap`.

Reviewing what we have in the RGB map

Now, its time to go ahead and analyze the information that our render has given us, starting first of all with the actual RGB render channel. Here, we see that although things are heading very much in the right direction quality-wise, there are still a number of issues that are present in the image that could do with our attention.

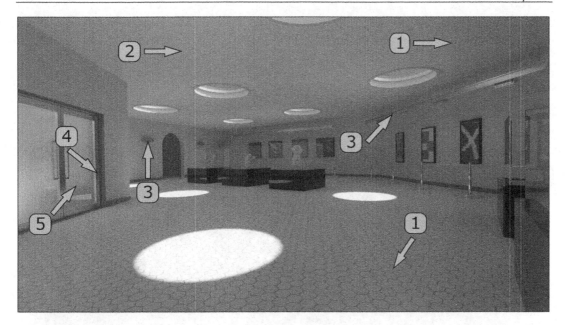

- The bump mapping on the ceiling and floor seems (on closer inspection) to be a little bit strong for my tastes and may need dialing back just a little.
- The color bleed or bounce that is now present in the scene actually looks pretty good to me, adding a little bit more of a natural and so photographic feel to the scene (this could, however, be dialed back somewhat using the **Saturation** control in the GI rollout at final render time if we desire so).
- One material that isn't looking too good at this moment is the blurry metal found on the light fixtures. This is actually looking quite dull and so could possibly be a little too blurry for its own good.
- An area causing quite a number of obvious problems is the glass and metal door. Both the metal frame and the frosted glass materials are producing quite a bit of noise between them.

Reviewing what we have in the Sample Rate map

Let's make a switch now and compare what we have learned from looking at the RGB render with what the Sample Rate VFB channel can tell us.

The premise of the **Sample Rate** channel is very simple; it is designed to show us where the available samples or rays (the number of which is controlled by the main image sampling options) are being used in the scene.

Dark blue denotes areas where a minimum or low number of samples are being employed, light blue through to green shows where a higher number of samples are being employed, while yellow to orange and then into red tell us that an increasingly high and ultimately maximum number of samples are having to be used. This means that image sampling is working very hard to try and resolve aliasing and noise issues, and where areas of pure red exist, there may actually not be enough samples available to adequately resolve the artifact problems.

The information in this image gives us the ability to fine tune the balance in the use of global samples (controlled by the global **Image sampler** settings) as opposed to the local or secondary samples coming from elements such as materials and lights for example (we have already mentioned this a couple of times in this chapter). Any areas where global sampling is being heavily employed (red pixels) are good candidates for increasing the local samples so as to balance out the load and improve the overall quality of the final image, often without noticeably increasing render times.

One instantly noticeable piece of information in the Sample Rate channel would be its agreement with our earlier observation from the RGB image that the frosted glass and metal frame of the door are quite noisy, since they were sampled quite substantially (as denoted by the green and even red colored areas).

The image also shows that our floor and wall materials are also require quite a bit of help from image sampling, which is perhaps not surprising given that they both have blurry reflections applied. So, we may want to look at increasing local subdivs there.

Seeing red around the edges of the direct light hotspots and in the bright reflections on the chrome is not really surprising as image sampling struggles to average out extremely bright pixel values. So, this is not necessarily something to be overly concerned about, although we could perhaps increase the samples being used for the chrome material.

To put all of those observations to work, let's first of all deal with our bump issues by performing the following steps:

1. Open up the material editor and select the **Ceiling** material from the list.

2. Scrolling down to the **Maps** rollout, we can set the value in the **Bump** spinner to **0.7**.

3. Next, we want to select the **Floor_Tile_Hexagon_White** and again scroll down to the **Bump** controls and set the value to **0.4**.

4. While in this material, we also want to scroll up to the **Reflection** rollout and set the **Subdivs** in the **Glossiness** section to **16**.

5. Next, we can select the **Doors_Blurred_Metal** material just above in the list and again set the **Subdivs** value in the **Reflection** section to **16**. We will repeat the same action for the **Barrier_Chrome** and **Walls** materials.

6. In the **Light_Fixture_Metal** material, we want to increase the **Glossiness** value to **0.9**, making them less blurry. And at the same time, set the **Subdivs** value there to **16**.

7. Finally, for the materials, let's select **Door_Glass** from the list and this time set both **Reflection** and **Refraction Subdiv** values to **16**.

Our last tweak to the quality settings will be to the reflection and refraction trace depth settings. These are currently being controlled locally, at the material level, with the total number of each interaction being set at a value of 5.

However, with so many reflections and refractions going on in the scene, we may possibly want to increase this setting so as to ensure that our materials are behaving appropriately. Now, we could do this one material at a time. In this instance though, I am going to apply a global increase, so let's perform the following steps:

1. In the **Global switches** rollout of the option editor, put a check in the **Max depth** option and set the spinner value to **10**.

2. We can also go into the **Color mapping** rollout and turn the **Don't affect colors** option back.

 Do keep in mind that this increase in realistic light behavior can impact render times significantly in some cases.

Outputting the final renders

With all of the quality control tweaks in place, I think we are pretty much ready to set things up for the output of our final render or renders. This will mean that we can then move into the post-production phase of our project and see what enhancements (if any) can be made.

Adding extra VFB channels

To give ourselves a little bit of extra flexibility in post, one thing that we can do here is add a few more V-Ray frame buffer channels to our output. To do that, let's perform the following steps:

1. Go back to the **VFB channels** rollout in the options editor and along with the already selected **RGB color**, (don't need Alpha) and **Sample Rate** channels, let's add **Reflection**, **Render ID** and also **Z Depth**. Our channel list should now have a total of 5 highlighted elements ready to be rendered out.

Setting the output format

Before we can hit the render button for one last time, we now need to decide which image file format we want to use when saving our renders to disk. To give ourselves the maximum amount of flexibility for image editing operations, we really need to output the maximum amount of pixel information possible, which for us means using a 32-bit file format (my preference being Open EXR). In the **Output** rollout of the options editor, let's perform the following steps:

1. Put a check in the **Save output** option.
2. Click on the browse button next to the **Output file** name field.
3. In the **Save Bitmap File** browser that appears, navigate to the location where we want to save our renders, in my case, the `Chapter_09` folder under `Exercise_Files | Final_Renders`.
4. Set a file name for the images. I will use `Materials_Final` (this will be applied as a prefix to the VFB channels that will also be saved). From the **Save as type** dropdown, select the **OpenEXR image file** option.
5. Finally, we can hit the render button one last time.

If the availability of sufficient storage space for rendered files is likely to become an issue, say for instance, we were rendering lots of files to disk such as in an animated sequence, then we may want to have the best of both worlds by opting to save to 16-bit (half float) files instead. This would still provide plenty of leeway in the post-production process, while using up only half the disk space of 32-bit files.

One last thing you may want to do before committing to a final render is perform a check to avoid a nasty problem that I have on rare occasions run into, which is the fact that maps assigned to material channels such as bump inside a material can sometimes suddenly get disconnected or lost. For this reason, it is a good idea at this point to just quickly go through the materials in the editor using the Preview option. and quickly check that everything is working as it should.

With our final render for this view done, we are ready to move on to the final post-production stage of our project and add the finishing touches to our render.

Determining the order of quality control steps

In order to give structure to the steps that we needed to take in this chapter, we have naturally had to perform our quality control tweaks in a specific order, taking renders of each step along the way so as to evaluate its effect before moving on. It does need to be noted though that the order in which we have taken these steps here is by no means a required nor sometimes efficient way in which to proceed.

For instance, rather than waiting until the end of the quality control process to balance out the sampling load, we may find it beneficial to add the Sample Rate VFB channel right from the start, leaving the less noise intensive GI clean up until later in the process. This would mean that subsequent test renders have already been optimized to deal with noise-related issues. It would also mean that we could combine tweaks to image sampling and materials, which would require us to take fewer test renders than we have here.

Ultimately, the type of work we do as well as the particular way in which our own brain prefers to work will help us settle on a workflow that is optimum for us. As long as all of the required quality control checks are in place, the order in which we do them can be one of personal choice.

Summary

Let's summarize what we have covered in this chapter with regard to fine tuning our scene.

Although our initial lighting setup hadn't left us with too much to do, the test renders taken did reveal areas of noise in both the Spot and Dome light contribution that required some attention to the sampling rates, especially so with the dome light.

The global illumination solution that we were producing still had visible noise (or splotches as render artists like to call them) that needed cleaning up and so we tweaked some parameters in both the **Irradiance map** and **Light cache** controls. We then learned how to save a calculated GI solution to disk and reuse it so as to drastically speed up subsequent renders. We were also able to demonstrate how to work with both global (image sampler) and local (materials and lights) subdiv values to get as much quality and speed from our final render as possible.

With all of that taken care of, we are now ready to move onto the final phase of the project, post-production. This is where we take our rendered output from V-Ray and turn it into something that has even more of a photographic feel.

10
Adding Photographic Touches in Post-production

In many ways, we come now to possibly the most important chapter of all in our quest to learn how we go about producing photographic renders in SketchUp and V-Ray, and ironically, we won't be using either of those applications. What we want to do now is to add some of the finishing touches to the good work that we have done up to this point in our 3D applications that will enhance or add to the photographic feel of our finished image.

Now, of course, a number of the steps that we will perform here could quite easily have been taken inside V-Ray itself, but for the sake of both speed and artistic flexibility, which of course are absolutely essential when working on commercial projects, we will handle them here instead.

Defining our goals

For one last time then, we want to define the goals that we are setting ourselves for this final portion of the project. Essentially, we want to layer up a number of subtle operations in our image that, when combined together, help push it towards a more photographic feel. At the same time, of course, we want to create our edits in such a way as to give ourselves the ability to go back and tweak or alter them anytime we want.

Setting up After Effects

As far as software tools are concerned, for the edits we want to perform here we could use any one of a number of high-quality post-production applications, a list of which would probably include Nuke (from The Foundry), Fusion (by eyeon Software), Composite (from Autodesk), or indeed the compositor mode that is built into the freely available Blender application.

For sheer ease of use though, we will make use of Adobe's After Effects package. This means that while the steps we take here are of course being applied to single images, we could just as easily apply them to an animated sequence and have the end result turn out exactly the same.

If you are an Adobe Photoshop user, then the good news is that it should be a fairly simple matter to transpose the steps we use here into that application as the two pieces of software share tools, terminology, and workflows (being layer-based) pretty closely.

The only drawback would be the need in Photoshop to drop down from using 32-bit files to 16-bit ones in order to perform some of the required steps. If we are working in a print-based, however, this may be a sacrifice that has to be made.

Before we get to work on our final render, we need to launch After Effects and make a couple of quick changes to the project settings simply to accommodate the workflow that we opted for when making our choices in V-Ray's color-mapping controls.

Once After Effects has opened, let's perform the following steps:

1. From the **File** menu, click to select the **Project Settings** option.
2. In the **Color Settings** section of the dialog box that appears, we need to access the drop-down menu and select the **32 bits per channel (float)** option that appears there and click on **OK**.

As we rendered floating point EXR files out of V-Ray, we need to be certain from the start of this post-production phase that we are going to get the fullest benefit from them. If we didn't make this change, we would still be working with all of the restrictions that are inherent in an 8-bit image workflow, meaning we would have a restricted level of image data with which we could work.

Bit depth is a way of describing the amount of information that is available in each of the R, G, and B (as well as possibly alpha) channels that combine to make up a composite RGB image.

An 8-bit image (2^8) is able to provide a maximum of 256 colors per pixel per channel, giving a total possible color count of almost 16.8 million colors in an image (1 million here is counted as a 1 followed by six zeros).

A 16-bit image (2^{16}) can give a maximum of 65,536 colors per pixel per channel, meaning there is a total possible color count of over 281 trillion colors in the image (1 trillion here is counted as a 1 followed by 12 zeros).

A 32-bit image (2^{32} 24 + Transparency), however, can give a maximum of 16,777,216 colors per pixel per channel, giving a total possible color count for the image of over 1 sextillion colors. (1 sextillion here is counted as a 1 followed by 21 zeros).

Visit www.math.com/tables/general/numnotation.htm for more information.

Another thing that we need to do is make certain that all of the math used to compute our editing operations will be as close to real-world light behavior as possible, thus enhancing the chances of our being able to produce a photographic-looking finished image. This can be done in one of two ways in After Effects.

We could simply enable the **Blend colors using 1.0 gamma** option, which temporarily converts color values used in blending modes to Gamma 1.0, meaning colors will blend in a more natural manner.

However, if we want to work in a genuine linearized environment, then the recommendation is to set the Working Space option to sRGB and then also enable the **Linearize Working Space** option.

This will ensure that not only blending modes, but also Image Re-Sampling and Motion Blur effects use gamma 1.0 in their calculations.

We have used the sRGB Working Space option here as our images are being viewed on an sRGB device, this being our computer monitor. If our project had some specific output requirements, then using one of the other color space options from the dropdown would be absolutely fine.

As we are dealing with neither a motion sequence nor audio here, we can ignore the rest of the options in the settings dialog box and simply click on **OK**.

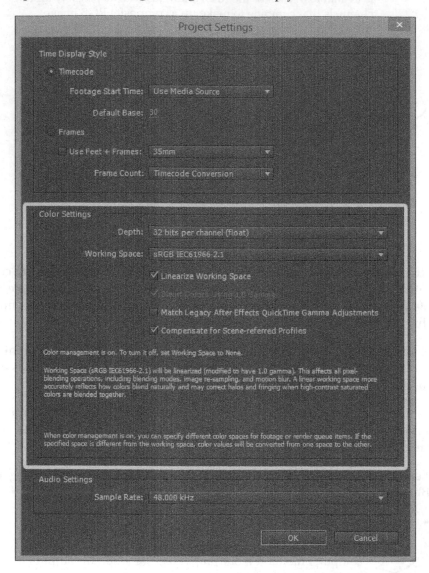

Importing our footage

Let's go ahead now and import our footage into After Effects so that we can start work on it in earnest. To do that, we can perform the following steps:

1. Go to the **File** menu, and from the **Import** flyout, choose the **File** option.

2. In the **Import File** dialog box that appears, we can either browse to our downloaded `Chapter_09` folder under `Exercise_Files | Final_Renders` and import the provided images from there or, alternatively, locate our own rendered versions if we have produced them.

The files we want to pull into After Effects (assuming we have followed the naming steps outlined in the previous chapter) will be as follows:

- `Materials_Final.exr`
- `Materials_Final.Reflection.exr`
- `Materials_Final.RenderID.exr`
- `Materials_Final.Sample_Rate.exr`
- `Materials_Final.ZDepth.exr`

Once imported, we can take a look at the finished RGB channel that came out of V-Ray by double-clicking on the `Materials_Final.exr` file, which will open up the image in a new **Footage** view window for us. Now, you may well be wondering at this point why we are seeing a gamma-corrected image as opposed to the much darker linear version that we rendered out of V-Ray.

> Remember in V-Ray we had to use the sRGB button on the frame buffer window in order to see how the gamma-corrected image would look. However, as the sRGB button affects only the V-Ray frame buffer and not the final image, we should be seeing the darker linear version that was rendered to disk.

The reason we get this visual discrepancy is due to one of After Effects' own default settings. To see what that is and how it works, we will need to perform the following steps:

1. Right-click on the **Materials_Final.exr** footage in the **Project** panel, and from the **Interpret Footage** flyout, choose the **Main** option.

2. In the **Interpret Footage** dialog box that appears, select the **Color Management** tab, where we will see the **Interpret as Linear Light** option.

This (as you can see) is set by default to **ON for 32 bpc** footage, meaning that when After Effects detects that an image has a linear profile embedded (as all floating point images should), it essentially applies an automatic gamma compensation to the viewer windows, which in turn means that the footage is seen correctly according to the Working Space profile that we have set up.

In fact, if I just set this to *off* from the dropdown, you will see in the following screenshot that we now have an image identical to that seen in the V-Ray frame buffer without sRGB compensation:

As we definitely want this option set to *on*, let's set that back to the default and exit by clicking on either **OK** or **Cancel**. To work on our footage in After Effects, we will need to place it inside a composition. We can do this by performing the following steps:

1. Drag the **Materials_Final.exr** RGB render down to the timeline panel (which automatically creates a new composition named after the footage itself, doing so on both the timeline and up in the **Projects** panel).

2. Finally, before we move on to any serious post-production work, we can save our After Effects project as `Chap10_AE_01.aep`. In my case, I will save this in the `Exercise_Files | After_Effects_Files` folder.

Dealing with the lighting hotspots

Possibly the first thing we will want to do here is deal with the lighting hotspots that are currently present in our image. We did say that we could have handled this in V-Ray itself by means of its **Color mapping** controls, which would have essentially clamped all the super bright (any brightness value higher than 1.0) at around the 1.0 mark.

Unfortunately, the color-mapping modes in V-Ray also affect other colors in the rendered image, shifting them around to a greater or lesser extent depending upon the particular mode chosen. Given that fact and taking into account that we can do exactly the same thing here in After Effects both very simply and with a much greater level of control, you will hopefully see why we are using this particular approach.

To do that, let's perform the following steps:

1. Over in the **Effects & Presets** panel, type HDR into the search field as shown in the following screenshot:

2. One of the options that appear in the list below will be the **HDR Highlight Compression** effect, so let's left-click to drag-and-drop this onto either the **Composition viewer** window or the **Materials_Final.exr** layer itself.

3. In the **Effect Controls** panel that opens, we can now set the suppression level to suit; in this instance, I will use a value of 90%:

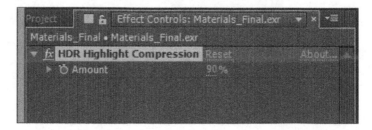

What we have accomplished here is to bring a little bit of the floor tile pattern back into these bright areas. Just how much we reintroduce is entirely down to our artistic choice, but the important thing here is that we now have complete and interactive control as we are now able to alter the effect at any point in the post-production process that we choose.

At this point, let's perform the following step:

1. Come up to the **File** menu; from the **Save As** flyout, choose the **Save As** option and save the project as Chap10_AE_02.aep.

Boosting the floor reflections

One thing that you will probably have noticed as you applied the **HDR Highlight Compression** effect was the fact that not only were the highlights affected, but to some extent, the entire image lost contrast and looked a little washed out, which of course is not going to help our pursuit of photographic quality. Now, while we could tackle this issue right now, this is generally a step that I prefer to leave until the end of the editing process, because it means we can apply a final correction effect to the additional layers that we will be adding as we move forward here.

One thing we do want to take care of at this point in time, however, is the fact that our floor reflections are looking a little dull for my tastes, not picking up any bright highlights from the exterior lighting as I would like and expect them to. What we need to do then is to boost them a little by means of the extra reflection pass that we rendered out of V-Ray.

All we theoretically need to do is apply a mask to our image that isolates the floor and allows us to apply a reflection boost to just that area of our image. However, we now run into the type of major problem that often crops up (sometimes on a number of occasions) throughout the course of a working project.

You see, ideally, we should be able to use the Render ID pass that we created in V-Ray as a mask, given that it assigns a unique color to every unique geometry element in the scene. Indeed, if we double-click on that element in the **Project** panel and take a look at it, you can see that we do have a unique color assigned to almost every element in the scene—everything, that is, except our floor, which due to the way that the model (quite deliberately, I must add) has been set up, has unfortunately been assigned the same ID color as the walls.

Now, we could spend some time experimenting with various ways of extracting a usable floor mask right here in After Effects, and certainly with a measure of trial and error, we would be able to come up with something usable. That, however, could potentially eat up a considerable amount of time, which again, in a commercial setting, is not generally a viable workflow to follow.

Instead, we should be prepared to backtrack a little at this point in time, jump back into V-Ray, and create a very quick but perfect floor mask for ourselves. To do that, let's launch SketchUp and open up the `DT_Interior_FloorMask_Start.skp` file from the `Chapter_10` folder in our `Exercise_Files` folder (this is just a copy of the finished scene file from *Chapter 9, Quality Control*).

There are, in fact, a few ways we could go about creating a mask in V-Ray, but seeing as in this instance we want to be as quick and efficient as possible, we will take what I think of as a brute-force approach. To do that, let's perform the following steps:

1. Open up the material editor, create a new standard material, and then right-click on it to rename it `Red`.

2. Right-click again on the newly-named material, and from the **Create Layer** flyout, choose **Emissive** (we will use this to give ourselves a self-illuminated material in the scene).

3. Triple-click on the floor geometry to select it from inside the group, and then right-click on the red material in the material editor to use the **Assign material to selection** function.

If we were to render at this moment, all we would get would be a very long wait that produced a render very similar to our existing final image—only with a red floor of course. What we want is a perfect mask; a render that has a bright red floor with every other piece of geometry in the scene completely black. To do that, let's open up the V-Ray option editor and perform the following steps:

1. In the **Global Switches** rollout, disable the **Lights** and **Shadows** options found in the **Lighting** section.

2. In the **Materials** section, we can uncheck everything.

3. In the **Camera** rollout, we need to uncheck the **On** option for the physical camera.

4. In the **Output** rollout, we can click on the **Output File** browse button and name our image `Floor_Mask.exr`, saving it to the `Exercise_Files | Final_Renders | Chapter_10` folder.

5. Finally, in the **Indirect Illumination** rollout, we can turn **GI** off and then hit the render button up on the V-Ray toolbar.

What we get is a very fast render of our scene with nothing but a red floor and black objects. This is a perfect mask for us to use, especially as the objects standing on the floor are perfectly separated from the floor color.

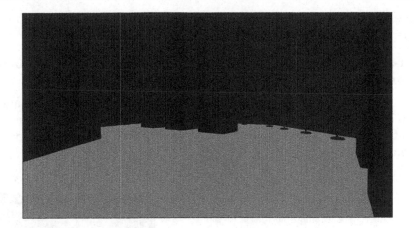

What we need to do now of course is to import this newly created piece of footage into After Effects, so let's go ahead and do that by performing the following steps:

1. Right-click in the **Project** panel, and using the `File` option under `Import`, browse to the `Chapter_10` folder under `Exercise_Files | Final_Renders` and select the **Floor_Mask.exr** file found there.

2. Once imported, we can drag both the mask and reflection renders down into the composition layer stack, making sure to place them above our current **Materials_Final.exr** layer.

3. Deselect both layers using the *Ctrl + Shift + A* keyboard combination, and then in the far-left column of the layer stack, click on the Visibility icon (the eyeball) for the Mask layer so as to turn it off.

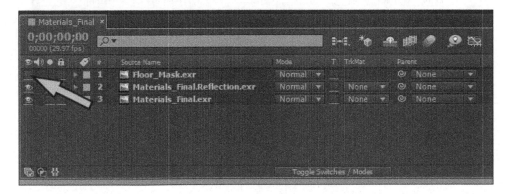

Next, we want to do some work on the reflection layer, so let's go ahead and set its Blend Mode to **Add** by performing the following steps:

1. Left-click on the **Mode** dropdown, and then keeping the mouse button down, select the **Add** option from the list.

2. Of course, we don't want to add extra reflections to the entire image, so with the reflection layer selected, let's come up to the **Effect** menu right at the top of the After Effects UI, and from the **Channel** flyout, select the **Set Matte** option.

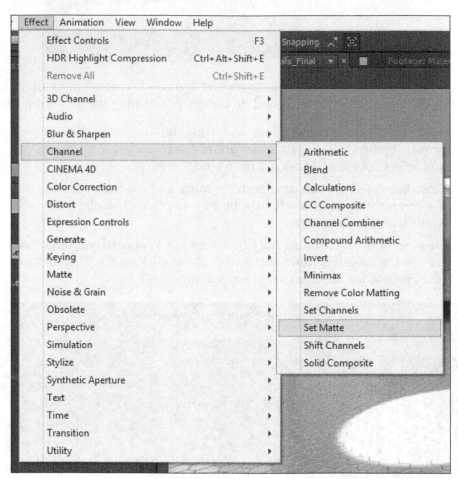

3. In the **Effect Controls** panel, access the **Take Matte From Layer** dropdown; select the **Floor_Mask.exr** option from the list and then in the **Use For Matte** dropdown, set the **Red Channel** option as shown in the following screenshot:

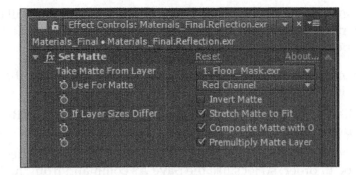

Now, straightaway we should spot a bit of a problem. Due to the image sampling that has been applied to our mask, we are getting some very bright fringing, or halo-ing, along the edges of some of the masked geometry, especially the chrome barriers and display cases closest to the camera. To fix this, let's perform the following steps:

1. Come over to the **Effects & Presets** tab, and in the search field, start to type the word simple.

2. In the search results area just below, we should now see the **32-bit Simple Choker** effect. Grab this and drop it onto the reflection layer, setting the **Choke Matte** value to **1.6**.

3. Finally, we can expand the reflection layer's **Transform** controls, and in there, set the **Opacity** level to **12%**.

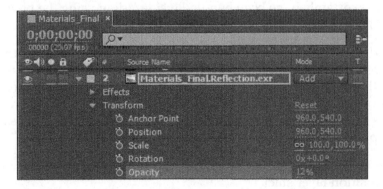

Toggling the layer off and on will show us the difference we have made to the floor reflections. It is a reasonably subtle boost for the moment, but keep in mind that we will be adding a final color correction at the end of the editing process that will also affect the look of our final reflections. Of course, you can feel free to adjust the reflection levels here so as to suit your own particular preference.

To keep our main AE composition neat and tidy, one of the things I like to do is separate out major edits by adding them to their own pre-comp. To do that, we can simply perform the following steps:

1. Control click to select all three current layers, right-click on them, and then choose the **Pre compose** option from the pop-up menu.

2. In the dialog box that appears, call this particular pre-comp **Reflections Adjustment**; then, click on **OK**.

3. At this point, I think saving another iteration of our After Effects project would be in order, so let's use the **Save As** command from the **File** menu and call this version Chap10_AE_03.aep.

Adding a subtle DOF to shift focus

The next adjustment that we want to make is to direct the viewers' attention inside the image a little. We did make a reasonable start at this by paying attention to camera placement and lens choices in *Chapter 8, Composition and Cameras*, but with an overview type wide shot in a fixed environment such as the one we are working with here, there really is only so much that we can do using composition.

So, a real-world photographer would probably further direct the viewers' attention here by introducing a little bit of depth of field to the shot, pushing the viewers' eye into the room and towards the exhibits on display there. Again, this is something that could most certainly have been handled inside V-Ray using the physical camera controls.

However, adding genuine 3D DOF to a render becomes very expensive time-wise, and of course, once it has been baked into the image, you are stuck with whatever settings you applied; there can be no tweaks or adjustments further down the production pipeline without having to re-render the whole thing again, which is why doing this in post makes for a much better workflow approach. To do this then, let's perform the following steps:

1. Come up to the **Project** panel and drag our Z depth render down into the composition layer stack.

2. For the edits we will make here to work correctly, we need to straightaway put this in its own nested composition by right-clicking on it and choosing **Pre compose** from the menu list.

3. To keep things recognizable and easy to work with, let's name it ZDepth_ Control and click on **OK**.

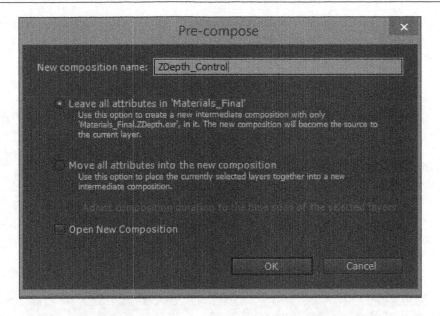

Now, when we added our Z Depth VFB channel to our rendered output back in V-Ray, you may have wondered why we didn't fine-tune the depth settings for the shot using the controls provided. Well, while we could most certainly have gone ahead and done that, but due to the fact that we were rendering out to floating point, this seemed like a redundant step, as again we can easily edit our depth settings in post. To do that, let's first of all double-click on the `ZDepth_Control` pre-comp in the layer stack to open it up and then perform the following steps:

1. Over in the **Effects & Presets** panel, type `invert` and then drop the 32-bit **Invert** effect that appears in the results area onto the **Materials_Final. ZDepth.exr** image (this gives us a white to medium-grey image as opposed to the medium-grey to white that we had).

2. Next, we need to shift the area of focus around a little, so again in the **Effects & Presets** panel, let's type out `levels` and then drop the 32-bit **Levels** effect onto the **Materials_Final.ZDepth** image as well.

3. In the **Effect Controls** panel, we want to set the **Input White** value for our **Levels** effect to `0.94` and then alter the **Gamma** value to read `0.05` (these settings will force the blur to appear quite close to the camera).

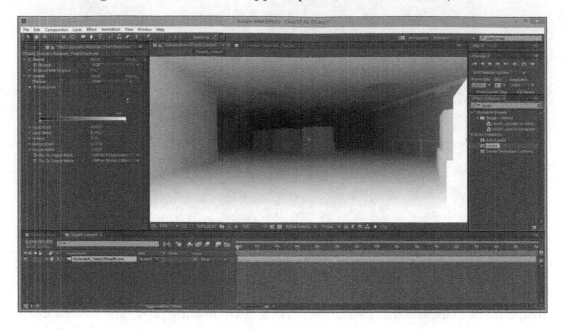

Our final edit for the `ZDepth_Control` pre-comp is to come back into the main composition and then click on the `ZDepth_Control` pre-comp eyeball icon to turn the layer's visibility off.

To get our pseudo DOF effect working, we need to perform the following steps:

1. Select our **Reflections Adjustment** pre-comp, and from the **Layer** menu at the top of the After Effects UI, choose the **New** option and then **Adjustment Layer** from the flyout.

2. Let's give this a clear descriptive name by right-clicking on the adjustment layer in the stack and then choosing the rename option from the pop-up menu.

3. Let's name it `Adj Layer - Camera lens Blur`.

4. We can now type `Camera` over in the **Effects & Presets** panel and add the **Camera Lens Blur** effect to the adjustment layer.

5. In the control options, set the Blur Radius to 2.5, leave the Shape option set to Hexagon, and in the Layer dropdown, set it to use the **ZDepth_Control** pre-comp.

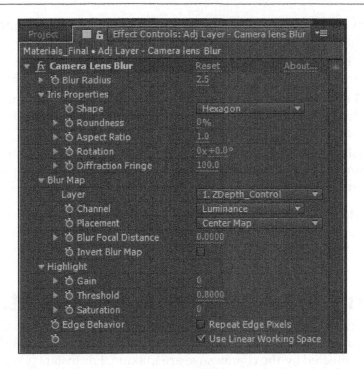

What we get now is a nice bit of defocusing blur at the front of the image that clears as the eye travels into the room. Again, you may want to make this effect a little stronger or a little weaker depending on your personal preferences. In fact, you may even want to experiment with slightly different focal distances by adjusting the levels control applied to the Z Depth render; all of which will help you set the effect the way you like it.

Again, this is a good time to save another iteration of our project, this time calling it `Chap10_AE_04.aep`.

Adding subtle relighting

Adding a DOF effect to the scene is not the only way that we can subtly focus or direct the viewers' attention in our image. Something else we can use our ZDepth pass for would be a gentle relighting of the scene. To see how this can be done, let's perform the following steps:

1. Drag another copy of our **Materials_Final.ZDepth.exr** image down into the composition layer stack, access the **Mode** dropdown for the layer, and set its blending mode to **Overlay** (this darkens the image down a little with the foreground being affected more than the background).

2. Next, we can twirl open the **Transform** options for the layer and adjust the **Opacity**, bringing it down to about **65%**.

3. As we don't want the overall brightness levels in the image to go down, let's come over to the **Effects & Presets** panel and add a **Levels** effect to the layer.

4. In the **Levels** controls, we can set the **Input Black** to 0.023, the **Input White** to 0.27, and **Gamma** to 2.55 (again, we can set the numbers here to suit our own particular view of what looks like a good effect).

5. To finish this effect off and tidy things up, let's add this layer to its own pre-comp by right-clicking on it, choosing the **Pre compose** option from the menu, and calling it Re Light.

The subtle gradation of brightness levels that we now have in the scene, going from dark to bright, again pulls the viewers' eyes towards the display cases sitting in the middle of the scene, adding to the feeling of being drawn into the image.

Boosting the glass reflections a little

Whenever we are working on an image or image sequence in post-production, one thing we absolutely must do is keep an eye on how the overall look and feel of the image is being affected by the changes we are making. For instance, one thing we see happening here is that our reflections, particularly the display cases closest to the camera, have lost some of their zing. To add a little bit of that back in, let's perform the following steps:

1. Drag another instance of the **Materials_Final.Reflection.exr** image into the main composition stack and set the blending **Mode** to **Add**.

2. Dial the effect back to suit by opening up the **Transforms** options and setting the layer's **Opacity** to 5%.

3. As before, we want to add this layer to its own pre-comp by right-clicking on it, choosing **Pre compose** from the menu, and calling it **Extra Reflections Zing**.

As this is another good time at which to save an iteration of our project, let's use the **Save As** function and call this iteration Chap10_AE_05.aep.

Final color corrections

It's time now to move on to our final color correction tweaks. Essentially, all we need to do now is add a little more life to the image by boosting the contrast range a little as well as perhaps adding a bit more life to the colors. To do that, we are going to use a very powerful color-grading plugin that ships as part of After Effects, mainly because the options we will use here have very obvious equivalents available in Photoshop also.

To apply the effect we want here, the first thing we will do is add a new adjustment layer to our composition by performing the following steps:

1. Come up to the **Layers** menu at the top of the After Effects UI and choose `Adjustment Layer` under `New`, moving it to the top of the layer stack (if it isn't already there).

2. To keep things neat, let's right-click on the layer and descriptively rename it `Color Finesse`.

3. Over in the **Effects & Presets** panel, type the words `color fin`, which will bring up the **Synthetic Apertures SA Color Finesse 3** plugin.

4. Apply this effect to the **Adjustment Layer** we have just created by dragging it onto it.

5. In the **Effect Controls** panel, twirl open the **Simplified Interface** rollout, and then close all other rollouts except for **HSL** and **Master**.

Now, while we could tweak away to our heart's content with the **Highlights**, **Midtone**, and **Shadow** controls, all we will do here is make some slight but nevertheless very effective alterations to the **Master** controls. In that rollout then, let's perform the following step:

1. Set **Vibrance** to a value of 10; set **Contrast** to 20; and set the overall **RGB Gain** to 1.1.

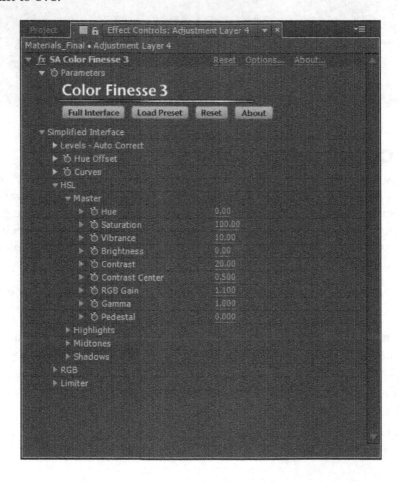

Again, we can set the values here to suit our own artistic preferences, but what you can see if you turn the Color Finesse effect off and on is that we have very obviously added quite a bit of life into our image.

It is true that we have undone a little bit of our earlier work in that we have now once again lost any real detail in our pools of direct sunlight, but if you hover your mouse cursor over them and check in the info panel, you should see that we are still currently at floating point values of just over 1.0, which is exactly where V-Ray's color mapping controls would have put them anyway.

The beauty here of course is that all of this setup is completely editable, and so we can still pull back or blow out the detail in these areas of the image as much as we like.

Adding a subtle vignette effect

The very last edit that we will make here is very much an optional one as we will simply add a vignette effect to mimic the edge darkening that many cameras inadvertently introduce as part of the photographic process. To do that, let's perform the following steps:

1. Come up to the **Layer** menu at the top of the UI and choose New | Solid.

2. In the **Solid Settings** dialog box that appears, let's name Vignette and make certain that the **Width** and **Height** settings match the comp as well as set the color to black; then finally, we can click on **OK** to close.

3. With the Ellipse tool selected up on the toolbar, we can either draw out a mask that cuts off the corners of the solid or simply double-click on the tool icon, which will fit an ellipse to the width of the current composition.

4. Down in the layer stack, we can twirl open the **Masks** rollout, check the **Inverted** option, and then set the **Mask Feather** value to 182 pixels.

5. Finally, we can adjust the **Mask Opacity** to suit; in this instance, we will go with a value of **20%**.

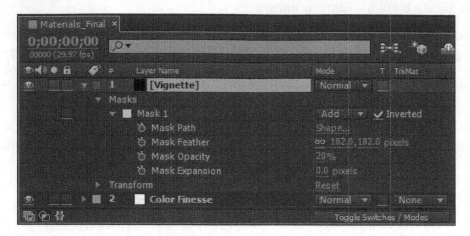

With that, we are finished with our post-production edits. If we just grab another copy of the **Materials_Final.exr** file from the **Projects** panel and place it at the top of the composition layer stack, turning it off and then back on again gives us a clear view of where our edits have brought us. The difference is not earth shattering, but more than enough for us to say that we now have a much more photographic and appealing final image (make sure to either delete or turn off this layer before moving on to the final steps).

The very last thing to do then is output our finished image to the desired file format, which in this instance will be a TIFF file that can be handed off to both printers and video editors alike. To save that out, let's perform the following steps:

1. Open up the **Composition** menu, and from the **Save Frame As** flyout, select the **File** option.

2. In the **Save** dialog box that appears, we need to give the file a name and location; in this instance, we will call it Gallery_Final and save it in the Final_Renders folder under Exercise_Files. All we need to do then is click on **Save** (don't worry that it is saving as a .psd file; we can fix that in a moment).

What we should get now is a new **Render Queue** panel open up in the timeline area of the After Effects UI. To make the swap from Photoshop file to .tiff format, all we need to do is perform the following steps:

1. Click on the **Photoshop** label next to the **Output Module** entry.

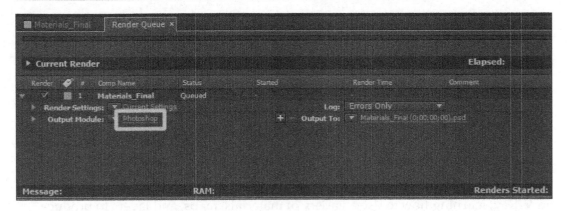

2. In the **Output Module Settings** dialog box that appears, change the setting in the **Format** dropdown from **Photoshop Sequence** to **Tiff Sequence** and click on **OK**.

3. If we want to check the current render settings, all we need to do is click on the **Current Settings** label just above. The **Render Settings** dialog box confirms that we are currently only rendering a single frame, so we can click on **OK** and are good to go.

4. All we need to do now is come over to the far right-hand side of the **Render Queue** panel and click on the **Render** button.

In our `final renders` folder, we should now have a single, finished TIFF file that has nicely captured all of our post production efforts.

Summary

Let's summarize the important elements of photorealistic rendering that we have covered during the course of our project.

First of all, we familiarized ourselves with the basic workflow in V-Ray by diving into a *Quick Start* tutorial that introduced us to camera composition, lighting, texturing, and then rendering an interior scene. We then set about using the provided scene files to create lighting rigs for daytime and nighttime interior shots as well as making good use of V-Ray's procedural day lighting system for an exterior set of shots.

We have spent quite a bit of time familiarizing ourselves with the texturing system in V-Ray, learning how to use a variety of materials, maps, and layers to produce realistic surface properties for our geometry.

Before moving on to producing our final output, we tweaked a variety of quality control settings in V-Ray, including Global illumination and Image Sampling settings in order to produce the quality level that our project required. Finally, having done all of that, using Adobe After Effects, we put the icing on the cake by utilizing a number of powerful compositing and post-production techniques to bring out the full potential of the images rendered inside V-Ray.

All that remains now is to take all of the lessons learned here and apply them to our own V-Ray rendering projects; such practice is after all the very best way to become skillful at any craft. In fact, as mentioned right at the outset, now would be a good time to make use of the SketchUp scene file provided with this book and turn it into a complete environment that can be rendered from any camera position at all.

If you would like feedback on any of the renders you create, feel free to drop me a line using the contact forms on the vrayelite.co.uk website or, alternatively, through my brian@vraylite.co.uk e-mail address. Take care and happy rendering.

Index

lighting setup, creating 78
  observation 79, 80
Interpret Footage dialog box 284
IOR 185
IOR values
  about 229

K

Kelvin color temperature scale 162
key light, interior daytime scene
  Sunlight 46
  V-Ray spotlight, using as 50-54
  V-Ray Sun, positioning 47-49

L

Lambertian model 223
Lambertian reflectance 224
light
  absorption 218
  interacting, with material 216
  reflection 218
  transmittance 219, 220
light, and material interaction
  glossiness, working 225-227
  light behavior 216, 217
  reflectivity 223-225
  transmittance effects 228-231
light behavior
  about 151
  exercise one 151
  exercise two 152-154
light decay
  exercise one 156
  exercise three 157, 158
  exercise two 156
  types 158-162
  understanding 155
light decay types
  in SketchUp V-Ray 158
light decay types, SketchUp V-Ray
  Inverse decay 160, 161
  Inverse Square decay 161, 162
  Linear decay options 159
  None decay options 159

light falloff. *See* light decay
lighting hotspots
  dealing with 285, 286
lighting process, exterior daylight scene
  initial exposure level, setting 119
  lighting tools 118
lighting process, interior nighttime scene
  artistic versus realistic approach 80, 81
  IES files 82-85
  key light 81, 82
light sources
  values 163
long shot. *See* wide shot
low shot
  using 242, 243

M

materials
  defining 174
  energy conserving materials 232, 233
  improving 271, 272
  interacting, with light 216
Materials_Final.exr footage 284
Materials List section 25
materials, RGB map
  reviewing 272, 273
materials, Sample Rate map
  reviewing 273-275
materials, V-Ray
  creating 25-27
  final lighting tweaks 34
  floor material, creating 27-30
  super bright whites 33
  surface properties, adding 31-33
maximum output resolution
  deciding 247-249
medium shot
  using 239
methods, vision defining
  artistic exercise 44
  definition, compiling 43, 44
  definition, painting 43
  definition, writing 43
  Gallery Interior definition 44, 45

Thank you for buying
Photographic Rendering with V-Ray for SketchUp

About Packt Publishing

Packt, pronounced 'packed', published its first book "*Mastering phpMyAdmin for Effective MySQL Management*" in April 2004 and subsequently continued to specialize in publishing highly focused books on specific technologies and solutions.

Our books and publications share the experiences of your fellow IT professionals in adapting and customizing today's systems, applications, and frameworks. Our solution based books give you the knowledge and power to customize the software and technologies you're using to get the job done. Packt books are more specific and less general than the IT books you have seen in the past. Our unique business model allows us to bring you more focused information, giving you more of what you need to know, and less of what you don't.

Packt is a modern, yet unique publishing company, which focuses on producing quality, cutting-edge books for communities of developers, administrators, and newbies alike. For more information, please visit our website: www.packtpub.com.

Writing for Packt

We welcome all inquiries from people who are interested in authoring. Book proposals should be sent to author@packtpub.com. If your book idea is still at an early stage and you would like to discuss it first before writing a formal book proposal, contact us; one of our commissioning editors will get in touch with you.

We're not just looking for published authors; if you have strong technical skills but no writing experience, our experienced editors can help you develop a writing career, or simply get some additional reward for your expertise.

Getting Started with Lumion 3D

ISBN: 978-1-84969-949-5   Paperback: 134 pages

Create a professional architectural visualization in minutes using Lumion 3D

1. A beginner's guide to architectural visualization.

2. Tips and tricks for modelling, texturing, and rendering using Lumion 3D.

3. Add a special touch to your images with Photoshop.

Direct3D Rendering Cookbook

ISBN: 978-1-84969-710-1   Paperback: 430 pages

50 practical recipes to guide you through the advanced rendering techniques in Direct3D to help bring your 3D graphics project to life

1. Learn and implement the advanced rendering techniques in Direct3D 11.2 and bring your 3D graphics project to life.

2. Study the source code and digital assets with a small rendering framework and explore the features of Direct3D 11.2.

3. A practical, example-driven, technical cookbook with numerous illustrations and example images to help demonstrate the techniques described.

Please check **www.PacktPub.com** for information on our titles

PUBLISHING

Blender Cycles: Lighting and Blender Cycles: Lighting and Rendering Cookbook

Over 50 recipes to help you master the lighting and rendering of different models in any scene using the Blender's Cycles engine

Bernardo Iraci

PACKT open source

Blender Cycles: Lighting and Rendering Cookbook

ISBN: 978-1-78216-460-9   Paperback: 274 pages

Over 50 recipes to help you master the Lighting and Rendering model using the Blender Cycles engine

1. Get acquainted with the lighting and rendering concepts of the Blender Cycles engine.

2. Learn the concepts behind nodes shader system and get the best out of Cycles in any situation.

3. Packed with illustrations and a lot of tips and tricks to make your scenes come to life.

Blender 2.6 Cycles, Materials and Textures Cookbook

Over 50 recipes to help you create stunning materials and textures using the Cycles rendering engine with Blender

Enrico Valenza

PACKT open source

Blender 2.6 Cycles, Materials and Textures Cookbook

ISBN: 978-1-78216-130-1   Paperback: 280 pages

Over 40 recipes to help you create stunning materials and textures using the Cycles rendering engine with Blender

1. Create naturalistic materials and textures - such as rock, snow, and ice - using Cycles.

2. Learn Cycle's node-based material system.

3. Get to grips with the powerful Cycles rendering engine.

Please check **www.PacktPub.com** for information on our titles

CPSIA information can be obtained at www.ICGtesting.com
Printed in the USA
LVOW03s1828141214

418774LV00010B/359/P